8-10-76

JOHN COURTNEY MURRAY

Theologian in Conflict

JOHN COURTNEY MURRAY
Theologian in Conflict

by

Donald E. Pelotte, S.S.S.

PAULIST PRESS
New York/Ramsey, N.J./Toronto

Library of Congress
Catalog Card Number: 76-18046

ISBN: 0-8091-0212-9 (Cloth)

Published by Paulist Press
Editorial Office: 1865 Broadway, N.Y., N.Y. 10023
Business Office: 545 Island Road, Ramsey, N.J. 07446

Printed and bound in the
United States of America.

1930594

Contents

Foreword

Catholics have been present in the northern part of the western hemisphere for almost half a millennium. And a third of a millennium has passed since they began to settle in one of the colonies that became part of the original United States. Through these years, millions of adherents have been served by leaders—bishops, saints, abbots, thinkers, doers—with names like John Carroll, Elizabeth Seton, James Gibbons, Dorothy Day, Thomas Merton, Isaac Hecker.

Not until the middle of the twentieth century, however, did a formal theological thinker tower above his fellows. How fitting it was that the tardy pioneer, Father John Courtney Murray, the subject of this book, should have spent so many of his energies on what might be called "the American theme," the part this land and its people play in unfolding patterns of civil and religious thought. Before him, men of many generations had spoken up for Catholicism, trying to demonstrate that the Church belonged in the United States, that it was not a misfit, that its members should not be held under suspicion for disloyalty.

Only the first bishop, John Carroll, anticipated some of the ways in which the American experience itself was to be listened to in Catholic formulation. And Carroll's voice was muffled, his impact largely forgotten; he is even slighted in the present work. Murray stands first among those whose voice was heard beyond Catholicism, who had to be reckoned with by public philosophers and political theorists. If Alfred Smith and John F. Kennedy were front-room participants in the political process, Murray was a "back-room" man, influential among elites, among "the influentials," the shapers of, and reflectors upon, the American process. As such he did not become as well known as the politicians, even though he was to come to *Time*-cover status. This book should help enlarge his reputation in the generation that might forget—might even *want* to forget—what he achieved.

Father Murray came along at the proper moment, and he helped make the proper moment. By the middle of this century it was clear to even the last of the nativists and the Klansmen that the tens of millions of American Roman Catholics could not be shipped back to Europe by the heirs of hostile old non-Catholic majorities in America. They could no longer be confined to Catholic ghettos. The new suburbs and the new campuses beckoned them. They would remain here. What was at issue now was the set of terms for their life in the larger society.

Murray helped provide those terms for the thoughtful ones. He taught them the meaning of a pluralistic society. It may even be plausibly argued that only the Jewish theologian and sociologist Will Herberg did as much as Murray to bring the very word "pluralism" into prominence in the religious context. Certainly, Murray made it possible for Catholics to be assured of the integrity of their Catholicism in the pluralist mixture more than anyone else.

Curiously enough, his chief enemies did not turn out to be antagonists in the Protestant-Jewish-Secularist camps at interfaith gatherings. They respected him as a dignified, clear, and formidable articulator of Catholic positions. As Donald Pelotte here shows, in chapters that even succeed in building up a sense of intrigue and suspense, Murray was countered and almost successfully suppressed by some of his fellow Catholics, both in Rome and in America.

One can read Pelotte's work, at least its first half, for the human drama that accompanied Murray's attempt to stake out a position. While the author spends little time using psychological tools, he does make available materials for analysis of Murray's inner man. Murray was a blend of angry man, pessimist, determined thinker, stalwart Jesuit, and friend to others. How misplaced was the opposition of the Old Guard on the Church-State front in Catholicism! Far from traducing the Catholic tradition, Murray reached deeper into its resources to advance theories congruent with its intentions and with much American republican thought. Not always do the custodians of a tradition know who its best friends are.

Shortly after the Second Vatican Council and *very* shortly after Murray's death there were those within Catholicism who discerned the traditional aspects of his thought. During those days of rage against anything traditional, the rejectors-from-within wanted to dismiss him as a conservative. They were more nearly correct than those who had wanted to describe him as a modernizer or a modernist.

Tradition and conservatism can mean many things. For Murray they meant being attentive to what the best of his antecedents had taught; being responsive to their intentions; examining what in that thought might be applicable in an emerging world. But if the emerging world did not "square" with Catholic faith as he knew it, so much the worse for that world. Those of us who knew him and contended with him also were well aware that he could be unyielding when he thought something basic to the faith was being jeopardized.

All of us will remember different aspects of his contribution. For me one of the most important was his successful demonstration that there was no neutral "American civil tradition." We all brought certain theological commitments to the understanding of the American propositions. Many of us "Protestantized" this understanding, engaged in Baptist readings of the First Amendment. Was the Thomist reading less respectable, he would ask? We might be positivists about law; was natural law less plausible?

Second, because he was never the optimist nor the sentimentalist—and his quoted letters in this book underscore that fact—he always introduced a note the realism to what could have been mushy interfaith occasions. He wanted to set the stage for disagreements based on a community of discourse, not agreements derived from a community of sentiments.

One is not likely to remember this work only as a chapter in recent Catholic history. The American proposition is still being elaborated, the American process still unfolds. We do not know, we really do not know, what to do or how to think about many of the basic features of religious and civil life in a society marked by the motto *E Pluribus Unum*. After a decade of life lived *Ex Uno Plures*, in which each of us has gotten better at asserting our own values, the motifs of our own tribes, we find it necessary to redevelop the community of discourse that Murray cherished. He offers models, motives, paradigms, and themes for the new generation's urgent task, and this book will serve better than any other guide I know to lead new readers and thinkers to the sources for a more intelligent and enlightened conflict and, one hopes, measures of resolution.

Martin E. Marty

The University of Chicago

Introduction

A man's thought can never properly be understood save in the context of his personal and environmental history and in light of the many elements that conditioned its development. With this principle in mind, the first three chapters of this book situate John Courtney Murray in an historical context.

The first chapter opens with a brief history of Murray's early life. It then examines those issues that contributed to the shaping of the theory of Church and State for which he became famous. Among those issues was the secularized humanism that emerged during and after World War II and affected every aspect of the American and Christian way of life. The need for prompt action in this situation provoked a general call for Christian cooperation among all men of goodwill. This appeal was based primarily on a plan outlined by Pius XII during the 1940s. This rallying call for intercredal cooperation caused concern in certain Catholic quarters, and especially in the circle that gravitated around *The American Ecclesiastical Review*. The latter viewed such cooperation as implicit doctrinal indifferentism and responded negatively. The discussion was further aggravated by the gradual emergence in Europe and in the United States of a "new theology" with "modern" theories concerning the nature of the Church. These ideas very often ran contrary to the "institutional model" of the Church embedded in Roman Catholic ecclesiology since the Counter-Reformation.

The second chapter studies the Church-State debate that engaged so much of Murray's time and energy during the 1950s. The debate led ultimately to a rebuke issued from Rome in late 1954. For a period of about four years Murray was virtually "silenced" on the Church-State issue. The enormous amount of personal correspondence between the key figures involved in the controversy are crucial to its understanding.

The third chapter examines the development of Murray's thought in the pre-Council and Council years, his contribution to the debate on religious liberty and to the writing of the Second Vatican Council's *Declaration on Religious Freedom*, which actually vindicated Murray's position. The chapter concludes with a brief survey of Murray's work from the end of the Vatican Council to his death in August, 1967.

On the basis of the historical exposition in the first three chapters, the fourth chapter provides a theoretical and systematic analysis of Murray's political philosophy. The American democratic experience more than any other factor appears to have influenced Murray's own mature position and indirectly the ecumenical Council's *Declaration on Religious Freedom.*

The fifth and final chapter situates Murray in the Americanist tradition. While the development of doctrine constituted the real theological problem, the specific issue of "Americanism" soon emerged as the chief point of theological disagreement between Murray and his opponents.

For American ecclesiology, the quarter of a century that began in the early 40s and ended with Murray's death represents a further process of Catholic assimilation into American life. This period was characterized by a strong drive on the part of American Catholics to overcome the limitations imposed by minority status. The reforms of Pope John and of the Second Vatican Council along with the election of John F. Kennedy contributed to the American Catholic's new acceptability. Murray's theological work, however, more than any other factor, was responsible for establishing the compatibility of American pluralism and Catholicism, and this in the eyes of both the Roman Catholic Church and of the American people. Murray's chief legacy to American Catholics was his demonstration that it is possible to be both an American and a Catholic without being disloyal to either.

1

The Early Years:
1940-1949

John Courtney Murray was born in New York City on September 12, 1904. His father, a Scottish-born lawyer, and his Irish mother were both Roman Catholics. As a young man, Murray expressed an interest in medicine, but want of money would not allow him to pursue this vocation. In 1920, at the age of sixteen, he joined the Society of Jesus and after receiving a B.A. from Weston College in 1926 and an M.A. from Boston College in 1927, he spent three years teaching Latin and English Literature at the Ateneo de Manila in the Philippines.

Returning to the United States in 1930, Murray studied theology for four years at Woodstock College in Woodstock, Maryland. After his ordination to the priesthood on June 25, 1933, he continued his studies at Rome's Gregorian University, which awarded him a doctorate in theology in 1937.[1] Murray then returned to Woodstock as a professor of theology specializing in the areas of grace and the Trinity. He held this post until his death in 1967.[2]

The Church that Murray had experienced as a child and the Church he faced as a young scholar were two very different realities. In 1899, only five years before Murray's birth, the American Church was shaken by the encyclical *Testem benevolentiae*, a warning from Pope Leo XIII concerning "Americanism." While the document was somewhat ambiguous with regard to the nature of the "Americanist" problem, it came at a time when it could not be dissociated from a series of papal initiatives against "Modernism." The Pope's warning had a dampening effect on creative thinking and Church leadership in America.

Before the Civil War, the pioneer clergy were seen as omnicompetent by their immigrant flocks. In their brick-and-mortar apostolates, however, priests built walls rather than bridges between their flocks and the American communities. After the Civil War, Catholics slowly moved closer to American intellectual society. The founding of the Catholic University of America in 1899 and a few excellent seminaries—which many would now term progressive—the launching of campus ministries, and the publication of a few new theological journals are illustrative of the trend. The most outstanding of these journals was the *New York Review*, inaugurated in 1905, and produced by three priest-professors of St. Joseph's Seminary, Dunwoodie, Yonkers, New York.

The *Review* was a scholarly periodical that published, for the most part, the work of leading European theologians; its orientation, contributions from Americans, and editorial policies, however, all point to the nascent intellectual life among American priests. The *Review*, and the movement to which it witnessed, died with Pope Pius X's condemnation of Modernism in 1907 in the encyclical *Pascendi dominici gregis*. A second renaissance would come only in the 40s and 50s when it was spearheaded by the pioneering work of men like John Murray and Gustave Weigel, his closest colleague in the Society of Jesus.

The condemnations of Americanism and Modernism were a major setback for the emerging intellectual life of the American Church. In actual fact, relatively few Americans proved to be affected by the heresy, but the overreaction of the Roman authorities to what many saw as a threat resulted in a climate of international suspicion toward "scientific" theology. As ecclesiastical witch-hunts replaced openness to scholarship, seminaries lapsed into a (manual) dogmatic slumber from which they awakened only with Vatican II. According to one American Catholic historian, the aftereffects of the Modernist purge on teaching in American seminaries were the principal cause for producing two generations of American priests who were isolated from the intellectual community of America and its standards.[3]

The last years of the First World War saw the gradual rise of Catholic interest in social thought under the leadership of Father John J. Burke, C.S.P., who had been editor of the *Catholic World* magazine since 1904. Burke spearheaded the creation of the National Catholic War Council, predecessor to the National Catholic Welfare Council. In 1919, when the latter was established, Monsignor John A. Ryan's program of Catholic social reconstruction provided the first signs of Catholic social progressivism.

Hostility toward Roman Catholics and a resulting defensive stance on the part of the Church characterized the period of the 1920s. The hostility was for the most part promoted by the temperance crusade and the campaign to restrict immigration. The organized bigotry of the Ku Klux Klan best exemplifies the anti-Catholic feeling of the time. The period ended in the bitterly fought presidential election of 1928 in which a Roman Catholic, Alfred E. Smith, lost his bid for the White House over the "religious issue."

Serious complications delayed the enactment of the National Origins Act passed by Congress in 1924. This Act was to limit the annual quota of immigrants from any country to 2 per cent of the number of individuals who had been born in that country and who were resident in the United States in 1890. The measure finally took effect on July 1, 1929. Its enactment marked a new era for the Church in America and the beginning of a long process of adjustment to a situation in which the immigrant no longer determined the Church's basic stance.

The 1930s brought a greater acceptance of Catholics in public life and a more serious concern within the Church for national problems. The Depression, the New Deal and then World War II wrought disruptions in American social order. These and the postwar "industrial revolution" greatly accelerated the normalization of America's large Catholic minority. The Crash, in particular, and the great Depression which followed were efficient causes of an increasing popular support for social reform in the 30s. The problems of unemployment and economic collapse stimulated a resurgence of both thought and action among Roman Catholics and other Americans.

In the Church itself new stirrings could be felt both here and abroad. Men like Etienne Gilson and Jacques Maritain were at work carefully developing a new interest in Thomistic philosophy. Called upon to lecture in various American universities, both had a profound influence on intellectual thought in America. Maritain's Neo-Thomism influenced Murray's writings, and secular thinkers like Mortimer Adler and President Robert M. Hutchins, of the University of Chicago, found Maritain's thought attractive.

In theology, the signs of new life were reflected in growing interest in the Church as the Body of Christ, in the revival of biblical studies, and in a newly awakened historical consciousness. The pre-Vatican II Church was in the initial process of rediscovering its roots. The first official steps at redefinition were taken by Pius XII in the momentous encyclical *Mystici corporis* (1943). The same Pope's *Divino afflante spiritu* (1943) became the Magna Carta of Roman Catholic biblical scholarship. Most important was the post-World War shift in Catholic attitudes toward history. The new attitude was characterized by a serious concern for historical research and a heightened awareness of the way in which the past inheres as a vital reality in the present. For instance, there was a renewed appreciation for John Henry Cardinal Newman's approach to development of Christian doctrine. Participation by some Catholic scholars in ecumenical discussions forced a reconsideration of the meaning of "tradition." At this time, Pierre Teilhard de Chardin (1881-1955), the Jesuit paleontologist, was hard at work developing his comprehensive evolutionary theology.

The important role of scholarly journals in this revival cannot be underestimated. *Commonweal*, founded in 1921 to promote American Catholic culture, had sufficiently proven its worth by redirecting the efforts of Catholics. Contributing articles from abroad came from Maritain, Gilson, Baron Friedrich von Hügel, the great English Catholic scholar, Romano Guardini, the German priest-theologian, and the Jesuits of the *Nouvelle Révue Théologique*. January, 1939 saw the appearance of the *Catholic Biblical Quarterly*.

Theological Studies, the quarterly of the combined Jesuit theological faculties in this country, was inaugurated in February, 1940, under the leadership of *America* magazine's editor, Francis X. Talbot, S.J. The *New York Review*, defunct since 1908, had finally been replaced. Under the editorship of William J. McGarry, S.J., formerly professor of theology at Weston College in Massachusetts, the journal was addressed "to those interested in the science of theology and the activities of contemporary theological minds." The aim of this new theological venture was "that of creating an organ through which theologian might speak to theologian, the latest research might be transmitted to research workers, a comprehensive coverage of current theological writing might be spread before the gaze of professors and students."[4]

According to an *America* editorial, the quarterly had "been launched with the knowledge that American theological scholarship has for years badly needed just such an outlet for current publication. This scholarship is rapidly growing in personnel and in quality. Its fruits are now available—not only to a few 'professionals,' but to any intelligent reader, lay or clergy."[5]

Articles in the first two issues dealt with such subjects as Saint Ignatius of Antioch and the Fourth Gospel, the Ecumenical Movement, and the problem of sexual morality. Each issue also contained two important features: a study on current theology and book reviews. Under Murray's leadership *Theological Studies* was to become the leading American Catholic journal of theology.

During the 1930s and 1940s Catholic theology and biblical studies began to recover some of the vitality that had characterized American Catholic thinking before the Modernist condemnation in 1907. Besides the appearance of new publications, there was a renewed interest in the subjects that had been popular at the turn of the century. Paralleling the appearance of the new publications was the founding of the Catholic Biblical Association of America in 1946. This was followed in the same year by the Catholic Theological Society of America (CTSA) under the leadership of Fathers Joseph C. Fenton, Francis J. Connell, C.SS.R. Eugene M. Burke, C.S.P., and Edmond D. Bernard, all associated with *The American Ecclesiastical Review*.

At the foundation meeting of the Society, held in New York City on June 25 and 26, 1946, Connell was elected the first President of CTSA, Fenton was chosen secretary and Murray was chosen for a two-year term to the Board of Directors. Subsequently the Board asked Murray "to initiate the writing of a publication or series of publications concerned with 'An Authoritative Church in a Democracy,' and to report progress at the next regular meeting of the Board of Directors."

The American Ecclesiastical Review, which published its last issue in December, 1975, had been founded in 1889. Its first editor was Father Herman J. Heuser, who intended the *Review* as a scholarly journal attractive to clergy and educated laity alike. In tact, however, it had little appeal to the laity.

The long theological debate about to break into the open on religious liberty represented, at least in large measure, a clash in theology between the theologians associated with *Theological Studies* and those with *The American Ecclesiastical Review.* Fenton became editor of *AER* in 1944 and, until his resignation in 1963, the journal became the mouthpiece of Catholic theological intransigence in the United States. A member of the Catholic University of America's faculty of theology, and professor of dogma, Fenton became dean of the theological faculty in 1952. Associated with him at *AER* was Redemptorist Father Francis J. Connell, also professor of theology at the Catholic University, and Father George Shea, professor of theology at the Immaculate Conception Seminary in New Jersey. Perhaps the best spokesman for the conservative Catholic position on Church and State was the previously mentioned Monsignor John A. Ryan, a leading progressive in Catholic economic thinking, labor action, and industrial concerns. For many years Ryan taught moral theology, political science, and industrial ethics at the Catholic University of America.[6]

Theological Interests

Murray did not emerge as an important figure in scholarly journals until the 1940s. In 1941 he became the editor of *Theological Studies* and, soon after, the religion editor of *America* magazine. To both journals he brought his keen interest in the problems of freedom, in the rights of conscience, and in the role of law. The situation of the Catholic Church in American life and the place of the American idea of freedom in Catholic life soon emerged as the central concerns of his writing.

In early March, 1943, Murray expressed doubt concerning "the importance of *Theological Studies* itself," and the significance of his role as editor. He subsequently requested permission to offer himself for service as a chaplain in the Army.[7] His request was denied.

An examination of Murray's relationship to his two editorial responsibilities, *Theological Studies* and *America,* provides important information regarding his interests in those early years. In particular they help partly to explain the various factors that led Murray to pursue the subject for which he would become so well known.

The problem raised in 1943 was again on Murray's mind as he wrote to Francis A. McQuade, his provincial, in April, 1946. "I take it that there are two questions: (1) the objective demands of two jobs, editor of *Theological Studies* and religion editor of *America*; (2) my own personal situation in regard to both of them." As Murray saw it, *Theological Studies* needed a full-time editor, who should be an outstanding theologian, "wholly devoted to the triple function of a member of a theological faculty—teaching, the direction of graduate research, scientific writing. In consequence, he should live in a house of studies, and have no other 'career,' no other major interest."

As for his relationship to *America*, Murray's job description outlined the need for a full-time religion editor whose field would be: "(1) what is called 'religion and society'—a very important field today; (2) current religious controversies; (3) doctrinal subjects, as they become topical, and relevant to current social issues. . . . Therefore, the religion editor's field is distinct from that of the professional theologian, at the same time that it is an extension of the latter's field, and would (ideally, I think) require professional training. It has its own possibilities of study, its own difficulties, its own apostolic value."

Murray then focused on the main point of his problem: "The editorship of *TS* and the religion editorship are, I think, not only two distinct jobs, but two distinct 'careers,' two different ways of life. If he wished fully to exploit their possibilities, no man could combine both." It seemed clear to Murray that he should be either editor of *Theological Studies* or religion editor of *America*, but not both—"(Correction: I could be both too! But not with any degree of satisfaction either to myself or anybody else.)"

Within this context Murray expressed his own personal interests and pointed to the major direction his work would take him:

> In the last four years or so, my predominant interests have tended away from technical theology as such into the field of what I have called "religion and society." Cf. the subjects I have written in: Catholic Action (I taught this at Woodstock); cooperation among men of goodwill; the papal peace program; the moral implications of atomic energy; freedom of religion (involving liberalism, Church and State, etc.). Add also: College religion, and theology for the laity.

The letter goes on to explain how he had also become rather seriously involved in the international student movement as a result of his interest in the theory of Catholic Action. "I have got fairly deeply in this field, to the extent of being regarded as an 'authority' by the NCWC people! In fact, they consult me most solemnly."[8]

In May, 1946, Archbishop Richard J. Cushing, then the chairman of the Youth Department of the National Catholic Welfare Conference, asked Murray to "recruit, prepare and lead to Europe a group of student representatives to participate in the several student congresses or conferences. . . ." Citing the need for "extraordinary actions" in this area Cushing expressed his evaluation about the need for such a project.

> The value of this project is not merely to meet the crises of the present hour. It must be treated as a radical step to begin quickly and effectively the preparation of our student leaders for the development of the future. In other words, the proposed group must come back prepared to spread information and to train others in this type of collaboration and international student action.[9]

Murray's reply to Cushing expressed enthusiasm for the project and the feeling "that something satisfactory, if not indeed ideal, can be done."[10]

According to the information Murray sent to McQuade, Murray's own name had been suggested to Cushing by the director of the NCWC Youth Department, Father John Bermingham. Murray had had fairly extensive contacts with the Youth Department chiefly with regard to problems of the international student movement and of Catholic Action theory in CYO work. But it was especially Murray's article, "Operation University" which had drawn NCWC's attention to the interest in the youth movement.[11]

Murray's response to Cushing was quickly followed by a letter to McQuade, in which he sought permission "to take the job." He wrote, "It seems to me a worthwhile project, and I think it can be managed. The trip could be combined with some 'field work' both for *TS* and for *America*. Furthermore, if I don't do the thing, it probably won't get done."[12]

Somewhat surprisingly, the provincial refused permission for the trip to Europe and participation in the International Assembly of Pax Romana in Fribourg, or the International Student Conference in Prague, both scheduled for August, 1946.[13]

In a frank reply to McQuade, Murray expressed concern about the decision.

> I don't want to argue against your decision, nor even to inquire into the reasons for it. (Though I am indeed curious to know the precise reason why you should be "fearful" of the proposal. To me, it looks like a difficult job, with delicate angles; but nothing to be fearful about. However, that is irrelevant.)

Murray then apologized for getting involved in the project.

You will say, of course, that I had no business starting all this.
And, unfortunately, you will be most horribly right. Apparently, I
have made a rather ghastly mistake. (Apparently, whenever I do
start something, it is a mistake. . . .)

After explaining briefly that he had been under pressure from events
and people to start the project, and secondly, that he frankly never expected a
"blanket refusal" from his superior, Murray again regretted his bad judgment:

At all events I made a mistake, I see that with quite horrible clarity. As I see that all my life I shall be, quite properly, a sucker for
an idea. And also, quite probably, too inclined to take personal initiatives.[14]

Besides revealing a fascinating aspect of Murray's personality, the attitude expressed in the above statements is highly indicative of his concerns in
those years. In the letter of April 22 to the provincial, Murray had also indicated that he felt pulled in the direction of "religion and society" "partly
under the pressure of circumstances (people asked me to do things they needed doing); partly under the will to give some contemporary flavor to TS; and
partly under the guidance of my own tastes, which are inclined to wander."[15]
Consequently, Murray's options were simple. With regard to the initial
problem raised he was either to resign from *America* and to redirect his interests into those channels that were proper to the editorship of *Theological
Studies* or he was to resign from the latter and confirm the present direction
of his interests by committing himself definitively to his work as religion editor of *America*. While he explained that his preference lay with the latter al-
ternative, he ultimately had to settle for the former. A quick perusal of *Theological Studies* during these years reveals to what extent his interests in
"religion and society" were channelled into its pages.
As early as 1945 Murray was being asked by American Church leaders
to express himself on important issues of the day affecting the Church and society. For instance, in April, 1945, Rev. Zacheus J. Maher, S.J., the American Assistant of the Society of Jesus, asked for Murray's opinion on what
should be the Jesuit policy on the admission of blacks to Jesuit-run schools,
universities and seminaries. The issue had come into public discussion over
the admission of blacks to St. Louis University. However, a dispute arose
about whether the black students might attend a university-sponsored student
prom. The authorities at St. Louis University seemed to have felt it would be
dangerous to permit it, but Father Claude Heithaus, S.J., leader of the
student movement that had helped to integrate the school, forced the issue into

the open. Black couples were permitted to attend the dance, but this resulted in Heithaus's transfer from the university.[16]

In this context, Maher asked Murray: "Will you kindly give me the opinion of some of the *graviores* as to the 'sinfulness' of excluding Negroes from the Student Conclave?"[17] Murray had already sent Maher a lengthy memorandum on the issue of admission of blacks to the Society of Jesus and added here that their admission would serve "the practical purpose of making the Society's [Society of Jesus] attitude unequivocally clear, and of being itself a blow at prejudice. . . ." In the light of subsequent developments Murray's response to the problem at St. Louis reflects some of the more limited attitudes of that period.

> For my part, I would be quite at a loss to detect any grounds for "sin" in the exclusion of Negroes from the dance. The issue is not between right and wrong, but between tact and stupidity in handling a delicate social situation. The values at stake seem to be social not moral. And I am inclined to think that it is distinctly unintelligent so to conduct things that the presence or non-presence of Negroes at a dance becomes a moral issue.
>
> On the other hand, I am also inclined to think that there is a certain amount of sinfulness involved in having let the whole affair become a subject of public notoriety, and especially in having the impression get abroad that there is schism in our own ranks over the question. Some fundamental loyalties were violated, and somewhere the prudential precepts with regard to the *usus linguae* went by the board. However, this is off the point about which you inquired—the "sinfulness" of excluding Negroes from the dance. As I said, I do not think the issue of "sin" comes up at all.
>
> It really comes up only if it could be proved that that form of social association was, at a given moment, a necessary part of a program of social justice, so that, if it were forbidden, the program itself would suffer seriously. But this could hardly be proved. Actually, what happened at St. Louis looks to me like a piece of sheer ineptitude in the way of handling things.[18]

In the September 21, 1945 issue, *Commonweal* published an article by Father George H. Dunne, S.J., entitled "The Sin of Segregation." It proved to be one of the most widely reprinted of *Commonweal* articles.

In early 1945, Archbishop Edward Mooney of Detroit and Monsignor Howard J. Carroll, General Secretary of NCWC, asked Murray and Father Wilfred Parsons, S.J., to join them in Washington for a meeting with a few Protestant representatives from the Joint Committee on Religious Liberty of the Federal Council of Churches and the Foreign Missions Conference of North America. "As you know," Murray reported to Maher, "our Protestant brethren are very excited over the issue of religious liberty." Archbishop Mooney had been impressed with Murray's criticism of the Protestant "Statement on Religious Liberty," which had appeared in the March, 1945 issue of *Theological Studies*. At the April 8 meeting in Washington, Mooney had designated Parsons and Murray "to carry on discussions with two appointees of the Federal Council." "With the view of getting the discussions moving on our own terms, it was thought advisable that I should write a full statement of Catholic theory—it will take three articles to do it. . . . The subject is extraordinarily difficult and delicate, and I have been having lots of trouble with it."[19]

The last few months of 1946 found Murray in a state of extreme fatigue and he is reported to have collapsed from exhaustion. In mid-February, 1947 Murray again petitioned his provincial to be replaced at *Theological Studies* and asked to be considered for some position with the Jesuit graduate students at Fordham University in New York. "I really think I need a new job and a new start!" And he added frankly:

> I say this from a personal standpoint, thinking of what *I* think would be good for me. Knowing, of course, that one is not the ultimate judge of one's own usefulness, etc., etc.
>
> The idea of needing a new start is not a new one. Two or more years ago—certainly about the time of my three-months undulant fever episode—it seemed to me that I had come to the end here at Woodstock. The *America* interlude was, of course, rather a mistake—that is definitely not my line. Before it, and after being ill, I was determined to have another shot; but now the good old determination does not seem to rise. At any rate, I seemed to fail rather signally to make the new start this year. Admittedly, the reason—and the fault—is in me. But there is the fact.
>
> Not to exaggerate: the situation is not at all desperate! I can go on being whatever use I am here. The only question is: is this my full usefulness? Perhaps others think it is—all right. I merely happen to think not. And my point is simply to say so. Because I rather feel that I must say so now, or forever shut up! I am, of course quite willing to be told to shut up—you needn't hesitate to tell me. That itself might end this long-standing, disturbing sensation of being in a stage of transition, from something I don't longer want to be, to something else.

Murray was obviously unhappy with his work at *Theological Studies* and at Woodstock and he honestly expressed his preference for working with graduate students. "There is nothing I would myself consider preferable to what I have and where I am." He concluded:

> I want to be a student (and there might be an advantage in having a student over students). And I want to write (my main "want"); and I want to do a bit of teaching (but not here). And I want an opportunity to further an interest into which half a dozen things I have done and thought about have led me—the furtherance of the lay intellectual apostolate among graduate students. In fine, I want to stay in my field, but get out of my rut! There you have it. . . . I have spoken my little piece! And feel the better for it, whatever happens, or whether nothing happens.[20]

Nothing happened. Apparently Murray's superiors felt he was indispensable at *Theological Studies.*

The Church-State Debate

In June, 1947, Murray was scheduled to deliver a paper on the theology of Church and State at the second annual meeting of the Catholic Theological Society of America taking place in Boston, but due to illness, he was unable to attend the convention. Ironically, it was Fenton who was chosen to deliver the paper in place of Murray. Praising Murray's brilliance but emphasizing the inadequacy of his own presentation, Fenton opened with the following comments:

> In a subject as delicate and complicated as that of the theology of Church and State there are bound to be some differences, at least in viewpoint or in stress, among the theologians. Thus, even if this paper turns out to manifest some attitudes distinct or divergent from those which will appear in Dr. Murray's forthcoming lecture, it may still be of some service. I believe that it will ultimately have been advantageous to the Society to have heard two approaches to this particular section of the theological field.[21]

At the third annual meeting held in Chicago the following year, Murray was well enough to deliver his paper on the "Governmental Repression of Heresy." Connell, as President of the Society, commented after the delivery. While praising Murray for "the painstaking research and the diligent study that were surely needed in the preparation of this paper," Connell criticized parts of the paper for being "out of harmony with the traditional belief and attitude of the Church for many centuries." "I for one," he added, "shall continue to hold the traditional view. . . ."[22] These were the first public signs of the theological clash about to take place on the theology of Church and State. Murray and Connell had already voiced written disagreement over each other's position on the related issue of intercredal cooperation.

Intercredal Cooperation

In fact, one of Murray's earliest areas of concern during those early years as editor of *Theological Studies* was that of intercredal cooperation. His first article on the subject, "Christian Cooperation: Current Theology," which appeared in September, 1942, was an attempt to synthesize the various theological positions on cooperation. Discussion on the subject was already well underway in European circles, particularly in France and England.[23]

Murray expressed the hope that *Theological Studies* might make some contribution to the complex discussion, at least in its theoretic aspects. While providing a summary of the recent theological thinking on cooperation "with a view to affording some documentation on the discussion," he promised further articles by Father John LaFarge S.J., and others on the historical, theological, and canonical aspects of the problem.

By clearly distinguishing between "Christian cooperation" and the larger and more complex problem of "Christian reunion," Murray pinpointed the critical issue. An article by Connell provided him with a point of departure. Murray quoted Connell:

In the United States up to comparatively recent times there was little danger of indifferentism to any great extent among Catholics. On the contrary, they were rather inclined to distrust adherents of other denominations and even to question their sincerity. . . . In recent years a strong reaction against the spirit of mutual distrust and antagonism has taken place among both Catholics and non-Catholics. . . . Now, however, the important question arises, whether some Catholics in their laudable efforts to be broadminded and charitable toward the members of non-Catholic religious bodies, are not becoming unduly tolerant toward their doctrines. Is not the pendulum swinging from bigotry to indifferentism? The question has its most practical application in the matter of "Interfaith" or "three-faith" meetings.[24]

Connell had cited the National Conference of Christians and Jews as an example of the kind of interdenominational organization that tended to encourage indifferentism. Murray was himself a member of this group and would ultimately be responsible for drafting the Catholic contribution to the organization's most important document of 1943: "The Catholic, Jewish, Protestant Declaration on World Peace."[25]

Connell was also concerned that cooperation might lead to a "watering down" of the Church's teaching on tolerance, on the relationship of Church and State, and on the scope of the Church's authority. Finally, participation in such organizations might lead to the danger of conceding to representatives of other religions a place of equality with the "True Church" in specifically religious capacities. Recognizing the prudence of Connell's warnings and insisting on the principle of "Catholic exclusivism," Murray suggested that further investigation was needed of "the actual effect on Catholics of the present cooperative movement."[26] He also insisted on: "the principle of charity, especially in its applications to the concrete, total situation existent in the world (and not only in America) today." "There is room for an exploration of the dangers to human life, national and international, involved in the failure of Catholics to cooperate with non-Catholics in the sphere of social reconstruction—dangers so great as to create a necessity for such cooperation."[27]

Commenting on Connell's suggestion for the need of educating the laity on the purposes and significance of such cooperation, Murray called for a "whole program of instruction, notably with regard to the great idea that Leo XIII constantly put forward, the mission of the Church in the temporal order." He added:

> I am inclined to think that the purpose and significance of Christian cooperation will not be grasped, nor the danger of indifferentism obliviated, unless the movement is seen by the people against a larger doctrinal background, and in the light of a genuine appreciation of the realities of the present world crisis.[28]

An analysis of the numerous articles appearing on this subject in *Theological Studies* and *The American Ecclesiastical Review* through the 1940s will show that the discussion of these two opposing sides never came anywhere near agreement. While Murray made every effort to clarify some of the issues involved and dangers to be avoided, Connell and his associates reiterated their warnings of "doctrinal indifferentism."[29]

The staff of *The American Ecclesiastical Review* was never persuaded by Murray's argumentation. Connell, for instance, responded to Murray's articles in *Theological Studies* of March, June, and September, 1943, with a reminder that Leo XIII, in an apostolic letter dated September 18, 1895, and addressed to Archbishop Francesco Satolli, Apostolic Delegate to the United States, had mildly rebuked those who had participated in the "World Parliament of Religions" at the Columbian Exposition held in Chicago in 1892-93. Because of the latitudinarianism expressed at the Parliament, Pope Leo had expressed disapproval over the participation of Catholics and had forbidden future activities of a similar nature. Granting the fact that Pius XII had later called for cooperation, Connell urged that theologians not overlook Leo's words of caution. For Connell, the spirit of religious indifferentism condemned by Leo XIII was still very prevalent in the United States and expressed itself particularly in the "attitude toward a diversity of religious beliefs engendered by conditions existing in our armed forces," and by "the emphasis that is nowadays laid on one of the 'four freedom's'—freedom of religious worship."[30] Underlying each of these problems was the Catholic position that Catholicism is the only true religion.

The importance of this early stage of Murray's theological reflection cannot be overemphasized. Through close examination and fuller clarification of his own thinking on the matter of cooperation, Murray was working at uncovering aspects of his Church-State theory. It mattered little to Murray whether one spoke of the relation between Church and State or of religious liberty or of cooperation. All three represented various ways of speaking about the same issue.[31]

Murray vs. Fenton

It was likewise this subject of intercredal cooperation which brought Murray into open disagreement with Fenton. Fenton represented the "traditionalist position" from the very beginning, and his willingness to engage in open discussion with the more "progressive" position forced Murray to clarify his own thinking.

As we shall discuss more fully in a later chapter, Fenton represented a point of view radically opposed to that of Murray. The differences in mentality were reflected in each man's understanding of theological reflection, and its role in the life of the Church. It affected their respective views of the nature of the Church and its relationship to the world. In a study entitled, "Before and after Modernism: The Intellectual Isolation of the American Priest," Michael V. Gannon says of this period:

> It seems to be the consensus among Catholic leaders today . . . that the Church in the United States should never again revert to the "separatism" espoused earlier in the century by Cardinal William O'Connell, Archbishop of Boston (1859-1944), or the "state of siege" which Father Joseph Clifford Fenton . . . thought was a perennial necessity on the grounds that Catholicism and modern culture were inevitably opposed.[32]

Murray was clearly opposed to this mentality and as Gannon says: "Murray lived out his own definition of the Catholic intellectual as a 'missionary' to the thickening secularist intellectual and spiritual milieu."[33] For him the task of such a missionary was

> that of undertaking a comprehensive analysis of the present intel-
> lectual, cultural, and spiritual situation in its totality. If we are to
> interpret the world, as we must, even to itself, our first duty is to
> understand it, in detail, with full realism under abnegation of the
> easy generalities with which the world is ordinarily denounced.[34]

Drift toward Secularism

As we have already noted, it was especially the drift toward a secularist
humanism that led Murray to take such a strong and unrelenting stand in
favor of Christian cooperation. "Reversing the Secularist Drift," perhaps one
of Murray's best summaries of the actual world situation and of the crisis in
this nation, partially explains the reasons for his anxious concern. Numerous
references in his articles during this period pointed to a "present cultural and
spiritual crisis." He viewed the crisis as a "drift toward an atheism that consciously sets out to be 'positive, organic, constructive,' a dynamic anti-Chris-
tianity and anti-theism, built on destroying the traditional concept of man,
and setting in its place a positive new ideal—a humanism without God."[35]

Murray perceived the simultaneous need to understand the situation
and to find ways to confront it. The Catholic scholar's responsibility in the
face of this need was to undertake a comprehensive and fully realistic analysis
of the intellectual, cultural and spiritual situation, and then to expend every
effort to enlighten the Christian intelligence that it might find ways of over-
coming the error.

The New Nativism

On another level, but closely related to the rise of secularism, was the
emergence of what Murray termed "the New Nativism." Following World
War II there was a renewed wave of anti-Catholicism typified most promin-
ently by Paul Blanshard. The birth in 1947 of a nondenominational group
known as Protestants and Other Americans United for Separation of Church
and State (POAU) revived a number of the features of earlier waves of anti-
Catholic feeling. While this was a serious attack on the Church, it lacked
what one historian calls "the preoccupation with foreignness and native puri-
ty that had characterized earlier movements of this type."[36] But Blanshard's
books were permeated with anti-Catholic bias and vitiated by a secularist-sta-
tist philosophy that was far more dangerous than any of the things in American Catholicism to which his books had called attention.

A comparison of attempted rebuttals of Blanshard's position shows that
Murray brought a particularly keen insight to the deeper problem posed by
Blanshard. While numerous Catholic scholars worked at answering Blan-

shard point by point,[37] Murray went immediately to the heart of the problem. "The newness of the Nativism," he said, "is revealed by the fact that it is *not* now Protestant but naturalist. The primary accusation is that Catholicism is anti-American because America is a democracy and democracy is necessarily based on a naturalist or secularist philosophy."[38] For Murray, Blanshard's use of the terms "American" and "un-American" as categories of ultimate value was a significant indicator of the contemporary drift toward a cultural monism, of the exclusive acceptance of the democratic state, and of a colossal national self-righteousness.

A Public Debate

Murray's attack against the "new nativism" made national headlines with *Time* magazine's coverage of a debate between Murray and Dean Walter Russell Bowie of New York's Union Theological Seminary. In this debate which appeared in the September, 1949, issue of *American Mercury*,[39] Bowie voiced admiration over various aspects of Roman Catholicism, and especially its fight against secularism. Nevertheless, he expressed concern over the Protestant's obligation to "believe that the clearly stated Roman Catholic purpose 'to make America Catholic,' would jeopardize the religious and civil liberties which have been the glory of Protestant countries and of Protestant culture."[40] His fear arose from the Catholic Church's claim to "dominance, wherever it can assert and maintain its claims. . . . Roman Catholicism, according to its own view, is not part of that larger and un-stereotyped fellowship of the spirit which includes Christians of different names with the Church of Christ."[41] Rather, it views everyone outside of the fold of Rome as schismatics and representing error. Bowie cited a number of examples to support his fears, for example, the situations in Italy, Argentina, and Spain; the teaching of papal statements such as *Immortale Dei* and *The Syllabus of Errors* and recently stated positions of F. Cavalli in *Civiltà Cattolica* and Francis J. Connell's position in *The American Ecclesiastical Review*.[42]

Murray's reply characterized Bowie's position as "faithfully following the familiar (Protestant) formula, with a literary accent that is, of course, quite Union Theological Seminary rather than Southern Baptist or Boston Methodist."[43] Further, he accused Bowie of "generalizations," "historical nonsense," "theological nonsense," and "epistemological and ethical nonsense," and of ignoring the context of each example supposedly indicative of totalitarianism. He likened Bowie's cited instances to "the bone or two out of which the Sunday-supplement archaeologist constructs the museum-piece prehistoric monster. Only Dr. Bowie wants to exhibit a monster of the future . . . a 'Catholic America' . . . exactly like contemporary Catholic Spain. . . ."[44]

It is always a bit difficult to convince anyone that a bogeyman does not exist, and the difficulty is greater here because . . . Dr. Bowie does indeed have his few scattered bones. . . . What one would have to do, therefore, would be to prove that it is impossible or illegitimate to construct out of them his fearsome monster. . . . As a Catholic theologian who knows a bit about political history, I have more sense than to regard past Catholic documents on Church and State as so many crystal balls in which to discern the exact shape of things to come.[45]

Murray concluded with a prediction which in retrospect more or less outlined the theological work that would be his for years to come: "If I were to venture a prophecy, it would be that the development of the genuinely Catholic and democratic State will mean the end of the concept, 'religion of the State' (or the Spanish or Cavalli model), as the constitutional form in which the doctrinal idea of the 'freedom of the Church' has historically found its expression."[46]

Murray received from the editor of *American Mercury* fifty-two letters in response to the debate and a request to offer "an overall comment"—to this he wrote an unpublished reply. In his reply, Murray admitted that his attempt to maintain a "certain lightness of tone" in the controversy was missed by most readers. He added, however, that the whole subject—"like life itself—is much too serious to be taken too seriously." He expressed the inability to take Bowie's thesis of "the Catholic peril" too seriously.

I suggested, and am prepared to maintain, that Protestants take it so seriously because of the "anti-Roman bias" inherent in their position. . . . The peril of "a Catholic America" is a chimera; the real peril is . . . secularism, as represented by Blanshard. Men more learned than Blanshard have given (the New Nativism) a philosophical armature which they call evolutionary scientific humanism. Other men more practical than he are endeavoring to give it political expression in what I should call "our Holy Mother the State," almighty (by democratic means, of course), creator of all things visible and invisible, even the dignity of man. Here, I think is the enemy. . . . In the presence of this enemy I consider Catholic-Protestant polemic to be an irrelevance.

Murray also responded to the accusation that he had been evasive in refusing to argue the Church-State issue with Bowie. He stated:

On the matter of Catholic doctrine with regard to Church-State relationships I flatly refuse to be what is called "simple," because the subject, historically and doctrinally, is enormously complex. Padre Cavalli was "simple" in the article cited by Dr. Bowie; I reject his theory of "unblushing intolerance" as a ruthless simplification that distorts the truth by ignoring the whole political dimension of the problem. Other Catholic polemists are "simple" when they seem to assert that the whole issue is settled by the axiom, "Error has no rights." I reject this false simplicity; the axiom is at best politically inoperative (it settles nothing about governmental repression of error) and at worst ethically meaningless (it merely asserts that error is error). I likewise reject all simplistic interpretations, whether Catholic or Protestant, of the *Syllabus of Errors*, which is a notoriously difficult document, and of the utterances of Leo XIII whose doctrine is greatly complex and delicately adjusted to a special historical context. I reject the simplifications of Protestant polemists who allege the Golden Rule as singly decisive in the whole matter, or argue that an authoritarian Church cannot be reconciled with a democratic society, or who assert (as indeed do some Catholic apologists) that the constitutional concept, "religion of the State," on the Spanish model, represents a "Catholic ideal," necessarily to be realized by inherent exigence of Catholic faith wherever there is a Catholic majority.

I refuse therefore to sum it all up in a few words, however much I wish I could! This is not dishonesty, as one correspondent implies, but its reverse.[47]

Secularism and the American Hierarchy

Murray was not alone in expressing fears about the effects of the rising secularism in this country. The November, 1948, statement of the Catholic hierarchy of the United States issued by the Administrative Board of the National Catholic Welfare Conference, and entitled, "The Catholic in Action," called for constructive efforts by Christians against secularism, which it called "the most deadly menace to our Christian and American way of living."[48] Among other things, the bishops referred to the Everson and McCollum decisions of the Supreme Court and warned that "within the past two years secularism has scored unprecedented victories in its opposition to governmental encouragement of religious and moral training."[49]

According to the bishops, when the Supreme Court ruled that no American public school system could directly cooperate with private religious groups, the justices adopted "an entirely novel and ominously extensive interpretation of the 'establishment of religion' clause of the First Amendment."[50] The bishops saw this as contrary to the understanding of the framers of the Constitution who publicly expressed their firm conviction that "religion and morality are the strong supports of national well-being."[51] They also explicitly encouraged the establishment of schools to teach religion and morality as "necessary to good government."[52] Announcing that they would "peacefully, patiently, and perseveringly work" to reverse the court rulings, the bishops urged religious-minded lawyers to strive for ". . . a reaffirmation of our original American tradition of free cooperation between government and religious bodies—a cooperation involving no special privilege to any group and no restriction on the religious liberty of any citizens." Lest, through misunderstanding, anyone should take alarm at this declared purpose, the bishops add: "We solemnly disclaim any intent or desire to alter this prudent and fair American policy of government in dealing with the delicate problems that have their source in the divided religious allegiance of our citizens."[53]

By the end of the 1940s and the beginning of the 1950s clear lines had been drawn for the battle that would soon break. Disappointed by the general lack of interest shown by Catholic scholars as well as average Catholics who failed to respond to the call for intercredal cooperation, Murray turned to other aspects of the same issue. The question now became: are American democracy and Roman Catholicism compatible? This far more difficult issue of Church-State relations would now elicit all of Murray's time and effort. With the clarification of his thought, Murray maintained that the Vatican should not only accept the pluralistic situation in the United States, but should approve it as a new system good in itself.

Notes

1. Murray's doctoral dissertation was on Matthias Scheeben (1835-1888) and was entitled: "Matthias Joseph Scheeben's Doctrine on Supernatural Divine Faith." For an excerpt of Murray's work: "The Root of Faith: The Doctrine of M. J. Scheeben," *Theological Studies*, IX (March, 1948), pp. 20-46. (Hereinafter referred to as *TS*.)

2. According to the "Woodstock College Kalendarii" Murray taught every year with the exception of 1950-1952 and 1954-1955.

3. Michael V. Gannon, "Before and After Modernism: The Intellectual Isolation of the American Priest," in John T. Ellis, ed. *The Catholic Priest in the United States: Historical Investigations* (Collegeville: St. John's University Press, 1971), pp. 293-383.

4. *America*, "Comments" 63 (May 4, 1940), p. 87.

5. *America*, "Comments" 62 (March 9, 1940), p. 591.
6. John A. Ryan and Moorhouse F.X. Millar. *The State and the Church* (New York: The Macmillan Company, 1922), Ryan and Francis J. Boland. *Catholic Principles of Politics* (New York, Macmillan Company, 1940).
7. Murray to James P. Sweeney, S.J., provincial superior, March 17, 1943, Archives of the New York Province of the Society of Jesus. "It is not a romantic impulse," he added, "but the result of lengthy thought, the conclusion of which is neither black nor white—till you make it one or the other! The offer is not motivated simply by a consideration of the general needs of the men in the service, which are grave and challenging enough, but can be met by others as well or better qualified than I. My specific motive, suggested by some remarks of Father Assistant, is a sense of possible usefulness in Europe when occupied—usefulness not only to the Army but perhaps also to the Society and the Church. (For this reason, I am not interested in the Navy.) For such work I think I have some particular qualifications: the 'feel' one gets for Europe and its peoples through having been there, and an adequate command of German and Italian." Archives of the New York Province of the Society of Jesus will hereinafter be referred to as ANYP.
8. Murray to McQuade, April 22, 1946, ANYP.
9. Cushing to Murray, May 1, 1946, ANYP.
10. Murray to Cushing, May 4, 1946, ANYP.
11. *America*, LXXV (April 13, 1946), pp. 28-29.
12. Murray to McQuade, May 4, 1946, ANYP.
13. McQuade's reply to Murray is not available. It is through Murray's further reply to McQuade that one finds that the permission was not granted.
14. Murray to McQuade, May 8, 1946, ANYP.
15. The attitude revealed here is not as evident in Murray's later life. However, he always suffered from an inability to say "no." For this reason he frequently worked himself to exhaustion.
16. Rodger Van Allen. *The Commonweal and American Catholicism* (Philadelphia: Fortress Press, 1974), pp. 94-95.
17. Maher to Murray, April 22, 1945. Murray Papers, Woodstock College Archives. (Hereinafter referred to as WCA.)
18. Murray to Maher, April 30, 1945.
19. *Ibid.*
20. Murray to McQuade, February 20, 1947, ANYP.
21. Fenton, "The Theology of the Church and the State," *Proceedings of the Second Annual Meeting of the Catholic Theological Society of America.* Boston, 1947, p. 15.
22. Connell, "Discussion on 'Governmental Repression of Heresy,'" *Proceedings of the Third Annual Meeting of the Catholic Theological Society of America.* Chicago, 1948, p. 100.
23. Murray made reference to the work of Jacques Maritain, "The Achievement of Cooperation among Men of Different Creeds." *Journal of Religion,* XXI (1941), and that of W. Butterfield, "Cooperation with non-Catholics," *Clergy Review,* XXII (1942). The influence of both of these individuals, particularly Maritain, is evident in Murray's thinking on the subject of cooperation.
24. Murray, "Christian Cooperation: Current Theology," *TS,* III (September, 1942), p. 414. The original quote can be found in: Connell, "Catholics and 'Interfaith' Groups," *The American Ecclesiastical Review,* CV (November, 1941), pp. 336-353. (Hereinafter referred to as *AER.*)

25. "The Catholic, Jewish, Protestant Declaration on World Peace" is published in excerpt in *Verbum* (Guatemala), Tuesday, January 9, 1945, as "La Cooperación Interconfessional Para la Paz." The U.S. publication appears as an appendix to "The Pattern for Peace and the Papal Peace Program," a pamphlet of the Catholic Association for International Peace, Washington, D.C., 32 pp., prepared by Murray and the Ethics committee of the Association. The Declaration was also published in *Vida: Revista de Orientación*, VII (1944), pp. 757-71. In his letter to Father McQuade, May 4, 1946, in which Murray requested to organize the youth project, there also was a request to attend a conference on religious liberty, which was to be held at Oxford, England, in August, 1946, under the joint sponsorship of the British Council of Christians and Jews and the American National Conference of Christian and Jews. The United States organization had offered to send Murray as its representative. Murray admitted being uncertain about the advisability of going, partly because "I know very well the Archdiocesan attitude in N.Y. toward the NCCJ (I don't think it is highly intelligent, but there it is)." He also wondered about the English hierarchy's attitude toward the conference. Apparently the provincial had refused this permission; Murray to McQuade, May 8, 1946, ANYP said: "I have no trouble in relinquishing all thought of the Oxford conference of Christians and Jews. In honesty, I should add that, unlike yourself, I have a certain sympathy with the project; moreover, I have no sympathy at all with the unintelligent attitude of the N.Y. Chancery. However, I see the practical difficulties. . . ."

26. Murray, "Christian Co-operation, Current Theology," p. 416.

27. *Ibid.*

28. *Ibid.* With regard to Murray's views on education of the laity, cf. "Towards a Theology For the Layman: The Problem of Its Finality," *TS*, V (March, 1944), pp. 43-75; "Towards a Theology for the Layman: The Pedagogical Problem," *TS*, V (September, 1944), pp. 340-76. In "Theology and Religion," *AER*, CXII (June, 1945), pp. 447-63, Joseph C. Fenton disagreed with Murray on special courses for laymen in theology, p. 462.

29. For further articles on the subject by Murray: "Cooperation: Some Further Views," *TS*, IV (March, 1943), pp. 100-111; "Intercredal Cooperation: Its Theory and Organization," *TS*, IV (June, 1943), pp. 257-86; exchange of letters with Father Paul Furfey, *TS*, IV (September, 1943), pp. 467-72; *Intercredal Cooperation*, Papers by Wilfred Parsons, S.J. and J.C. Murray, and the Ethics Committee (Catholic Association for International Peace, 1944); "On the Problem of Cooperation: Some Clarifications," *AER*, CXII (March, 1945), pp. 194-214. This last article is a reply to Furfey's: "Intercredal Cooperation: Its Limitations," *AER*, CXI (September, 1944), pp. 161-75. It is in this reply to Furfey that Murray suggested dropping the use of the term "intercredal," since some have objected to it. "It was my own coinage, *faute de mieux*; in order to avoid verbal disputes, I no longer use the term; if anyone can find a better term, we could agree to adopt it," p. 194. A further article by Furfey: "Why Does Rome Discourage Socio-Religious Intercredalism?" *AER*, CXII (May, 1945), pp. 364-74. Also: Francis J. Connell, "Answers to Questions: The National Conference of Christians and Jews," *AER*, CXXXI (October, 1949), pp. 341-42. Finally three articles by J. C. Fenton: "The Catholic and the Church," *AER*, CXIII (November, 1945), pp. 377-84, esp. p. 383; "The Church and the World," *AER*, CIXX (September, 1948), pp. 202-14, esp. p. 211ff.; "Factors in Church Unity," *AER*, CXIX (November, 1948); pp. 375-83, esp. pp. 382-83.

30. F. J. Connell, "Pope Leo XIII's Message to America," *AER*, CIX (October, 1943), pp. 254-55.

31. Murray, "Fredom of Religion, I: The Ethical Problem," *TS*, VI (June, 1945), pp. 229-86 and "The Problem of State Religion," *TS*, XII (June, 1951), pp. 155-78. See also Thomas T. Love. *John Courtney Murray: Contemporary Church-State Theory* (New York: Doubleday, 1965), pp. 40-41. The latter is a published dissertation in political science from Princeton University by a Protestant theologian. Love examines Murray's writings on the subject of Church and State, considered in chronological order as a gradually developing theory, in the context of contemporary criticism and contrary statement of theory within the Catholic community. He assigns three stages to the development: The first period was one of dissatisfaction with the adequacy of current Catholic formulations, 1942-46. The second period was one of criticism of the so-called conservative position and some constructive effort, 1948-49. During the final period Murray systematically restated and defended his view, 1951-54. While the study is impressive it overlooks the development and maturity that took place in Murray's thinking between 1956-60 and finally during the Council years. Nevertheless it provides a framework in which to study Murray's political thought from an historical and theological point of view.

32. In John Tracy Ellis, ed. *The Catholic Priest in the United States: Historical Investigations* (Collegeville: St. John's University Press, 1971), p. 363. See J. C. Fenton, "The Church and the State of Siege," *AER*, LX (January, 1945), pp. 54-63. "The Church, the City of God, has always been, and until the end of time will be beset by enemies. . . . She has always been perfectly correct in judging the mass of mankind outside the fold as hostile to her interests," p. 63.

33. Gannon, in Ellis, *The Catholic Priest in the United States*, p. 362.

34. Murray, "Reversing the Secularist Drift," *Thought*, XXIV (March, 1949), p. 37.

35. *Ibid.*, p. 36.

36. David J. O'Brien. *The Renewal of American Catholicism* (New York: Oxford University Press, 1972), p. 114; Paul Blanshard. *American Freedom and Catholic Power* (Boston: Beacon Press, 1951); *Communism, Democracy, and Catholic Power* (Boston: Beacon Press, 1951); *The Irish and Catholic Power* (Boston: Beacon Press, 1953).

37. Everett R. Clinchy, president of the National Conference of Christians and Jews, "A Letter in Answer to Paul Blanshard," *America* (May 7, 1949), p. 200; Francis J. Connell, C.SS.R., "Review of 'American Freedom and Catholic Power,'" *Cornell Law Quarterly* (Spring, 1950), pp. 196-98; George H. Dunne, "Paul Blanshard and the Catholic Church": I—"Preface to Criticism," *America*, LXXXI (June 4, 1949), pp. 309-11; II—"The Great Catholic Conspiracy" (June 11, 1949), pp. 339-41; III—"Church and Democracy" (June 18, 1949), pp. 359-61; IV—"Catholic Schools" (June 25, 1949), pp. 379-81; V—"Church and Medicine" (July 16, 1949), pp. 438-40; VI—"The Church and Science" (July 23, 1949), pp. 459-61; VII "Church and State" (July 30, 1949), pp. 477-79; Robert C. Hartnett, S.J., "Debate With Blanshard," *Catholic Mind*, XLVIII (May, 1950), pp. 262-70; Will Herberg, "Review of 'American Freedom and Catholic Power,'" *Commentary* (August, 1949), pp. 235, 265.

On answering Blanshard "officially," a series of exchanges between Francis Cardinal Spellman of New York and Monsignor Giovanni B. Montini (Pope Paul VI) then at the Vatican Secretariat of State can be found in the Spellman Papers, Archives of the Archdiocese of New York, Saint Joseph's Seminary, Dunwoodie, Yonkers, New York. Not all the correspondence is available, but the following will provide information about the hierarchy's concern over Blanshard. In a letter to Montini on May 22, 1953, Spellman writes: "In further reference to our correspondence beginning with my letter of February 7th which your Excellency answered on March 12th and regarding which I commented in my letter to you of April 17th concerning the matter of answering attacks on the Holy See, I am enclosing herewith an article which appears in the *Christian Century* by Paul Blanshard entitled 'The Case of Archbishop O'Hara.'

"Since Mr. Blanshard makes very specific points I should like to refute him point by point and would appreciate your assistance." Montini replied on June 8, 1953: "I am authorized to inform Your Eminence that the laudable intention manifested by refuting the statements made in this article is appreciated by His Holiness. . . . It is felt, however, in view of the past history and known dispositions of the person in question, that entering into a controversy with a writer of this kind, thereby giving him further importance and publicity, would be of doubtful value at this time; and would in all likelihood bring about a new attack upon the Church, with the rallying again of its adversaries to his support. The remedy will be that of avoiding the nomination of American ecclesiastics as representatives of the Holy See. . . ."

Spellman's reply to Montini, July 27, 1953, thanks him for his letter ". . . in which you counsel me not to reply to Paul Blanshard's attack on the Church. We have had a distinguished layman, Mr. O'Neill, reply to him in the Christian Century. . . ." James N. O'Neill. *Catholicism and American Freedom* (New York: Harper & Brothers, 1952) is a detailed refutation of Blanshard. He was apparently chosen to give the "official" reply to the Blanshard attacks. Professor O'Neill was the chairman of the Department of Speech at Brooklyn College, and also author of: *Religion and Education under the Constitution* (New York: Harper & Brothers, 1949).

38. Murray, "Paul Blanshard and the New Nativism," *The Month*, 191 (April, 1951), p. 216.

39. "Across the Gulf," *Time*, September 12, 1949; Rev. W. Russell Bowie, "Protestant Concern Over Catholicism," *American Mercury*, LXIX (September, 1949), pp. 261-73; Murray, "The Catholic Position—A Reply," pp. 274-83.

40. Bowie, "Protestant Concern Over Catholicism," p. 262.

41. *Ibid.*

42. Bowie is referring to F. Cavalli, "La Condizione dei Protestanti in Spagna," *La Civiltà Cattolica*, II (April, 1948), pp. 29-47. I quote in full Bowie's excerpt from this article because it reveals the position held by the official Church in Rome and the reason for concern by Protestants here in the United States: "The Roman Catholic Church, convinced, through its divine prerogatives, of being the only true church, must demand the right to freedom for herself alone, because such a right can only be possessed by truth, never by error. As to other religions, the Church will certainly never draw the sword, but she will require that by legitimate means they shall not be allowed to propagate false doctrine. Consequently, in a State where the majority of the people are Catholic, the Church will require that legal existence be denied to error, and that if religious minorities actually exist, they shall have only a *de facto* existence, without opportunity to spread their beliefs. If, however, actual circumstances . . . make the complete application of this principle impossible, then the Church will require for herself all possible concessions. . . .

In some countries, Catholics will be obliged to ask full religious freedom for all, resigned at being forced to cohabitate where they alone should rightfully be allowed to live. But in doing this the Church does not renounce her thesis . . . but merely adapts herself. . . . Hence arises the great scandal among Protestants. . . . We ask Protestants to understand that the Catholic Church would betray her trust if she were to proclaim . . . that error can have the same rights as truth. . . . The Church cannot blush for her own want of tolerance, as she asserts it in principle and applies it in practice"; Bowie, "Protestant Concern Over Catholicism," p. 264. Bowie's reference to Connell is "Preserving the Faith Inviolate," *AER*, CXIV (January, 1946), pp. 34-47.

43. Murray, "The Catholic Position—A Reply," p. 274.

44. *Ibid.*, p. 281.

45. *Ibid.* As far as Murray is concerned it is not possible to prove Bowie's position by quoting from Cavalli's article, "a tag or two from Leo XIII, a proposition from the *Syllabus*, a fragment from a Spanish catechism ..." p. 281. Just ten years later when Murray is seeking permission from his superiors to publish an article on his position in *La Civiltà Cattolica* he makes reference to Cavalli's article: "You may remember that most curiously dreadful article in the *Civiltà* in 1948 that was widely publicized as official Catholic doctrine. Its most wonderful tenet was that Catholics alone have the right to exist and that they allow others to coexist with them only when they are forced to do so. I wonder if the editors still hold this view. And if they don't, I further wonder if perhaps they do not owe a debt to the world to say so, in some fashion!" Murray to Vincent McCormick, S.J., July 22, 1958, WCA.

46. Murray, "The Catholic Position—A Reply," p. 282.

47. "Letter to the Editor of *American Mercury*," September 9, 1949, WCA.

48. *Catholic Action*, XXX (December, 1948), p. 3.

49. *Ibid.*, p. 14.

50. *Ibid.*

51. *Ibid.*, p. 13.

52. *Ibid.*

53. *Ibid.*, p. 15. Murray evidently was influential in helping NCWC work out a clear position on this complex issue. In a letter to Very Rev. Ferdinand C. Wheeler, of Woodstock College, December 3, 1947, Archbishop John T. McNicholas of Cincinnati expressed gratitude for Murray's valuable contribution: "On behalf of the Administrative Board of The National Catholic Welfare Conference, I wish to express our gratitude for your kindness in permitting Father John Courtney Murray, S.J., to assist our Education and Legal Departments in the preparation of briefs for the Everson and Champaign cases. Father Murray has been most generous in his cooperation with the members of our staff, and has contributed substantially to our success in developing a working principle of Church and State in educational matters. His scholarly analysis of Church-State relations is acknowledged by our staff as a valuable contribution toward winning the Everson decision.

As the Church-State issue continues to be a matter of considerable concern to the Welfare Conference, we shall have further need of Father Murray's services during the coming months. Please be assured that we shall be most grateful for your continued kindness in permitting Father Murray to meet from time to time with the members of our staff"; WCA. Archbishop McNicholas was probably the foremost leader and subscriber of the Murray position on Church-State relations. See: McNicholas, "The Catholic Church in American Democracy," Press Release (Washington: National Catholic Welfare Conference, 1948).

2

Opposition and Rebuke:
1950-1959

For American Catholics, as for the country at large, perhaps the most divisive force of the 1950s was the anti-Communist campaign led by Senator Joseph R. McCarthy, a Catholic from Wisconsin, and an alumnus of Marquette University in Milwaukee. McCarthy's public charges of treason against the State Department and his attack on civil liberties won significant support among Catholics in many of the large cities of the nation.

A speedy switch from alliance with Russia to militant hostility toward Communism characterized the period after the Second World War both here and abroad. The Church had long been an opponent of Communism and would now play a significant role in the development of the Cold War. In the minds of many Catholics, tired of having their true Americanism and patriotism challenged, McCarthy provided an occasion to show that they were as authentically American and patriotic as they were Catholic.

Catholics were nearly as divided over McCarthy as the rest of the nation. While a larger percentage of Catholics favored McCarthy than did Protestants, and while Catholic McCarthyites outnumbered Catholic anti-McCarthyites, the Senator's Catholic strength was not as great as it often seemed. According to Donald F. Crosby, S.J., a large body of Catholics remained passive, indifferent, and only intermittently involved in the controversy. The Catholics who were deeply committed for him or against him were always small minorities. Furthermore, Catholic opinion on McCarthy rose and fell in exact conjunction with his national popularity, thus indicating that Catholic opinion tended to follow that of the rest of the country. In elections during this period, Catholics tended to vote their party, not their religion. The division in Catholic ranks extended to the press, Catholic universities, and the hierarchy.

For the most part, the Catholic debate over McCarthy occurred mostly on an elite level, with Catholic editors, politicians, clerics, writers, businessmen, and educators, carrying on most of the argument. With the exception of *Commonweal* and *America* magazines, the Catholic press was generally unanimously in support of McCarthy throughout the 1950-1954 period. In dealing with Communist action in the Cold War, *Commonweal*, for instance, sought a middle way between the careless smearing of honest liberals and ignoring the dangers of Communist infiltration.

Intensifying the fierce war of rhetoric between the Catholic McCarthyites and their opponents was the tendency of both sides to appeal to patriotism to support their theses. According to Crosby, the controversy worsened relations between Catholics and Protestants, many of whom feared that Catholics were "using" McCarthy to put them at a disadvantage. The activities of the Catholic McCarthyites, meanwhile, reinforced the belief of many American liberals that Catholics were illiberal, anti-civil libertarian, and undemocratic.[1] The result of McCarthyism was that it "rekindled the specter of a monolithic Catholic bloc."[2]

While Murray was himself not publicly involved in the McCarthy debate, he expressed to a friend: "I sometimes think that even our opposition to Communism lacks the depths and the seriousness and the intellectual appreciation of the issues involved which would be altogether desirable."[3]

Some years later Murray wondered whether "we prove our Americanism and our Catholicism simply by being vociferously anti-Communist." "In an anxiety to 'prove' our Americanism and our Catholicism," he questioned, "have we simplified the problem of the United States down to the problem of internal subversion by Communists, especially in our universities?"[4] For Murray the more positive task was for the American to learn the inner principles of American institutions, their public philosophy. And he seriously questioned whether Americans were "spiritually and intellectually equipped to meet the Communist threat at its deepest level."[5] He called our engagement with Communism on the domestic scene a "basic fiasco." "The anti-Communist movement, centering on the issue of internal subversion, probably compounded the confusion by transforming issues of stupidity into issues of 'disloyalty.'" And he added: "Whatever its effect on public emotion, the anti-Communist movement has been fairly spectacular in its failure to contribute to public understanding."[6]

> . . . The issue of Communism, if I understand it at all, is an issue first, of understanding, and secondly of action based upon understanding. Moreover, all this tribal cultivation of loyalty leads to a

stupidity that is itself dangerous. I mean the stupidity of mistaking the real domestic issue. Who is the real enemy within the gates of the city?

I suggest that the real enemy within the gates of the city is not the Communist, but the idiot.

Here Murray was using the word "idiot" not in its customary, contemporary vernacular usage of one who is mentally deficient. Rather he was going back to the primitive Greek usage where the idiot meant, first of all, the private person, and then came to mean the man who does not possess the public philosophy, the man who is not master of the knowledge and the skills that underlie the life of the civilized city. The idiot, to the Greek, was just one stage removed from the barbarian. He was the man who was ignorant of the meaning of the word "civility." In this context, Murray asked:

What is our contemporary idiocy? What is the enemy within the city? If I had to give it a name, I think I would call it "technological secularism." The idiot today is the technological secularist who knows everything. He's the man who knows everything about the organization of all the instruments and techniques of power that are available in the contemporary world and who, at the same time, understands nothing about the nature of man or about the nature of true civilization.

And if this country is to be overthrown from within or from without, I would suggest that it will not be overthrown by Communism. It will be overthrown because it will have made an impossible experiment. It will have undertaken to establish a technological order of most marvelous intricacy, which will have been constructed and will operate without relations to true political ends; and this technological order will hang, as it were, suspended over a moral confusion; and this moral confusion will itself be suspended over a spiritual vacuum. This would be the real danger, resulting from a type of fallacious, fictitious, fragile unity that could be created among us.[7]

Thus during the fifties, Catholic liberals like Murray and John Cogley of *Commonweal* would have to show that the American Church possessed a wide variety of attitudes, especially on political and social issues. O'Brien is correct when he asserts that "these men tried to offer reasonable arguments for the Catholic position on outstanding issues" as aid to parochial schools, birth control, censorship, Communism, "however irrational or unseemingly the partisanship and polemics of other Catholics might be."[8]

In particular, there was the important need of correcting the non-Catholic image of the Church and of promoting among Catholics a sense of authentic American values. According to Cogley: "At least we were trying to take those values which are American values—e.g. civil liberties, the Bill of Rights, the separation of Church and State—and to offer a rationale for them which would be comfortable to Catholic doctrine."[9]

But, as we shall see, McCarthy's fear of alien liberal ideas in American politics was paralleled by the Vatican's fear of new and liberal ideas in Roman Catholicism. The attempt on the part of liberals like Murray and Cogley to work out "the conformity between Catholicism as a religious philosophy and what might be called in a good sense 'Americanism' as a political commitment"[10] was bound to provoke suspicion and hostility from reactionaries like McCarthy and his counterparts in Rome.

Because of this the 1950s brought Murray both fame and trouble. In particular, he argued vigorously that America's brand of Church-State relations was actually more consistent with the best in Catholic political theory than the Church's ancient claims to preferred status. In so doing, he attracted "suspicion" in Roman quarters. His published works on Church and State began to draw the first "warnings" from conservative churchmen who feared the freedom, pluralism, and openness of his views.[11] At the same time he was being accepted at home and abroad as a speculative theologian of the first magnitude. His expertise earned him the admiration of his academic peers. Invitations to lecture came from government agencies, and from Yale, Harvard, Brown, and other major non-Catholic universities.

Invitation to Germany

In 1950, when McCarthy was just beginning his attack on the State Department, Murray was named consultant for the United States government in the Public Affairs Section of the Office of the U.S. High Commissioner of Germany. In March, he was invited to spend three months there to "explain to the Germans how Church-State relations should be arranged in a democracy"![12] In seeking permission for the project, Murray characterized it as worth pursuing since it would benefit him immensely by providing him with an opportunity to pursue studies in the field of Church and State. He added: "I shall strenuously endeavor to do no positive harm!"[13]

Murray's name had been recommended to the State Department by the National Catholic Welfare Conference in the belief that participation by Catholics in such programs would be in the best interests of the Church. The State Department and the High Commissioner would thereby be encouraged to cooperate with the authorities of the Catholic Church in Germany. The project included visits to the German bishops, lectures or conferences at major Catholic seminaries in the three Länder, and conferences with German leaders connected with the formation of the Western German State. The State Department hoped that, as an American, Murray might represent and interpret to American authorities the German and Catholic points of view on Church-State relationships. Murray's report, summarizing his activities, was sent to the State Department on his return.[14]

The Yale Professorship

In September, 1951, Murray became Visiting Professor of Philosophy at Yale University. Emmet John Hughes considered this year as one of the most important experiences in Murray's life. "As the first Catholic priest to be so honored, he shattered all precedent—and some prejudice—by spending the year . . . at Yale University. It was a period when he rejoiced in his self-appointed labor of proving that Catholic learning could stand tall beside secular learning in America. . . ."[15]

Other scholars who were there at the time reflected on his qualities and on the enthusiasm with which he was received at Yale. George A. Lindbeck, who was Murray's graduate assistant during that year, recalled:

I remember especially how he agonized over a series of public lectures which he gave. . . . But what I remember best is seeing him in his undershirt after a night largely spent getting ready for a lecture, tense yet courtly, driven by a perfectionist urge, and trapped by his own difficulty in scheduling his work into a major loss of sleep.[16]

James Shannon, former auxiliary bishop of St. Paul, Minnesota, who was a graduate student at Yale in those years wrote:

In that period, I came to know personally his great kindness, his enormous erudition, his wholeness as a person, and his subtle, perceptive, often devastating wit. One of the fringe benefits of that year of grace was the pure pleasure of evening long conversations in his home on campus. Students, professors, writers, visitors, newsmen came to see him, to listen, to learn and to be refreshed and encouraged by his wisdom, his compassion and his great courtesy. The young priests and other scholars who sought his counsel, academic and otherwise, always found him helpful and generous with his time and talent.[17]

An examination of the correspondence between Yale and Murray and between Murray and his superiors provides information as to why Murray had been chosen for this position as well as the important implications seen

by him in this appointment. For years Yale had been searching for a professor of medieval philosophy and had made countless efforts to attract Etienne
Gilson to the post. Gilson, however, had pledged his remaining years to the
Medieval Institute at Toronto. In view of this, Yale turned to Murray. To
maintain the appointment in line with Murray's work at the time, Charles
W. Hendel, Chairman of the Department of Philosophy, suggested the
broader topic of "Medieval Philosophy and Culture." "You have done work
of which we know the great value, on the relation of Church and State in the
medieval period. . . . What we want from you . . . is whatever you are
yourself studying and writing about that is itself of general interest."[18]

A few days after receiving the invitation from Hendel, Murray contacted his provincial superior, informing him of the invitation but without indicating any preference for or against acceptance. "I have not," he wrote,
"been able to consider all the aspects of the matter."[19] The lengthy memorandum that followed but a few days later, however, indicated Murray's
great interest in the appointment and presented the reasons why Murray felt
the invitation should be accepted.

In a rather curious departure from the enthusiasm he showed concerning the appointment, Murray wrote to John Tracy Ellis on September 3,
1951:

> Actually, this Yale job is not one that I myself particularly wanted,
> since it carries me rather out of my own field; I cannot in any
> sense pretend to be a professional Philosopher. However, it seemed
> necessary to accept the invitation, and I shall endeavor to do no
> positive harm!

And in another letter addressed to Monsignor Joseph Fenton, September 4,
1951, Murray said: "Personally, I did not want the job, but it was judged
best that I should accept the invitation."[20]

In a list of reasons in favor of an affirmative response that he addressed
to his provincial John J. McMahon, he expressed continuing interest in the
need for the Church to work closely with secular society. Admitting the unusual nature of the offer, he feared that a refusal would mean the defeat of
the goodwill effort on the part of Yale University. More importantly he saw
the "apostolic opportunity involved in this appointment" as the principal
reason for an affirmative answer to the request. He wrote to McMahon:

> I am myself convinced that there is great need today for this par-
> ticular type of intellectual apostolate within the secular University.
> The moment is one of crisis. It has been discovered that there has

taken place a great "treason of the clerks" within the University. This has created a new openness to Catholic Philosophy and Faith. On the other hand, there has been a hardening of the naturalist opposition to the Catholic Faith. This is particularly evident in the effort to portray the Church as the "totalitarianism of the right," balanced by Communism, "the totalitarianism of the Left." (Witness the success of Mr. Blanshard's book *Communism, Catholicism and Democracy.*) At this juncture a Catholic priest can do a special work in the secular University.

He recognized the fact that the offer was given to him personally because he was known at Yale. Refusal would mean the loss of a major opportunity for himself and for the Church. In addition, he felt personally prepared for this kind of work.

I have exercised this type of apostolate on occasion and have acquired a sense of the mentality. For this kind of work there is needed a man who is not simply a technical philosopher, but also a theologian, and one acquainted with contemporary aspirations and currents of thought. Many things that I have done have equipped me in this sense. I am confident that I could handle the job adequately.

To reinforce his already clearly stated opinion that the Church ought to be at work in secular society he added: "I would like to emphasize the fact that the 'absence' of the Church from the American secular University is something of a scandal. One might hope that the example of Yale would be followed by other Universities and a new and valuable field of teaching opened to the Church." While admitting that the appointment would mean a temporary change of "careers," Murray characterized his present "career" as "already ambiguous, inasmuch as I am half-scholar and half-operator." But the new position would provide the occasion to pursue his interests in the area of Church and State. Since the graduate teaching would be done on medieval political theory, or on the Church-State problem in the Middle Ages, he saw the offer as an opportunity to perfect his knowledge in his own field.

One year at Yale University would give me an experience much more valuable for the work that I want to do, especially in the field of Church-State relationship, than in teaching in a Catholic Graduate School, because it would be an opportunity to acquaint myself at first hand with opinions in this field and the attitude to the Church's doctrine entertained by non-Catholic seculars.[21]

The only personal evaluation that can be found of Murray's year at Yale appears in a letter to Vincent McCormick, S.J., American assistant at the Jesuit Generalate in Rome. "I have returned from the land of the infidel without doing any serious harm (I hope). What good was done it is hard to say. One cannot measure such things as that. However, all in all, it was a useful experience for me, and I believe that my sheer presence in that environment was of some value."[22]

The Church-State Debate

Soon after his return to Woodstock from Yale, Murray began a systematic formulation and defense of his position on Church and State. His articles in various journals on Church-State relations became more frequent. Particularly important were four major articles in *Theological Studies* that provided a thorough analysis of Pope Leo XIII's position on the subject.

These writings were to bring increasingly more serious rebukes from such conservative centers as the Holy Office in Rome, the Apostolic Delegation in Washington, and the Catholic University of America. The Church-State controversy is extremely important in that it gives us an insight into the clash on methods and ecclesiologies prevalent in Europe and America at that time. By 1955, it brought on Murray's submission to strict censorship and the abandonment of any further writing on Church-State matters.

An analysis of the correspondence between Murray and his Jesuit superiors in Rome, J. C. Fenton and John Tracy Ellis, is enlightening in that it provides unpublished answers to a number of questions. Who was responsible for Murray's being silenced? What was the real point of contention? Was Murray actually considered a heretic in Rome? Finally, an examination of Murray's attitude during these years gives a clearer picture of his personal character.

The first piece of important correspondence available that reflects the kind of relationship Murray would have with his immediate Jesuit superiors in Rome is dated April 24, 1951. Significantly the topic of the letter is *Humani generis*.[23]

"Delighted" by the praise from the superior general of Father Cyril Vollert's *Theological Studies* article on *Humani generis*, Murray reported that "here in the United States, among Catholics and also to some extent among non-Catholics, this Papal utterance has commanded more attention than any others certainly within my memory."[24] Murray also confessed some displeasure with the forthcoming article on the background of the encyclical by Father Gustave Weigel,[25] but believed "he is entitled to have his say." He inquired from McCormick about what

happened to the memorandum that I wrote Msgr. Montini on the

Church-State Problem. My only information was that it had been called to the attention of the Holy Father by Msgr. Montini himself, and had been committed to the hands of "experts." Heaven help it, and me. . . . If you should chance to hear any rumors or rumblings about it, I would of course be glad to be informed.[26]

Finally, Murray reported that two of his articles were forthcoming in *The American Ecclesiastical Review* in answer to the "superficial" article of "last September." "The first attempts to sketch, only in outline, the theory that I think might be regarded as tenable. The second will deal specifically with Leo XIII."[27]

Disturbed by Murray's comment on Weigel's article, McCormick wrote that "In such a controverted question and after the supreme authority has spoken, there can be only one 'say.' "[28] He also suggested that Murray save Weigel from "any vagaries of an over-sympathetic heart."[29] A few weeks later Murray responded and gave assurances in regard to Weigel that he will "be most careful" and that the superior general's letter on the encyclical "will be accepted with complete loyalty, as the guide of our thinking."[30]

Correspondence with Joseph C. Fenton[31]   1930594

Outside of an annual report on *Theological Studies* and a brief evaluation of his Yale project in the same letter,[32] Murray did not correspond again with McCormick until August, 1953. His personal correspondence with Fenton began in August, 1951. Ten letters span the months from August 16, 1951, to June 5, 1953. The initial 1951 exchange was angry and tense. Murray sent Fenton a reply to a Connell article demanding no "editor's comment" if it is published.[33] Fenton scorned the "lofty lecture" of Murray's letter and deplored his running of the second part of his reply to Shea on "The Problem of State Religion," in *Theological Studies* rather than in *The American Ecclesiastical Review*.[34]

Murray's exchanges with Fenton ceased while he was at Yale, September, 1951-June, 1952. But in the summer of 1952 an article by Gustave Weigel, "The Church and the Democratic State" appeared in *Thought* discussing the two principal theories of Church-State relations.[35] Weigel's characterization of Fenton and his associates as the "static expositors" as opposed to Murray's position as representative of the "dynamic expositors" did not help to clear up what initially appeared to have been but a "misunderstanding."

On April 4, 1953, Fenton derided Murray's effort to make him a "whipping boy" in the controversy. He referred to the *Thought* article by Weigel as "irresponsibly vicious and mendacious" and expressed strong disapproval of "the inexcusably false charges" made by the editor of *America* "last Fall" in his comments on the publication of the Holy Office letter, "compelling" a reply by Fenton in *The American Ecclesiastical Review* of October, 1952.[36]

In April, 1953, Murray was hospitalized for what was diagnosed as "extreme fatigue, rooted in a cardiac insufficiency."[37] After his release from the Mercy Hospital in Baltimore, Murray was ordered to take an indefinite period of rest. It lasted until September of that year. In April, May, and June, 1953, months which coincided with Murray's illness, the last exchanges between him and Fenton suddenly soften into "Dear John" and "Dear Joe." On April 11, Murray suggested to Fenton that it "would be readily possible to clear up whatever misunderstandings have arisen. They distress me and I should like to do away with them." He added:

> It may well be that I write in a somewhat abrupt and at times perhaps careless fashion, and this may contribute somewhat to misunderstandings and bad impression. I shall be in touch with you later about the possibility of a meeting. For the moment . . . let me say that I had no desire to make you any sort of "whipping boy." My only intention is to get things straight. And I had most certainly no intention of being personal in any bad sense. If my letter was hurtful, I offer you my apologies.[38]

Fenton replied on April 17 expressing the desire "to meet soon," saying:

> It will be a pleasure to sit around and laugh at a correspondence which, in retrospect, looks anything but edifying or even serious.
>
> Looking back on it, I suppose I was terribly nettled, and that I showed it in my first reply to you. I have horror of printed controversies between priests, especially when these controversies tend to be personal. The bitter personal attacks against me in *Thought* and in *America* were distressing to me, but not half as distressing as my own reply to the editor of *America*, a reply which I was compelled to make.
>
> A printed charge that I misrepresented your teaching would be equally disagreeable, especially since it is completely evident that such a charge would be absolutely untrue. If, however, such a charge does appear, I shall have to face it, without rancor or bitterness.[39]

Presumably by odd coincidence, Murray began his correspondence with John Tracy Ellis in June, 1953, precisely when he ended his two-year exchange with Fenton.[40]

Ellis was at this time managing editor of *The Catholic Historical Review* at the Catholic University of America while Fenton edited *The American Ecclesiastical Review*. The correspondence shows that Ellis was as much in sympathy with Murray as Fenton was not. The exchanges are noteworthy in that they reflect Murray's sanguine expectations with regard to Rome, despite Alfredo Cardinal Ottaviani's speech on Church-State relations on the previous March 2, 1953; his lack of hope in the American bishops, including what Ellis always called "Chicago" (Samuel Cardinal Stritch); and his optimistic reaction to Pope Pius XII's important address, *Ci riesce*, given to a group of jurists and dated December 6, 1953. This address directly set the stage for the bold speech delivered by Murray at the Catholic University of America on March 25, 1954.

On June 25, 1953, Ellis wrote to Murray and praised him for an article which appeared in the June, 1953, issue of *Theological Studies*.[41] He referred to it as a "magnificent" and "masterly synthesis of Leo XIII's thought" and the "strikingly new—at least for me—interpretations which are drawn from it."[42] On July 13 Murray replied with a reference to Ottaviani's speech:[43]

> The discourse by Cardinal Ottaviani in the spring may possibly precipitate something in Rome. As you doubtless know, it was a purely private utterance, possessing no official significance, either formal or informal. Moreover, I have it on the highest authority that our Holy Father was not pleased by the discourse, and did not consider that it represented the true and full mind of the Church. It is a curious thing that the views that I have tentatively put forward have been received with more sympathy in theological circles in Europe than in the United States.[44]

Ellis responded with delight to the heartening news from Murray and expressed hope that some outward indication would be given from Rome to offset the impression left by Ottaviani's March speech. He also enclosed a "reaction of Michael Cardinal Browne, O.P. to the 1948 statement of Archbishop McNicholas," and commented: "It certainly would not improve our position if this were made public."[45] Ellis likewise enclosed an article he had written for *Harper's Magazine*[46] and in view of the Ottaviani speech deliberately withheld from publication, fearing he might "do the cause more harm than good if I went ahead." Now he asked Murray for criticism and advice on it. On July 20, Murray called the article "Very Good" while he honestly expressed to Ellis his feelings about the lack of leadership from the American bishops: "The curious thing is that we no longer seem to have any American Catholic bishops—like Carroll, England, Hughes, Ireland, et al. Now they are all Roman Catholics—You will rightly understand what I mean."[47] In trying to explain the reason for some of the hedging, Murray explained that Archbishop McNicholas's statement was not well received "in 'Rome,' i.e., a certain part of Rome." He added "The subject came up in a conversation I had with Msgr. Montini in Rome in 1950. He was personally sympathetic with my 'orientations' and rather wanted his hand to be strengthened— but . . ." (*sic* in original).

In Response to Ellis's *Harper's* article, Murray attempted to explain exactly what he would like to see come out of the controversy.

> I should myself want to see the "American tradition," which you have ably stated, enforced. But I must say that it seems to me vulnerable to no adversaries, inside and outside the Church, until what time it is reinforced. I mean, it is vulnerable to the assertion, "Spain is 'the ideal,' the U.S. constitution is a *pis aller*." Present day thought is still cast in terms of the post-Reformation "Catholic nation-state." I do not indeed want the American situation canonized as "ideal." It would be enough if it could be defended as legitimate in principle, as standing *aequo jure* with the Spanish situation—each representing an important realization of principle in divergent concrete historical contexts. Are we to suppose that 30,000,000 Catholics must live perpetually in a state of "hypothesis"?

Suggesting that Ellis publish the article and take the risk that the American bishops might be labelled "opportunist," Murray wondered, "How many present-day bishops would be as forthright as the men you cite?"[48]

A few days later on July 22, 1953, Ellis expressed full agreement with Murray's comments on episcopal leadership. In his view, "something fine and bracing has gone out of the American Church and it is difficult to see how it can be regained." Now willing to risk the reaction that might result from the *Harper's* article, Ellis stated his intention:

> . . . My sole concern is to further in whatever small way I can a reasonable and possible *modus vivendi* for Catholics here in opposition to the extreme and unrealistic teaching of a few on both sides of the ocean. I understand perfectly the sense in which you speak of the "American Catholic bishops" of several generations ago, and I share your view entirely. If that be "Americanism" let them make the most of it![49]

In late August, McCormick sent Murray an anonymous French polemic against liberal influences and advised Murray: "Go cautiously but with calm courage."[50] Murray voiced "amazement"[51] over the French document and vowed that "I shall do my best with God's grace" to follow McCormick's counsel. He reported having written nothing since his hospitalization in April, an "interlude" which had allowed him time "to gain some perspective": "I was getting too intent" . . . but "anginal pains" persist.[52]

On November 15, 1953, McCormick wrote an unclear *mandatum* to John J. McMahon, the provincial, which, as will be explained below, involved *America* magazine and Clare Boothe Luce, American ambassador to Italy. McMahon relayed it on November 21 to Murray, quoting in full:

> Read Can.2316. If I assist a man to come to Italy for that purpose knowing that is why he is coming do I fall under the penalty? Our highest superior—I was with him last month—thinks so, unless excused by ignorance. *America* might know that. I think the time has come for Fr. Murray to put down in simple, clear statements his full, present position regarding this Church-State question and to send it to me for Father General. Sic mandatum.[53]

Murray's swift response to McCormick, which was dated November 23, 1953, asked for time to reply to the *mandatum*, while he worked at completing the last article in the series on Leo XIII. "It so happens that I haven't yet the energy to undertake more than one major task at a time. And it would be a major task to formulate the 'statements' requested." He suggested he had less a "position" than a "purpose" of inquiry. He also expressed perplexity over the first part of the *mandatum* and asked McCormick to be a "bit less cryptic" as to whether he is "*suspectus de haeresi* or simply the object of interest." Murray also wanted to know whether McCormick and the General were also "suspect" because of the "encouragement" they had given him.

Murray promised that he would answer honestly, "trying to distinguish the varying degrees of firmness and tentativeness with which I have different things." "It would help," he added, "to know whether I am speaking into a Roman climate of hostility or receptivity." With regard to the reference to "assisting a man to Italy" Murray wondered if the reference was to the past or to the future admitting that he was not aware that he had propagated heresy in Italy in 1950. "Did I?" he asked. He continued by reporting on his four-hour dinner of November 16 with Cardinals Edward Mooney and Samuel Stritch, a meeting arranged at the invitation of the former. Murray reflected at length on this meeting:

> Cardinal Mooney of course is my good friend and very sympathetic. His idea, as he put it to me privately, was "to do a job on"

H.E. [His Eminence] of Chicago. I've never been quite sure whether Cardinal S. [Stritch] is my friend or not. In any event, he was most friendly that evening, and the discussion was full and free.

Cardinal S. [Stritch] has scruples (he is natively a scrupulous man in many directions: e.g., he was worried about his discourse at the American College affair, and seemed glad of my assurances that he had not "gone too far"). He brought forward his difficulties—really only two: on freedom of religious propaganda, and on the concept of a "religion of the state." And he listened—with some sympathy, I thought—to my discussion of them, during which I tried to bring out the fact that I am not inclined to be dogmatic, but that I feel that these points present real theological and political issues which have not yet been satisfactorily argued out.

The evening ended on this note, as I went down the corridor with Cardinal S. [Stritch]: that, as a member of the magisterium he was obliged personally to be cautious, but that he was glad someone was attempting to cope, on the broad theological, political, and historical basis with these points, which are a genuine source of difficulty to American Catholics (during the evening Cardinal M. [Mooney] had constantly insisted on this point of "American difficulties").[54]

Thus, while Murray reported that Stritch was nervous over the whole Church-State issue, Stritch was also "heartened by Monsignor Montini's assurances" that "the famous discourse of Cardinal O. [Ottaviani]" was a "purely private utterance." Murray added: "Stritch went so far as to say that the *sensus fidelium* in the U.S. is definitely against the canonical thesis insofar as it asserts governmental and legal favor and protection of Catholicism and denies religious freedom as a civil right."[55]

A few hours later in a second letter, Murray reported a "delayed brainwave" and asked if the problem of Italian travelers and McCormick's enigmatic sentences about "assisting people into Italy to foment heresy" referred not to him at all but to the American Ambassador, Clare Boothe Luce, and the agitation of the Texan Pentecostals in Italy.[56]

Murray reported that before Mrs. Luce left for Rome he had prepared her statement for a Senate Committee before which she had to appear "on how a Catholic frames his support of separation of Church and State." He also lamented the implications that might be left by Mrs. Luce's reading of the President's Thanksgiving Proclamation in a Protestant church.

Doubtless this has been the customary practice of former Ambas-

sadors; and I hope the thing ranks as a civil ceremony or that passive assistance, *ratione officii*, at an ensuing religious ceremony will
be tolerated. But I don't like the symbolism—that America is
Protestant. It isn't; it is pluralist. When she returns in December I
could do some more briefing, if I know what's what.

In an additional postscript he wondered if McCormick's reference to
America in the *mandatum* meant the magazine's critique of the Spanish
Church-State formula.[57] While defending the validity of both the Spanish
and the American formula as different adaptations to "peculiar conditions of
religio-social fact," Murray deplored the controversy. "Spanish law," he
noted, "is not going to be liberalized, at least not until the next revolution."
    McCormick's speedy reply urged Murray to "put aside all anxiety." He
promised to warn him "at once and clearly" of any direct threat. He further
assured Murray that the *mandatum* merely followed the General's desire for
Murray's views apropos the *America* position and the *Ecclesia* polemic. Mc-
Cormick then quoted the Superior General: "One does not know what
Madrid might do next. But Rome has not expressed any fear for the orthodoxy of Fr. Murray, though not everybody in Rome, I presume, accepts his
writings." Finally McCormick confirmed Clare Boothe Luce's problem with
the Pope, who was "almost wroth" over her aid to the "dishonest and dis-
reputable Pentecostals, himself citing the canon against her, and also resent-
ing her failure to ask for an audience." McCormick's conclusion was warm
and encouraging: "So calm, and peace be your fruits of the Spirit, and may
He continue to enlighten the path you are opening up. Work without fear.
Fear, worry cripple a man in such work as you have undertaken."[58]
    On November 19, 1953, Murray wrote Ellis sending reprints of the
June *Theological Studies* article and one of the March article for Ellis's
friend, Joseph P. Walshe, Ambassador of Ireland to the Holy See. He added
a note about his meeting with Stritch and Mooney.

I had dinner the other night with Cardinals Mooney and Stritch;
among other more encouraging things the former said: "None of
us today could go as far as Gibbons went." This is for yourself. I
was dying to ask: "Why not?" But did not, being on my good behavior. Actually, the evening was, I thought, useful and satisfactory. But Chicago [Stritch] is frightened by his appurtenance to the
magisterium. Understandable, no doubt.[59]

On November 23, Ellis said he had sent the Murray reprints to Walshe
and "confidentially" informed him of his fellow countryman, Michael
Browne, O.P., and the future of Church-State relations in the United States.

Ellis reported Walshe also had stated that, "fortunately, the thesis in question is now disavowed by the majority of those in high places here, [Rome] but not yet in public." Ellis's more realistic evaluation, however, was that it would take considerable time before that position was generally believed either inside or outside the Church. In commenting on Murray's report on the dinner in Washington, Ellis wrote:

> The question that occurred to your mind to ask your dinner companions is altogether pertinent. Walshe termed Chicago's Roman speech of October 15 "the perfect and well turned answer" to the gentleman of March 2 [Ottaviani]. Surely it *was* a fine speech and in the right direction, but again there is a distance which separates them from Gibbons—and McNicholas in 1948—that must be traversed before unquiet minds will be set at ease.

In a postscript Ellis noted:

> I have been informed that a fellow editor here on the Campus [Fenton] declares that my "tradition" in *Harper's* is quite wrong. It's given me no concern, for in the realm of historical fact (where alone I feel at home) I would defy anyone to find any other tradition among the bishops of the United States.[60]

In some of the final correspondence of 1953 it became evident that Murray had the support of his superiors in the United States and in Rome. On December 6, 1953, Joseph F. Murphy, S.J., Rector of Woodstock, wrote to the Provincial, John J. McMahon, informing him of an important letter from the Superior General regarding Murray. In his semiannual report to the General, Murphy had spoken of Murray's illness that spring and referred to the "unfortunate Roman statement [Cardinal Ottaviani's] of last March" as at least a contributing factor in that illness. Murphy reported the General to have written the following in a letter dated August 7, 1953:

> Longe abest ne P. Joannes C. Murray a Sancta Sede reprehendatur. Nihilominus passu cauto et bene ponderato prosequatur in suis studiis et investigationibus perficiendis, aliorum peritorum consilio libenter audito. . . .[61]

Murphy noted that Murray was informed of the General's feeling and that the latter was grateful for the approval of his work, adding that "this is the only direct assurance he has had from Very Reverend Father General." Murphy told McMahon that Murray "has acted and does act with the prescribed caution." He also reported to the provincial about Murray's dinner-meeting with Mooney and Stritch on the occasion of the bishops' Washington meeting.

> Recently . . . Father Murray was invited to dinner and a long evening of discussion with Cardinal Mooney and Cardinal Stritch. Cardinal Mooney was host. He has long approved the line of thought which Father Murray is pursuing. His purpose in staging the meeting was to have Cardinal Stritch, still scrupulous as to whether or not his statement on American Church-State relations at the dedication of the North American College, was all that it should be, discuss the problem with Father Murray.
>
> The evening was very satisfactory and very heartening to Father Murray. On his return, he noted that his feeling of security in answering questions on his position was greatly bolstered by Father General's words of approval quoted above. This occasions my bringing that approval to your attention.[62]

A few days later, Murray's optimism was evident in a letter to Ellis. He exploded with delight over Pope Pius XII's December 6, *Ci riesce* discourse to a group of Italian jurists.[63]

> It will be interesting to see what our fellow editor [Fenton] will have to say about the recent discourse of the Pope to a group of Italian jurists. I have not yet seen the full text, but it is clearly the Pope's own reply to the famous discourse of Cardinal Ottaviani. And it is an important disavowal of the position taken by the latter.

Murray also reported that Cardinal Stritch had told him in a recent letter that he had been much reassured by the general approval given to his speech at the North American College dedication in Rome. Murray added:

> As you know, he tends to be very anxious and scrupulous. But I somehow got the impression from him that he would be willing to go farther, if only someone would prepare the way for him. This is as it should be—in any case, this is the way things are at the moment. It seems that we do not or cannot now look for leadership from American bishops. Hence the only thing is, with all reverence, to do a bit of leading. It seems to me that at the moment things are moving a bit quickly, and in the right direction. For instance, the Pope's recent discourse seems to accept the principle

that the problem of religious freedom must receive some manner of international solution, or of solution within the context of the international community as it is presently coming into existence. I have long felt that this is one of the necessary steps in development. After the Reformation the Church accepted the fact of pluralism within the international community—that is, the distinction between "Catholic states" and "non-Catholic states." But this distinction, insofar as it is still at all valid, is not sufficient for the present day situation.[64]

Ellis's prompt reply to Murray a few days later encouraged him to "bend your best efforts to blaze the trail" for Stritch.[65] Despite excessive optimism about Rome, Murray's December 19 response to Ellis was oddly cautious and doubtful on the American bishops. He challenged Ambassador Walshe's optimism "on the possibilities of Chicago," which Ellis had previously related:

The best that we can hope for from that quarter is that he will not get in the way. Perhaps this is actually the limit of legitimate expectations. I agree with you that the average American bishop is so harassed by problems of administration that he has neither time nor inclination to tackle problems of high thought.

And with a "please don't quote me" caution, Murray generalized with some daring:

Sometimes I almost wish that Gallicanism had somehow passed over this country. . . . The French hierarchy are always disposed to close ranks and to defend the things French. . . . Moreover, they will be prepared to defend the freedom of the theological fraternity to investigate these difficult subjects. I cannot help but wish that a similar disposition was present here in this country.[66]

1954

The new year brought the controversy into "open warfare." Early in January, Ellis wrote ominously: "Just before the holidays I met the editor of the AER at a little Christmas party . . . and he said that after the new year he was going to 'open his guns.' I did not ask: on whom?" To reinforce the belief that Pius XII's Ci riesce speech was indeed what Murray understood it to be, Ellis reported having received word from his friend, Ambassador Walshe, stating that he had had a chat with a Father Joseph Delos, O.P., after the papal address of December 6, "and the Dominican was of the firm opinion that it was a reversal of the Ottaviani thesis." Ellis concluded: "Matters are moving in the right direction, surely."[67]

All the news did point in that direction. With the firm backing of his general a few months earlier and a clear indication of the Pope's stand on the issue, Murray felt secure in speaking his position in the controversy loudly and clearly. But he obviously misread the extent of the power and influence of a few key figures in Rome and in America, namely, Ottaviani and Fenton.[68]

Just a few weeks following the *Ci riesce* discourse a controversy over its interpretation began to take place in the theological journals in America. Gustave Weigel took the lead with his article "Religious Toleration in a World Society." Mentioning the fact that religion has most often been a "stumbling block to world reunion," Weigel termed Pius XII's *Ci riesce* as "the juridical solution of the problem of religious disunion." Weigel found a number of significant points in the December 6 discourse. According to Pius XII, the position of the new juridical order in the matter of religion would be friendly and cordial. ". . . The new world reunion would be tolerant of different and theoretically conflicting religions. . . . The new society would not try to impose one definite religion on all men nor make such religious uniformity a condition for the new federation." Governments would be obligated to practice such toleration. The discourse of the Pope "certainly clarifies the obscurities lurking in the minds of so many of our non-Catholic brethren who feel that the Catholic Church is a conspiracy to rob them of their right to follow conscience in their religious decisions." *Ci riesce* "will end the accusation of not a few who assert that the Catholic Church has a double norm for solving Church-State relationships." Thus the position expressed by the Pope was radically different from the position where "the Church demands liberty for personal religious belief in countries where Catholics constitute a minority, while Catholic uniformity is imposed on all citizens in lands where Catholics form a political majority."[69]

Fenton had his own definite interpretation of *Ci riesce*. While bemoaning the fact that the first reports on the *Ci riesce* were not accompanied by the full text, he pointed to the fact that "there were comments and explanations based upon citations which had been taken out of context, and some of these comments and explanations were inadequate and misleading."[70] According to Fenton's interpretation, Pius XII's discourse "insists that the Church 'in principle or as a thesis *(per principio ossia in tesi)* cannot approve the complete separation between the two powers (Church and State),' " although under certain conditions "a *limited* separation of Church and State may be and sometimes is licit."[71] Furthermore, the teachings of *Ci riesce* affected the discussion of "the past several years" regarding "matters of theology and public ecclesiastical law on the subject of Church and State." From the latter point, Fenton drew three conclusions. First, it would henceforth be "idle to maintain" that the term "Catholic State" "is inept or that it has no clear meaning, or that it can legitimately refer only to civil societies or kingdoms of times past." Second, there should be no further "objections raised against the teaching or the terminology of writers who hold that, in itself, error has no rights." Third,

> it is certainly no longer feasible to reprove the teaching that, objectively, a complete separation of Church and State is an evil. Likewise it would appear that henceforth the legitimacy of the explanation of relations between Church and State in terms of thesis and hypothesis will be acknowledged.[72]

Murray's Confrontation With Rome

On March 25, Murray delivered a forceful lecture on *Ci riesce* at the Catholic University of America in Washington. It set the stage for the rebuke from Rome. While no full text was prepared, there are three documentary sources for information on this crucial speech: the NCWC news summary; Murray's nine-page typewritten transcript of his detailed notes; and these same notes in longhand along with an extensive amount of other notes of comment on Pius XII's *Ci riesce* of December 6, 1953.

The NCWC Release

Murray expressed praise for the "recent Papal discourses" which have "rescued the question of religious tolerance from the wretched morass of expedience in which, unfortunately, even some Catholic writers have involved it." He hailed the Pope for having "criticized and rejected" a regrettably "rather widely held" theory that legal tolerance of other religions was, in Catholic doctrine, either mere expediency or "a reluctant concession to force." He stressed that the problem of religious liberty can no longer be studied as the problem of a single nation but only in the broader context of mankind's search for political unity. "Political unity may possibly, in God's providence," he said, "be the preparation for religious unity." In weighing the whole problem of religious pluralism, he emphasized: "the highest good is a peaceful life for the Church and for divided humanity—the good of world harmony." Finally, he pointed out that Pius XII had demolished "the false idea" that the Spanish system stood for a "thesis" and the American system merely for a "hypothesis." The NCWC release contained no reference to Cardinal Ottaviani.

The Murray Notes

Murray's typed notes followed one set of his written notes, and even here some references to Ottaviani were omitted. He placed his whole analysis of *Ci riesce* in the context of Pius XII's deliberate rejection of Ottaviani's position: (1) "*Ci riesce* is the Pope's public correction of impressions left by Ottaviani's construction . . ."; (2) "Ottaviani evoked protests in diplomatic circles," i.e., French, Irish, Swiss, and German; (3) the Pope's "first point" was to stress that "only" he is "competent to speak in the last instance on such vital questions touching international life." Hence, "exit auctoritas Emissimi"; [sic] and (4) therefore: "anyone whose theory is that of Ottaviani is under necessity of reversing his views."

His pencilled notes (whether they were spoken or not) included, in addition to some further direct reference to Ottaviani, the statement: "I informed [sic] of fact directly by close adviser in June—5 page, single-spaced letter"— the "fact" being the papal displeasure with Ottaviani's March 2 statement. Elsewhere in Murray's notes the author of the letter is identified as Robert Leiber, S.J., private secretary to the Pope. Murray's notes continue with a quote from Leiber: "reflects private view of Cardinal [Privatensicht]" with "no sort of official or even semi-official" authority. Murray's summary of the Leiber report continues:

> Pope wanted this publicly known—displeased by appeals to discourse as official. . . . Expressed disagreement. . . . Disagreement doctrinal. . . . O. notified by consultant of H.O. . . . Pope would take occasion for public statement. . . . Outlined position substantially that of *Ci riesce* (my informant a collaborator).[73]

The reaction to Murray's speech was varied. Ellis, who had attended the lecture, wrote him a few days later: "Your lecture was splendid in every way, a true university performance, as I remarked to several people. It has stirred a great deal of discussion on the campus which is all to the good. Hold yourself to a reasonable pace now so that you may be with us for a long time to come."[74] But the reaction of Murray's nonsympathizers would prove fateful. Murray's outright and public criticism of Ottaviani would prove to be the real turning point in the controversy. The argument with Rome on the Church and State issue might have followed in any event. But this made it inevitable and, for Ottaviani, made it personal.

On April 1, a week after the lecture, Ottaviani, in a letter to Francis Cardinal Spellman, enquired about Murray.[75] Thanking Ottaviani for bringing the matter to his attention, Spellman promised to "take up the matter which you bring to my attention with the Rector of the University." But, he added, "I would appreciate it if you will give more details of what Father Murray said in his lecture that was offensive to you and just what quotation he made from any address of His Holiness and what interpretations were given to the words of our Holy Father."[76]

The most vehement attack on Murray's Catholic University lecture came from Fenton. In a postscript to "Toleration and the Church-State Controversy," Fenton characterized Murray's attempt as either giving the impression that the Holy Father's allocution constituted a repudiation of the teachings of Ottaviani or contending that because of *Ci riesce* those accepting the teaching of Ottaviani were obliged to reverse their position to avoid coming into opposition with the Pope's teaching—a contention which Fenton described as "utterly baseless and incorrect."

> Any careful, honest, and competent examination of the text of the *Ci riesce* and that of Cardinal Ottaviani's article will show that there is absolutely no point on which these two documents contradict one another. There is no statement in the article, "Church and State: Some Present Problems in the Light of the Teaching of Pope Pius XII," in any way contradicted, rejected, or repudiated in the text of *Ci riesce*. There is no statement in either document which could in any way legitimately be interpreted as opposed to the spirit of the other."

Expressing his complete sympathy with Ottaviani's teaching, Fenton explained why it could and should be accepted: because of the "notably adequate theological evidence in its favor." For Fenton it was "the only acceptable" position. Calling Murray's claim "fantastic," Fenton expressed difficulty in understanding the opposition to Ottaviani's position, since it was "traditional teaching," and was "simply what is contained and what has been contained in the great body of manuals in theology and in public ecclesiastical law which deal with this particular subject, the teaching of the *magisterium* itself."

Fenton's final point is crucial in that he clearly saw the point of contention between the two interpretations:

> Those who would like to believe and to have others believe that authoritative pontifical teaching on this and other subjects has changed or "developed" in such a way that some things presented as true by Popes like Pius IX and Leo XIII have been completely or partially denied by more recent Pontiffs would not like what the Cardinal had to say on this subject. The *Ci riesce*, however, gives no support to their opposition, on this point or on any other.[78]

For Fenton, *Ci riesce* gave no support to the position that change or development had taken place.

In the following issue of *The American Ecclesiastical Review* another article appeared: "*Ci riesce* and Cardinal Ottaviani's Discourse," by Giuseppe Di Meglio, calling Murray's contention "devoid of foundation" and "disrespectful." "Such a judgment," he said, "deserves to be rejected immediately. . . ."[79] In August, McCormick advised Murray to "ignore" Di Meglio's article "whether in writing or in speech." However, McCormick added: "It is thought here, that it should be answered, 'perche non e vero.' " While asking for a suggestion as to who might do this, McCormick expressed the wish that "it were well for someone, whose competency would be respected, to give a very exact and brief and clear explanation of just what the Holy Father said: that He enunciated a principle of universal application."[80]

Murray's reply indicated he had paid no attention to the Di Meglio article and had not even bothered to read it until McCormick had brought it to his attention. He suggested that an answer should be given, preferably by someone in Rome, and ideally a non-Jesuit—"because it would be unfortunate to reinforce the impression which my friend at the Catholic University has tried to create, that this is a 'battle against the Jesuits.' " Murray's reply also made mention of a personal, no longer extant letter of Murray to Ottaviani, "in the nature of a personal apology" which "he lacked the grace to accept . . ." and of a letter of Father General with "instructions" that Murray was told he would soon receive from Rome. After this he confessed "pessimism" and "no heart" to complete the final Leonine article on government and the order of religion.[81]

Shortly after this the pressure could be felt from Rome. In a series of reflective notes on this incident, Walter Burghardt, a close associate of Murray's, pointed out that the head of the Holy Cross Order in Rome was urged to get Theodore M. Hesburgh, President of the University of Notre Dame, to dissuade Murray from appearing at Notre Dame. There was also the issue of *The Catholic Church in World Affairs*, published by Notre Dame Press and edited by Waldemar Gurian and M. A. Fitzsimons. Burghardt correctly surmised the book was withdrawn because of Murray's essay, "On the Structure of the Church-State Problem."[82] Murray had written to Fitzsimons a fortnight after getting instructions from his superior general to ask him both to add an explanatory note "to any second edition and to supply even 'a pageinsert' " if the first edition was still in stock.[83]

Meanwhile at the Catholic University of America, Fenton and his associates chastised the local head of the American Association of University Professors for sponsoring the crucial Murray lecture.[84]

As a further indication of where the power was at this time and Fenton's own influence both here and in Rome, an important incident in Ellis's life should be mentioned.[85] Ellis had told Murray, in a letter no longer extant, of an invitation he had just received to deliver a lecture at the Tenth International Congress of Historical Sciences scheduled for Rome in September, 1955, on the subject: "The Catholic Church and Church-State Relations in the United States." Murray wrote Ellis:

> Your confidential information about the lecture in Rome was rather dismaying. I should have thought that this would have been an excellent opportunity for a good American Catholic utterance. It is difficult for me to see why there should be grounds for any timidity. My own impression is that such a lecture as you would give would be well received, perhaps not universally, but in certain important quarters. I shall hope, somewhat against hope, that you may yet have the opportunity. Please do some fast talking![86]

Ellis, out of courtesy, sought permission to give the lecture from his ordinary, Archbishop Patrick O'Boyle of Washington. The initial response from the chancellor of the archdiocese, Monsignor Philip M. Hannan, seemed positive. Hannan's letter to Ellis expressed confidence that permission from the Archbishop would be forthcoming since Ellis had assured them that the paper was merely "dealing with history, not philosophy or public law."[87] Ellis responded to O'Boyle enclosing a rough draft of the main points he would treat: "I would have in mind to illustrate the various points with examples taken from Church-State relations in the United States such as the letter to Carroll from Madison in 1806. . . ."[88] O'Boyle's reply to Ellis was a simple recognition of the receipt of his letter, with the promise that he would take up the matter with the rector of the Catholic University, Bishop Bryan J. McEntegart, within a matter of days.

Reflecting on the incident many years later, in a letter to Walter Burghardt, Ellis provided further information on why the permission was not granted and the reason for O'Boyle's reservations. The Archbishop was prepared to grant the request and had assured Monsignor Hannan, "I can be talked into this." Ellis explained, however, that O'Boyle "was nervous about the subject, especially since it would be given in Rome, and he was casting about, as it were, for support from others." Ellis seemed certain he had Hannan's support, but O'Boyle needed more reassurance, and therefore, sought the counsel of the rector of the University. After discussing the matter with Bishop McEntegart, O'Boyle phoned and met with Ellis "and in the course of his remarks which were stated more in the form of asking if I would be willing to forego the paper—to which I readily assented since, I said, as my superior I felt I should do that—he mentioned *en passant*, 'you know there is Monsignor Fenton, *The American Ecclesiastical Review*, and all that sort of thing.'" Ellis added his own interpretation to this:

In other words, the Archbishop was fearful of how Monsignor Fenton would react were he to learn of my paper and that I had had permission from O'Boyle to deliver it. It was a clear case of asking permission where it would have been better not to do so: he was initially well disposed to the idea, but the more he thought of it the more fretful he grew, it would seem.[89]

By the end of 1954 the move to silence Murray and anyone else showing any kind of creativity was well underway. Such an attitude only helped to reinforce the "ghetto mentality" so abhorrent to the Catholic liberals here in the United States. Pius XII's ambiguity on crucial theological issues very often led to a misinterpretation of his thinking. In spite of assertions to the contrary from people close to the Pope, like Montini and Leiber, his receptivity to the "théologie nouvelle" and to the new Catholic vision of the world was certainly unclear. It was not that Pius XII disregarded completely the necessity to open up the Church to modern development, as was the case with Pius X. Pius XII's later utterances showed that he was well aware of this need. However, he was fearful that things would get out of hand if he supported the new trends.[90] Though he took some liberal positions, as for instance, in Ci riesce, various and divergent interpretations always emerged. As we shall see in the last chapter, the question was one of interpretation, and the theological method employed in studying the papal allocutions. Until clarity could be reached on such a crucial issue, those who represented the more traditional position, and very often those who held the key positions of influence in and with Rome, would win the day.

1955

While in relation to Rome 1955 would prove to be Murray's year of defeat, in America St. Louis University would be granting him an honorary degree of Doctor of Laws for developing "a profound mastery of theological scholarship with which he combines an unusual sensitivity to the problems of current culture. . . . His teaching, his learned publications, his lecturing, his controversies have brought Father Murray to the very first rank of American theologians and religious spokesmen."

After August, 1954, one has to wonder what impelled Murray to regain "heart" for the final Leonine article. In January he wrote to McCormick indicating he had nearly finished it. He reported having sent to the Superior General, in October, a reprint of his *Thought* article on "The Problem of Pluralism in America," "with the request that it be examined," but "I have heard nothing." He concluded on a note of pessimism expressing little hope and a kind of "indifference to the outcome" of the controversy.[91]

McCormick's reply indicated that he was himself responsible for the silence on the *Thought* article as he saw no reason to "stir up the embers" by raising the issue. "The flash had subsided; and *His* [the Jesuit Superior General's] mind, I knew, was: let's forget it all now: the one little error had been noted, the mildest admonition had been given; let that simple, clear error be corrected, avoided, and for the present let us talk of the organist of the Gesù." McCormick advised Murray, however, that there was to be no reprint of the *Thought* article until approved by Rome.[92]

In March the Maryland provincial's office received an unsigned cable from Rome approving the Murray reprint. A few days later, McCormick wrote Murray of the cabled approval and enclosed the censor's no longer extant report on the article. While saying that he thought the General would approve the Murray request for a trip to Rome, McCormick questioned its wisdom since: "Some will say you have been summoned" and "I see no good to be gained by contacting his Em. O [Eminence Ottaviani]. He has been too badly hurt by this whole affair by what happened there and here."[93]

McCormick wrote Murray again in early July. Worrying whether Murray had controlled his patience and still thought "kindly of us," he reported the Roman reaction to two issues. First, reminding him that the Holy Office should not be provoked, since "just now it is rather on edge," he gave permission for the publication of the Murray chapter for "the Armed Forces book,"[94] in accordance with the censor's comments for revision and with the approval of "superiors over there." But he asked: "Why should you . . . take space to pay tribute to the spiritual influence of Jew and Protestant religion? Personally I do not see." The scope of the article "is to show what and how the Catholic religion helps the country." Second, he apparently enclosed the censor's report for the last of the Leonine articles and stated: "The article, as you see, cannot be published." Approving the censor's "prudence," he said, "these men have your interests at heart, and they know the scene over here." He then quoted the feeling of one of the censors:

> Textum bis ex toto perlustrato, censeo: textum prout est publici iuris fieri non posse; accusaretur auctor sine mora a suis "amicis" in America et hic Romae apud S. officium. Nihilominus non pauca in MS sunt perbene dicta.

With this McCormick concluded: "It seems to me a mistake to wish to carry on with that controverted question under present circumstances," and nothing could be gained "by provoking those who will not be appeased. Fr. General agrees with the final verdict, although not with every comment of the censors." He added: "Leave Spain out of it. So, fiat. Time will bring changes."[95]

A week later Murray answered McCormick "with a few words of gratitude" to thank him for his "delicate way of saying, 'You're through!' " He concluded tersely: "Since I am natively of a pessimistic turn of mind, the result was not unexpected. But the whole thing represents a defeat and a failure of the first order."⁹⁶ McCormick's prompt reply brought more unhappy news. He found he had exceeded his power in the last letter and asked that the chapter for "the Armed Forces book" be sent directly to Rome for approval "to give you all the protection possible." In an attempt to encourage Murray he wrote: "You are far from through, I hope: but let the State-Church question rest for the present."⁹⁷ Murray's reply was pessimistic:

> It was kind of you to say, "You are far from through, I hope." I
> do not share the hope. (Except perhaps in the general sense of hoping that I may still somehow fulfil the injunction of the Examen Generale, "se utilem exhibeat"!) All the books on Church and State and on allied topics have been cleared from my room, in symbol of retirement, which I expect to be permanent. When Frank Sheed returns, I shall cancel the agreement I had with him to edit and revise the articles on Church and State for a book. Fortunately, my gloomy prescience impelled me to refuse an invitation to give the Walgreen Lectures at the U. of Chicago. And all other practical measures will be taken to close the door on the past ten years, leaving all their mistakenesses to God. (At that, I do not believe that I was mistaken on the central issue—the need for a unitary theory.)

Along with these remarks, Murray enclosed the corrected pages of the "Armed Forces chapter" as requested by McCormick. His argumentation, he said, was "based on the premise that civil peace, ensured by laws that are just in the circumstances, is the highest end of the political ruler." My point is that civil peace, thus ensured, is a source of moral strength in the American community. And most importantly, he added: "I do not see that this argument raises the issue of 'indifferentism.' "⁹⁸

Evidently responding to Murray's queries, which are now missing, McCormick promised to ask the Superior General about the extent of restraint on his writing. Meanwhile, he advised: "I suppose you may write poetry. Between harmless poetry and Church-State problems, what fields are taboo I don't know; but ordinary prudence will give the answer. We'll try to keep out of controversy for the present."⁹⁹

Defeated on the Church-State issue, Murray did not completely give up writing or lecturing. In an address delivered at St. Louis University in November he discussed the role of the Catholic university in a pluralist society as a "ministry of clarification" and a "work of discernment."[100] His writing began to deal more with the topic of the role of Catholicism in America. His "Catholics in America: A Creative Minority" challenged Catholics to contribute something to America through their creativity as a minority group.[101] "Challenges Confronting the American Catholic," appearing in the December issue of *Life* magazine, was perhaps one of Murray's most important articles in this area. In stressing that the "Catholic community belongs to America" and to "the definition of the American way," Murray outlined a number of tasks that relate to the Catholic "belongingness" here.[102]

Meanwhile, in *The American Ecclesiastical Review*, Fenton continued his relentless attack on those opposing the Ottaviani thesis on Church and State,[103] and using a more recent allocution of Pius XII on the subject, characterized the traditional position as the Church's official teaching "normative for all future teaching and writing on Church-State relations by Catholics."[104] Pius XII's discourse illicited no response from Murray.

1956-1959

At the beginning of 1956 Murray was in a mood of disenchantment. This is evident in a letter to McCormick. While recognizing that "the issue of Church and State still flames," he admitted "that to me at the moment it is a nuisance and a bore. I couldn't care less." Promising to carry out any instructions McCormick might give, he sent for approval the text of a lecture given at the Kent School in the course of a seminar there on the idea of Christian education.[105] Murray likewise referred to a letter from a Paul Botta, editor of the German journal, *Dokumente*, asking permission to reprint passages from the *Thought* article: "The Problem of Pluralism in America." Realizing the difficulty he had already had with Rome on this article, Murray asked McCormick how to answer the letter.[106] On February 3, Murray acknowledged to McCormick the arrival of a cabled veto on the *Dokumente* article.[107] The same day McCormick explained the veto. If extracts carried "the opinion or thesis that came under censure," he said, and "was declared untenable in Fr. Murray's writings," either Rome or the German bishops would respond; "and so the public here and elsewhere is informed of the S.O. [Holy Office's] action." McCormick did not see how Murray "could escape responsibility for a grave imprudence, to say nothing more, in permitting an editor to republish what the S.O. [Holy Office] censured." McCormick also reported that his conversation with Father Leiber revealed that:

> There is a strong movement in Germany against a Concordat; Rome is absolutely firm in wanting the Concordat as the sole means of safe-guarding Catholic education. Without it there will be State schools with no religion and all will be forced to attend

them. Conditions there are very different from the U.S.A. It does look as though *Dokumente* might be wanting to use you to boost the American Church-State separation plan for Germany. Hence Fr. L [Leiber] recommended you hold off, defer granting permission until you have the leisure to examine the matter more thoroughly.[108]

In reply Murray assured McCormick that "I altogether agree" with his cautions on the German situation and added: "Europeans rather like to 'use' Americans when it suits their purposes." But he reported that his letter of refusal to the magazine arrived too late to stop the publication.[109] He had not seen the published version, he said, but felt that it was not likely "there will be trouble coming from Germany: but one never knows." Referring to Fenton, Murray noted: "It was interesting to see in one of Msgr. F's [Fenton] latest articles a direct quotation (but not in quotes) from one of the H.O.'s [Holy Office's] propositions. I have not seen it verbally in print anywhere else, not even in anything of mine. It is not unlikely that he wrote the four of them."[110]

On February 29, Murray reported to McCormick that he had read the *Dokumente* text and sent McCormick a copy of the letter he wrote the editor as "a form of fire insurance."[111] The letter to Botta reflected Murray's attempt to clarify the matter especially regarding concordats. "If you should hear of any such misunderstandings," he said, "I would appreciate any efforts you might personally make toward clearing them up."[112]

Until August there was no significant correspondence between Murray and McCormick. But on August 18, McCormick sent a letter to him reporting that Bishop William A. Scully of Albany, episcopal chairman of the NCWC Motion Picture Committee, felt Murray's address on censorship "strikes a severe blow at the Legion of Decency." McCormick promised to call on Scully personally when he went to Albany and suggested that Murray try to contact him before the November bishops' meeting.[113]

It would seem that while under censorship by Rome on the subject of Church and State, Murray was turning much of his attention to the subject of public morality and particularly to the moral role of Catholicism in a pluralistic society.[114] Murray began to invest more time in American public affairs and in the subject of public argument. At this time he served as a consulter on the President's Atomic Energy Commission. He became deeply involved with setting up a group that "is going to try to take a broad approach —not just Church and State in the legal sense, but the whole relation of religion to a free society."[115] This project was led by Robert Hutchins and the members of the Fund for the Republic, Inc. In these years he was also actively involved in the National Conference of Christians and Jews and with the

Foundation for Religious Action in the Social and Civil Order.[116] His public lectures were more frequent and dealt with the subject of good public argument. He delivered a most important lecture for the Red Mass in Boston on September 29, 1956, entitled "The Next Liberal Task for America."[117] An address given at Rockhurst, New York, dealt with the subject "Religion and Government in the United States: The Argument That is Not Going on."[118]

The respite from controversy with Rome allowed Murray time to rethink the subject of Church and State. He confessed spending the summer of 1956 "going through the various things I have written on the Church-State problem, with a view to making the revisions, corrections, etc. necessary before putting out all the matter in book form. Confessing that he was not completely satisfied with everything he had written he asked the Rev. John Castelot, who was seeking copyright permissions, not to quote from his "least satisfactory article, since it is the one most in need of revision. . . . I am unwilling to let it stand as in any way a definitive statement of my own position."[119]

Indicating exactly what he felt was the heart of the problem in the controversy, Murray criticized Castelot's letter to him for construing his position as a denial of the proposition held by Francis Connell that "a Catholic state is *per se* bound to profess the one true religion, Catholicism." In this, Murray expressed belief but called for a distinction in the word "profess." "Is it a matter of religious acts of social worship according to the faith and rules of the Catholic Church?" he asked Castelot. "Or is it a question of the legislative act of legal establishment of Catholicism as the religion of the State?" He asserted that the two questions were not identical, even in the text of Leo XIII.

By late March, 1957, Murray appeared more certain about his position and began to share his further thinking on the subject of Church and State with a number of close associates. He sent galleys of the last unpublished Leonine article to a Father Murphy with a letter granting permission for Murphy "to use any of the substance of the article for any purpose (whether acceptance or refutation)" while prohibiting any "direct quotation, much less any reference to this article which, as it were, does not exist!" He added: "You will tell me (and I shall agree) that this is no way to carry on theological argument. However, that's the way it is. Even so, one is not forbidden to make friendly gestures. And this letter, and the MS, is in the nature of a friendly gesture."[120]

From this date until July, 1958, there is little correspondence available.[121] But the latter date marked a highpoint in Murray's effort to clarify his position on Church and State. Murray wrote to Donald Wolf, S.J., at Georgetown University expressing admiration at Wolf's "careful reconstruction of a lot of scattered ideas of mine." The essay is done "with admirable intelligence," he said, and added comments and suggested corrections "of a minor kind."[122] Murray suggested Wolf use "unitary theory" rather than unitary norm in the explanation of his position. "I use the term 'unitary' to characterize the theory as whole," he said, "that is, there is one theory to be applied to all situations (this against the disjunctive theory)." Regarding the relation of religious unity to political unity he suggested that it would be well to note that, although the former is possible without the latter, the presence of the latter in fact would represent the highest level of social consensus. But he qualified: "The thing we have not yet proved in the U.S. is that the social consensus, as at least moral, can be maintained in the absence of religious unity, sc., in the presence of radical divisions. There are signs that the consensus is eroding."

To the question whether Murray's "unitary theory" would allay fears of Protestants in the country, Murray answered:

> I don't think any theory, even my own, would do much to allay Protestant fears and suspicions. These have other roots and are dubiously accessible to reason in any form. The problem is historical and psychological. In trying to elaborate a theory I never had in view this emotional aspect of the matter. It is external to the problem as such, which concerns the inner integrity of the Catholic conscience as such and the legitimate terms on which it can affirm Catholic existence within the American constitutional commonwealth. It is we who need the theory for our own sakes. Whether anybody else is calmed by it is a secondary matter, and a problem more in charity and virtue than in truth.

Murray concluded by stressing his concern about Wolf's anxious desire to see his work in print. "The trouble is that I am not!" Murray frankly stated. And he explained the reason:

> It happens that his Eminence the Pro-Secretary of the Holy Office is a most convinced advocate of the "disjunctive" theory and an equally convinced adversary of my "unitary" theory. He has not taken kindly to my past disagreements with him. In fact, he seems to be rather gunning for me. In consequence, I was advised by Father General over two years ago not to continue my advocacy of my own views in print. The result, he felt, would be trouble. This is why I never let my last article get farther than galley proof. I had sent it to Rome for censorship. The judgment was favorable from a doctrinal point of view. But the two censors added their

view that it would be "inopportune" to publish the thing. And Fr.
General concurred and told me, in the nicest possible way, to keep
my big mouth shut.

Suggesting to Wolf that if this was the mandate by which he had to
abide, "I think it also holds for you. Perhaps a fortiori, since it might be
thought I was continuing my advocacy *per alium*. And that would not do at
all." He concluded on a hopeful note: "I am sorry that you are thus stuck,
after all the work you did. But I feel it necessary to let you know that you are
stuck! Everything will come unstuck one fine day—but not yet. . . . It is too
bad it has to end in some frustration; but in that you at least have company
—my company!"[123]

Soon after, Murray wrote McCormick indicating that he was eager to
see the matter "come unstuck" sooner than he had promised Wolf. Noting
that "it is some time since I have bothered you," he stated that within two
weeks he would send an article entitled "Unica Status Religio" along with
the Italian translation. He requested that the article be published in the
Civiltà Cattolica and "since this cannot be done without prior approval of
the Holy Father, I want that too." He recognized that this was a large, but
necessary, request, for "there is an occasion for it, and also a reason." The
crucial reason was the problem of John F. Kennedy, whose office requested
Murray for help on the Catholic constitutional problem. The second reason
he saw as "more important than the occasion": "The present confused state
of Catholic thought" inhibiting American Catholics from confidently asserting that "within the total religio-political situation of the U.S., the First
Amendment is good law, that can be defended by Catholics in principle, that
is, in terms of the structured ensemble of principles that govern human legis-
lation with regard to the relations of religion and government." Murray
summarized the Holy Office's "disjunctive theory" condemning "dises-
tablishment" and tolerating the First Amendment only as *"minus malum"*
bearable only until "the passage of governmental power into Catholic
hands." He explained that the purpose of his article was "to put a footing of
doctrinal argument under the assertion that the First Amendment was good
law and could be defended in principle. He therefore insisted that it appear
in the *Civiltà Cattolica* and that it have the explicit approval of Pius XII,
since in this matter "no one can bring clarity and unity to Catholic thought
except the Holy Father himself."[124]

Murray asserted that his own "unitary theory," explained in the article,
avoided direct "refutation" of the disjunctive theory—"I try not to repeat my
mistakes"—but was merely an "extension of the Holy Father's own line of
thought." He added that: "If the interpretation is incorrect, or the extension

illegitimate, I want to know the fact, and the reasons. But if the interpretation and extension are valid, it would promote the cause of truth if they were published. In the circumstances it would seem that only the Holy Father himself can be the judge." In conclusion he recalled the "dreadful" *Civiltà Cattolica* article of 1948[125] arguing that "Catholics alone have the right to exist and that they allow others to coexist with them only when they are forced to do so." Murray wondered if the editors of *Civiltà Cattolica* still held this view. If they did not, he suggested they perhaps owed "a debt to the world to say so, in some fashion!"

Murray's final point was clear and to the point. He did not adduce as the reason for making the proposal "a desire to clear up my own ambiguous situation," he said, but

> I would most heartily welcome such a clarification, one way or the other, since at the moment I do not know whether I am right or wrong. It seems fair to state that no effective guidance has come from Rome. Five propositions were sent, none of them unambiguous and none of them held by me. For the rest, a counsel of prudence to keep silent. I have observed the counsel, under assent to its prudence. Only now I wonder whether the time has come for counsels of prudence to cede to the claims of truth.[126]

Without waiting for Murray's article "Unica Status Religio," McCormick answered Murray and said he would "speak frankly."

> I am afraid you do not know that Rome of today. I very seriously doubt that there would be any chance of the Civiltà accepting an article by you on the subject of Church-State relations. No; we must be patient; some people never forget; if the possible, political situation in the USA should put the Civiltà et al on the defensive, then would be the time for some explaining to be done over here, and a clearer and perhaps authoritative statement of the Church's essential teaching on the matter might be made. I really think that you must wait for that, not expose yourself by trying to hasten it. In the end what is correct in your stand will be justified. Meanwhile be content to stay on the sidelines, unless the hierarchy forces you into play: deepen and clarify your own position, and be ready with your solution approved, when the opportune time comes. That is not coming in the present Roman atmosphere.[127]

Only a few months later Pius XII would be dead (October 8, 1958), and the seemingly harmless Angelo Cardinal Roncalli would be succeeding to the papacy as an "interim Pope."

Notes

1. Donald F. Crosby, S.J., "The Angry Catholics: American Catholics and Senator Joseph R. McCarthy, 1950-1957." Unpublished dissertation, Brandeis University, 1973. For an excellent article see: Vincent P. De Santis, "American Catholics and McCarthyism," *The Catholic Historical Review,* LI (April, 1965), pp. 1-30.

2. David J. O'Brien, *The Renewal of American Catholicism* (New York, Oxford University Press, 1972), p. 141.

3. Murray to John Tracy Ellis, December 19, 1953, WCA.

4. Murray, "Catholics in America—A Creative Minority?" *The Catholic Mind* (October, 1955), p. 595.

5. Murray, "The Freedom of Man in the Freedom of the Church," *Modern Age: A Conservative Review,* I (Fall, 1957), p. 142.

6. Murray. *Foreign Policy and the Free Society,* ed. by J.C. Murray and Walter Millis (New York: Oceana Publications, 1958), p. 37.

7. Murray, "The Return to Tribalism," *The Catholic Mind,* LX (January, 1962), pp. 6-7.

8. O'Brien. *The Renewal of American Catholicism,* p. 141.

9. Cogley, "Looking Backward, Looking Ahead: Fortieth Anniversary Symposium," *Commonweal,* LXXXI (November 20, 1964), p. 264.

10. Cogley. *Religion in America* (New York, 1958), p. 269.

11. John Tracy Ellis, in his *American Catholicism* (2d ed. rev.; Chicago: The University of Chicago Press, 1969), rightly describes the 1950s as a period of widespread suppression of freedom of thought and expression for Catholics. The tone of the decade, he says, "had to some extent been set by the cautionary and warning words of Pius XII's encyclical, *Humani generis,* of August 12, 1950. In the years that followed, prominent Catholic scholars both in Europe and in the Americas . . . were frustrated and discouraged by the fact that repeated admonitions from ecclesiastical authorities had made openness and freedom conspicuous by their absence"; pp. 220-21.

12. Murray to Thomas E. Henneberry, provincial superior, March 2, 1950, ANYP.

13. Murray to Henneberry, March 21, 1950, ANYP.

14. The twenty-five page report was entitled: "Project: Church and State in Germany." It was submitted to "The Chief, Religious Affairs Branch of the Educational and Cultural Division of the Office of Public Affairs of the Office of the High Commissioner for Germany."

After giving a brief summary of the history of the Church-State situation in Germany, and of the ideas that went into the development of its various forms, Murray distinguished between the system of partial separation of Church and State under the Weimar Constitution and the complete separation in the United States. He warned against an American effort to model German society on the cultural as well as political pattern of the United States. He pointed to strong German hostility toward any American effort that would establish in Germany a system of radical and complete separation such as exists in the United States.

Among Murray's recommendations were the following: first, to continue the present American policy of avoiding all acts that might create an impression that the

United States was directly or indirectly aiming at the secularization of the German state; secondly, that contacts between Germans and Americans ought to be multiplied, particularly on the intellectual level; finally that a strengthening of the spiritual bonds between all people with whom the United States hoped to make common cause was in the essential interests of the United States government and people. "In the last analysis," he concluded, "there is only one German question today: Will Germany go West or East—or lie down? Religious forces will be a potent factor in influencing the fateful choice towards active resistance to Soviet Communism and active alliance with the Western nations." Copy, WCA.

15. Emmet John Hughes, "A Man For Our Season," *The Priest*, XXV, No. 7 (July-August, 1969), p. 390.

16. George A. Lindbeck, Yale University, to Rev. Thomas Ambrogi, Woodstock, Maryland, September 6, 1967. WCA.

17. James Shannon, "Tribute to John Courtney Murray," *Catholic Bulletin*, Archdiocese of Minneapolis-St. Paul Minnesota Weekly, September 7, 1967, p. 3.

18. Letter of Charles W. Hendel, Chairman of Yale University Philosophy Department, to Murray, June 5, 1951, WCA.

19. Murray to Very Rev. John J. McMahon, June 8, 1951, ANYP.

20. Murray to Ellis, September 3, 1951; Murray to Fenton, September 4, 1951, WCA. It is not clear why Murray would have felt this way when every other piece of correspondence with Yale and his superiors express a contrary attitude. It probably expresses an apparent lack of self-confidence and uncertainty about his work that emerged occasionally in Murray's life.

21. "Memorandum for Very Rev. Father Provincial with Regard to Visiting Professorship at Yale University," Murray to John J. McMahon, June 12, 1951, ANYP.

22. Murray to McCormick, January 31, 1953, Copy WCA.

23. The encyclical letter, *Humani generis*, was published on August 12, 1950, and it named and rejected such new trends as historicism, the false theory of evolution, existentialism, the Catholic feeling of inferiority with regard to modern science, the tendency to minimize the differences among the churches, the importance of theological concepts. The encyclical initiated a kind of neo-Modernist persecution running through the 1950s and right up into the first sessions of Vatican II. Among its victims, along with Murray, would be Yves Congar, Henri De Lubac, Teilhard de Chardin, and most of the outstanding minds of that time. In this country *The American Ecclesiastical Review* under the editorship of Joseph Fenton provided the greatest support to Pius XII's effort at checking the liberal movement throughout this period. This development was not entirely unexpected. Some of the allocutions Pius XII had given in the late 1940s had foreshadowed it. The real purpose of *Humani generis* was clearly stated in its title: "Concerning certain false opinions that threaten to undermine the basis of Catholic teaching." With this came a strong emphasis on conservatism throughout the Church and Pius X's canonization in 1954 came as a confirmation of the conservative trend.

24. Murray to McCormick, April 24, 1951, Copy WCA; Vollert, " 'Humani generis' and the Limits of Theology," *TS*, XII (March, 1951), pp. 3-23.

25. Weigel, "The Historical Background of the Encyclical 'Humani generis,' " *TS*, XII (June, 1951), pp. 208-30.

26. None of the correspondence between Murray and Msgr. Montini (Paul VI) can be found in the Murray Papers. Montini was then sub-secretary of State and thus very closely associated with Pius XII. Further, Murray's correspondence indicates

Montini's sympathy with his position and apparent actual encouragement of the development of his thought.

27. The reference to the "superficial" article of September is to Fr. George W. Shea's, "Catholic Doctrine and 'The Religion of the State,'" *AER*, CXXIII (September, 1950), pp. 161-74, which objected to Murray's rejection of the traditional concept of "the religion of the State." Murray's first reply: "The Problem of 'The Religion of the State,'" Part I, appears in *AER*, CXXIV (May, 1951), pp. 327-52, and is accompanied by an unusual editorial note from Fenton: "In its September 1950 issue, *The American Ecclesiastical Review* carried an article in which Fr. George W. Shea stated and explained his unwillingness to accept certain theses on Church and State contained in the writings of Fr. John Courtney Murray, S.J. Thus, since Fr. Murray's teachings on the subject have not been published previously in the *Review*, the editor considers it only fair to allot him space to present his own views and reasons on the pages of this magazine." And Fenton added: "The editor likewise believes that it is only fair to add that he does not share Fr. Murray's views on the subject of this article," p. 327. This so dismayed and angered Murray that he refused to publish Part II of the article in *AER*. It appeared in *TS*, XII (June, 1951), pp. 155-78, under the title "The Problem of State Religion."

28. In his *The Papacy and The Modern World* (New York: McGraw-Hill, 1970), Karl Otmar von Aretin has some very interesting comments about the absolutist rule of Pius XII. According to von Aretin, Pius XII, in an overestimation of his office, regarded his many addresses "not as contributions for discussion but as utterances of a binding nature for Catholics." He put it very clearly in his *Humani generis* when he said: "When the popes explicitly pronounce judgment on a hitherto controversial question, it is a clear indication to all of us that, according to the intention and will of the popes, it should no longer be subject to free discussion by theologians." Von Aretin comments: "The addresses of Pius XII therefore evoked no discussion inside the church, nor, thoughtful as they were, and in retrospect sometimes even prophetic, did they have any influence. When he died, the Catholic Church found herself in the same fossilized state as she had been at the death of Leo XIII." p. 227.

29. McCormick to Murray, May 14, 1951, WCA.

30. Murray to McCormick, June 1, 1951, Copy, WCA. The Superior General's circular letter is dated February 11, 1951, and published by the Woodstock College Press, 1952, for private circulation under the title: "Letter of Very Rev. Father General John Baptist Janssens on the Encyclical 'Humani Generis' of Pius XII." Murray was personally convinced that Weigel's article would cause no difficulty from the standpoint of the text and the doctrine of *Humani generis*, since it was concerned simply with the background and context of the encyclical. His chief fear, however, was that the Jesuits in France might not like the imputation that they stood under the influence of existentialist thought. Weigel's article also contained "one or two suggestions about the nature of the theological task that might be questionable." And he added in the same June 1 letter to McCormick: "Given the seriousness of the situation and the evident preoccupation both of the Holy See and of Very Reverend Father General, I shall, of course, be most careful about anything we publish dealing with the Encyclical. Perhaps I should say that Father Weigel himself is not in any sense inclined to minimize the content of the Encyclical or to be oversympathetic with the ideas that are disapproved in it and in the letter of Father General. We have all studied Father General's letter carefully, and it will be accepted, with complete loyalty, as the guide of our thinking and very particularly of the editorial policy of *Theological Studies*."

31. This writer tried to locate the Fenton Papers in March, 1974. The executor of Fenton's estate, the Reverend Robert Trasher of East Springfield, Mass., responded by saying that Fenton left no theological notes, diaries, or personal letters that would be pertinent to the subject of this book.

32. Murray to McCormick, January 31, 1953, Copy, WCA.

33. Murray to Fenton, August 16, 1951, Copy, WCA. The article Murray is replying to: Francis J. Connell, "The Theory of the 'Lay State,'" *AER*, CXXV (July, 1951), pp. 7-18. Connell objects to Murray's theory as "a very definite and radical departure from what has hitherto been commonly regarded as Catholic doctrine ..." pp. 17-18. Murray's reply to Connell: "For the Freedom and Transcendence of the Church," *AER*, CXXVI (January, 1952), pp. 28-48.

34. Fenton to Murray, August 27, 1951, WCA. As was mentioned previously, Murray was annoyed at Fenton's appending an editorial disagreeing with Murray's reply to Shea. Murray considered this a violation of editorial protocol and advised Fenton that he saw no use in attempting "to carry on a full dress discussion on the Church-State problem in the pages of *The American Ecclesiastical Review*." Murray to Fenton, September 4, 1951, Copy, WCA.

35. Weigel, *Thought*, XXVII (Summer, 1952), pp. 165-84. The article was originally a paper read at the College of St. Thomas, St. Paul, Minnesota, on November 15, 1951, as one of the lectures in the Archbishop Ireland series on Church and State.

36. Fenton to Murray, April 4, 1953, WCA. In "A Reply to Father Hartnett," *AER*, CXVII (October, 1952), pp. 286-99, Fenton accused Robert C. Hartnett, S.J., editor of *America*, of "deceptive oversimplification of the Holy Office's letter *Suprema Haec* and Fenton's own review of James M. O'Neill's *Catholicism and American Freedom* which treat the same subject of the Church's necessity for salvation." (O'Neill has already been identified in Chap. I. n. 37, p. 24, as the person officially designated by Cardinal Spellman to answer Paul Blanshard's attacks on Catholicism.) In his *America* editorial, Vol. LXXXVII (September 20, 1952), Hartnett suggested that Father Leonard Feeney and his followers at St. Benedict were subjected to ecclesiastical censure because they had contended that persons dying outside the Church could not be saved. Fenton denied this interpretation and criticized O'Neill for the same erroneous interpretation. The text of *Suprema Haec*, the Holy Office's letter to Cardinal Richard Cushing of Boston on the Feeney case, can be found in: *AER*, CXXVII (October, 1952), Latin text: pp. 307-11; official English translation: pp. 311-15.

37. Joseph F. Murphy, Rector of Woodstock College, to Fenton, April 21, 1953, WCA. For the remaining years of his life, Murray would suffer the pains of a weak heart, a bad back, and acute bursitis. His inability to regulate carefully his work schedule and slow down occasionally was a problem he never solved. It would ultimately lead to his death in 1967.

38. Murray to Fenton, April 11, 1953, Copy, WCA.

39. Fenton to Murray, April 17, 1953, WCA. The meeting never took place. Murray's last letter to Fenton, May 25, 1953, from Blue Ridge Summit, Pa., where he was in recuperation from his illness, suggested a meeting after the summer; Fenton to Murray, June 5, 1953: "agrees," but by the end of that summer the controversy would take a different direction.

40. From here on the debate between Murray and Fenton took place in the pages of *AER* and *TS*. The final chapter of this study will undertake an analysis of their disagreement over the Church-State formula particularly as it relates to the issue

of Americanism.

41. "Leo XIII: Separation of Church and State," *TS*, XIV (June, 1953), pp. 145-214.

42. Ellis to Murray, June 25, 1953, WCA.

43. The Ottaviani discourse referred to here is "Church and State: Some Present Problems in the Light of Teachings of Pope Pius XII," given by the Cardinal at the Lateran University on March 2, 1953, on the occasion of the anniversary of Pius XII's elevation to the Pontificate. A shortened version appears under the same title in *AER*, CXXVIII (May, 1953), pp. 321-34. Fenton, in "Toleration and the Church-State Controversy," *AER*, CXXX (May, 1954), pp. 340-41, called the article "a shortened but completely accurate expression" of the original discourse. The interpretation of this discourse, its "authority" and its relationship to Pius XII's *Ci riesce* address of December 6, 1953, played an important part in the Church-State controversy from here on in. An interesting reference is made to it in a letter from John Fearns, the Archdiocese of New York Censor of Books, Dunwoodie, N.Y., to Francis Cardinal Spellman, April 20, 1953 (Spellman Archives, Dunwoodie, New York): "I was very much interested in reading the discourse of His Eminence Alfredo Cardinal Ottaviani.

"I referred to his book *Institutiones iuris publici ecclesiastici* and found that this discourse in principle repeats what he has there and what he taught.

"There are applications that, of course, are not in the text book, Spain, Father Murray's thesis, the activities of the Evangelicals in Italy. I suspect that it is with the last that his interest particularly lies and that he is at pains to justify the action that has been taken. His explanation is direct and logical, but it is doubtful that it would be convincing to those who have not studied or read the theses preceding, on which it is based." See: Ottaviani, *Institutiones iuris publici ecclesiastici*, Vol. I, 1947; Vol. II, *Ius publicum externum*. Editio tertia, Typis Polyglottis Vaticanis. A review by J. C. Fenton appears in *AER*, CXIX (December, 1948), pp. 471-72.

44. Murray to Ellis, July 13, 1953, Copy, WCA. Murray was writing from Ridgefield, Connecticut, where he was acting as assistant pastor of St. Mary's Church. The letter expressed his hope that the touch of pastoral life would help complete his recovery. He also reported having put aside his final article on Leo XIII until his recovery, though he saw the delay as perhaps "providential." This period of convalescence gave him time to read Ellis's two volumes on Gibbons: "I am left completely in admiration. It was most interesting reading and high scholarship." Regarding the information that Ottaviani's speech of March 2, 1953, was "a purely private utterance, possessing no official significance," the only source up to that time seems to have been Fr. Robert Leiber, S.J., who was then private secretary of Pius XII. In a German letter to Murray (Rome, Piazza della Pilotta, June 12, 1953), Leiber writes: "In short, about the conference of Cardinal Ottaviani: You know and you can use it, it only represents the private views of the Cardinal. It has no official or semi-official character. Your Reverence would do well, in my humble opinion, at least in a personal letter to the Cardinal, to correct what he erroneously characterizes as your opinion. You would do well to leave out of this matter the personal qualities of Msgr. Fenton." Leiber to Murray, WCA.

45. Ellis to Murray, July 16, 1953, Copy, WCA. The McNicholas statement of January 25, 1948, "The Catholic Church in American Democracy," referred to previously in Chap. I, n. 53, p. 26, is at issue here. The full text of the press release is not available. Ellis quotes the most important part of it in "Church and State; An American Catholic Tradition," *Harper's*, CCVII (July-December, 1953, p. 67) and

Perspectives in American Catholicism (Baltimore: Helicon, 1963, pp. 7-8). "No group in America is seeking union of church and state; and least of all are Catholics. We deny absolutely and without qualification that the Catholic bishops of the United States are seeking a union of church and state by any endeavors whatsoever, either proximate or remote. If tomorrow Catholics constitute a majority in our country, they would not seek a union of church and state. They would then, as now, uphold the Constitution and all its Amendments, recognizing the moral obligations imposed on all Catholics to observe and defend the Constitution and its Amendments."

46. This is the article referred to in n. 1, above. In it Ellis speaks of the following bishops as representatives of this tradition: John Carroll, John England, John Hughes, James Gibbons, John Lancaster Spalding, John Ireland, John J. Keane, Richard J. Cushing, John T. McNicholas.

47. Murray to Ellis, July 20, 1953, Copy, WCA.

48. *Ibid.*

49. Ellis to Murray, July 22, 1953, WCA.

50. McCormick to Murray, August 21, 1953, Copy, WCA.

51. Murray expressed his amazement in this way: "I think it quite shocking to find out that Freemasonry has penetrated the Curia, and I tremble for your 'security'! Seriously, it is a bit alarming to see abroad in the Church the mentality represented by this document. In a way, the most astonishing statement was . . . where there is mention of 'absolute fidelity to the teachings of the Popes and of St. Thomas, which is the same thing.' I happen to be acquainted with some of the South American literature on Maritain, and some of it borders closely on the vicious. However, it is somehow instructive to read this kind of literature. It makes one realize more and more the necessity of serenity and charity in controversy." Murray to McCormick, September 9, 1953, WCA.

52. *Ibid.*

53. McCormick to John J. McMahon, November 15, 1953, ANYP. Canon 2316 reads: "Qui quoque modo haeresis propagationem sponte et scienter iuvat, aut qui communicat in divinis cum haereticis contra praescriptum can. 1258, suspectus de haeresi est." Canon 1258 reads: "1. Haud licitum est fidelibus quovis modo active assistere seu partem habere in sacris acatholicorum. 2. Tolerari potest praesentia passiva seu mere materialis, civilis officii vel honoris causa, ob gravem rationem ab Episcopo in casu dubii probandam, in acatholicorum funeribus, nuptiis similibusque solemniis, dummodo perversionis et scandali periculum absit." *Codex Iuris Canonici*, Typis Polyglottis Vaticanis, MDCCCCXLVII.

54. Murray to McCormick, November 23, 1953, Copy, WCA. On December 7, 1953, Stritch wrote to Murray expressing gratitude over their meeting: "Our conversation in Washington was a satisfaction to me of a desire which I have had for a long time. If I was frank in stating my difficulties I assure you that I was just trying to find an answer to them. I have thought and worked on this problem and what I said in Rome was the expression of what I hold to be the teaching of the Church. It is a satisfaction that in the aftermath of my address as far as I can discover many whose judgment I esteem approved of what I said. As was said to you, we must go along prudently and thoughtfully in these studies and seek the advice of competent scholars. It pleases me immensely that you are willing to help me and I want you to send me from time to time your further studies on this important question." WCA.

The above reference to Stritch's "discourse at the American College Affair" is to the address the Cardinal gave in the presence of Pius XII, on October 14, 1953, on the occasion of the dedication of the new North American College in Rome. In his address he reminded Americans of the ideals upon which their country was established, referring basically to the recognition of the dignity which God has given to man. "For us our country above everything else is a land of freemen, conscious of their rights and dignity, collaborating together in a brotherly spirit for the common good of all." Quoted in: Maria Cecilia Buehrle. *The Cardinal Stritch Story* (Milwaukee: Bruce, 1959), p. 114.

55. From the same letter of Murray to McCormick, November 23, 1953. This is the second indication from someone at the Vatican that Ottaviani's discourse had no official status. The first, previously mentioned, came from Father Robert Leiber. It is important to mention this fact since this information gave Murray the confidence he needed to strike out against the Ottaviani position in March, 1954.

56. On this point Murray was very specific in this same November 23 letter to McCormick: "The affair of the Pentecostals from Texas was at the moment in the news. And I remember telling her that she might protest arbitrary acts of violence against American citizens, but that she had no right, either as Ambassador and still less as a Catholic, to interfere with the just application of existent Italian laws. There was no mention of Canon 2316 (I carry only a limited number of canons in my head!)." He also added: "One thing is certain: she never heard of Canon 2316. And I rather hope that, if there is to be a reprimand, it will be given gently, preferably by the 'highest superior' himself. She is doctrinally all right in the faith, but has a woman's idea—maybe some men's idea—of positive law. Moreover . . . she can be stubborn and even rebellious."

57. The reference is to a series of exchanges between the editor of *America*, Robert Hartnett, S.J., and the Archbishop of Seville, Pedro Cardinal Segura y Saenz. In a Lenten pastoral, Segura had rejected a remark by President Harry Truman that expressed dislike for the present Spanish government (*New York Times*, February 8, 1952). The Cardinal feared that American pressure would force the Spanish government to permit religious freedom for Protestants in Spain. At first *America* tried to dismiss the controversy by pointing out that Truman had said the wrong thing. But a few weeks later after seeing the full text of the pastoral, *America* changed its opinion and criticized the Cardinal for completely ignoring political philosophy, for grouping Protestants in the same category as rationalists and Communists, for limiting religious liberty to Catholics alone. *America* saw this as going contrary to Pius XII's 1942 Christmas message which spoke of "The right to worship God in private and public and to carry on religious works of charity" as a fundamental right. Finally the *America* editorial rejected the Cardinal's claim that religious liberty in Spain would be contrary to divine law (*America*, LXXXVII [1952], 1). The Spanish journal *Ecclesia* answered with the claim that the editorials in *America* were in doctrinal error and contrary to the teaching of papal encyclicals. *Herder-Korrespondenz*, VI (1951-1952), p. 376. While this debate was in progress, the Vatican was negotiating a new concordat with the Spanish government. Consequently, the Church-State formula suggested by Murray and *America* magazine had political ramifications. In this context, the reaction of the Vatican and the Spanish hierarchy to Murray's philosophy is comprehensible. The new concordat was signed on August 27, 1953. It permitted closer cooperation between the Church and State and a stronger governmental influence in episcopal appointments than in the other concordats concluded since 1918. Yet, it did not mark a return to the *Patronato Real* of the old Spanish monarchy. See: "Inter Sanctam Sedem et Hispaniam sollemnes conventiones [Italian and Spanish texts], *Acta Apostolicae Sedis*, XLV (October 27, 1953), pp. 625-55; "Spanish concordat," *America*, LXXXIX (September 12, 1953), p. 567.

58. McCormick to Murray, November 27, 1953, WCA.

59. Murray to Ellis, November 19, 1953, Copy, WCA.

60. Ellis to Murray, November 23, 1953, WCA.

61. Janssens to Murphy, quoted in Murphy to McMahon, December 6, 1953, ANYP.

62. Murphy to McMahon, December 6, 1953, ANYP.

63. This discourse of Pius XII directly set the stage for Murray's bold speech at the Catholic University of America on March 25 of the following spring. *Ci riesce* will be analyzed in the next section.

64. Murray to Ellis, December 12, 1953, Copy, WCA.

65. Ellis to Murray, December 16, 1952, WCA.

66. Murray to Ellis, December 19, 1953, Copy, WCA.

67. Ellis to Murray, January 8, 1954, WCA.

68. The extent of the Curia's influence became evident when the European theologian, Yves Congar, was silenced by his superiors in early 1954. It was Congar's particular interest in ecumenical questions which had inspired his revolutionary thinking on the relationship between the Church and the world. He was particularly concerned with the role of the laity in the Church, to which theme he had devoted his famous *Jalons pour une théologie du laïcat, Unam Sanctam,* Vol. XXIII (Paris: Edition du Cerf, 1953).

69. *America,* XC (January 9, 1954), pp. 375-76.

70. "The Teachings of *Ci riesce,*" *AER,* CXXX (February, 1954), p. 114.

71. *Ibid.,* p. 120.

72. *Ibid.,* pp. 122-23.

73. Murray Papers, WCA.

74. Ellis to Murray, March 30, 1954, WCA.

75. Alfredo Cardinal Ottaviani to Francis Cardinal Spellman, April 1, 1954, Archives of the Archdiocese of New York.

76. Spellman to Ottaviani, April 5, 1954, Archives of the Archdiocese of New York.

77. *AER,* CXXX (May, 1954), p. 341.

78. *Ibid.,* pp. 342-43.

79. *AER,* CXXX (June, 1954), p. 384.

80. McCormick to Murray, August 8, 1954, WCA.

81. Murray to McCormick, August 18, 1954, Copy, WCA. Since the above-mentioned letter from the general and "instructions" are missing from the Murray Papers it is difficult to know what message they contained. An attempt on my part to get copies of the above from the Jesuit Curia General in Rome proved unsuccessful.

82. Notes of Walter Burghardt, WCA.

83. Murray to M. A. Fitzsimons, September 13, 1954, Copy, WCA. The letter is important in that it indicates somewhat the message of the missing letter and "instructions" from his superior general. Murray said to Fitzsimons: "You perhaps know that there are people who are after my head—preferably not attached to the neck. I had a private communication from my Father General in Rome to this effect. He is concerned about my head, and quite sympathetic. The net of it is this: (1) the most informed circles in Rome are now thinking about the Church-State problem in terms of these categories: principles, the application of principles, and the principles that govern the application of principles; (2) there is some concern lest I be misunderstood, sc., lest I be understood to be talking about 'principles' when in fact I am talking about the 'application of principles' or the realization of principles in history; (3)

my essay in your book might possibly give rise to this misapprehension." Murray explained that if there was to be a second printing he hoped to get the matter straight, by a note to the effect that he was "giving an historical analysis, not a doctrinal-juridical statement." He indicated to Fitzsimons that there was nothing in the book to be retracted. It was more a matter of protecting himself and the book. He referred to a review of the book in the September issue of *AER*, adding that the review was "importantly part of the general situation." He assured Fitzsimons that there was no question of any public "condemnation" and that the matter was to be kept secret and confidential! ". . . My Father General wants the matter kept secret." Finally Murray gave his personal evaluation of the matter: ". . . I seem presently to be caught in a rather taut Roman situation. For my part, I believe and hope that it will resolve itself in a manner favorable to me and my friends. But for the moment one treads on the well-known eggs . . . I have a price on my head. And such as it is, I have a perhaps forgivable interest in that article or any otherwise expendable organism. . . ."

84. Burghardt notes.

85. This matter is dealt with in the letters sent by Ellis to Walter Burghardt for inclusion in the Murray Papers; Ellis to Burghardt, October 15, 1968, WCA; Ellis to Burghardt, October 17, 1968, WCA.

86. Murray to Ellis, August 12, 1954, Copy, WCA.

87. Msgr. Philip M. Hannan, Chancellor, Archdiocese of Washington, D.C., to Ellis, July 28, 1954, Copy, WCA.

88. Ellis to Archbishop Patrick O'Boyle, August 14, 1954, Copy, WCA. Ellis also informed O'Boyle of the program for the Fourteenth Conference on Science, Philosophy, and Religion in their Relation to the Democratic Way of Life, which was to be held at Harvard later in the month. He commented: "It is good to see the names of nine or ten Catholics listed in the program. Not infrequently we have been criticized for our 'ghetto' mentality and, perhaps, rightly so. Participation of this type will, I think, do something to help us break through the barriers that separate us from fellow scholars of other religious beliefs."

89. Ellis to Walter Burghardt, October 15, 1968, Copy, WCA. In this same letter to Burghardt, Ellis reported that he accepted O'Boyle's decision and raised no further question. However, when Murray and three other theologians were banned from lecturing at the Catholic University of America in February, 1963, Ellis was contacted and asked his opinion of the matter. "I deplored," he said, "the banning, needless to say, and then added something along the lines: 'But that sort of thing has been going on at this University for over a decade.' This remark gave the deepest offense to Bishop McEntegart, Archbishop O'Boyle *et al.*, and from that day to this relations between my ordinary and myself have ever been distant and cool, to put it mildly."

90. von Aretin, *The Papacy and the Modern World*, p. 225.

91. Murray to McCormick, January 14, 1955, WCA. "The Problem of Pluralism in America" originally appeared in *Thought*, XXIX (Summer, 1954), pp. 165-208. It also appeared in *Catholicism in American Culture* (College of New Rochelle, 1955), and was reprinted in *The Catholic Mind*, LVII (May-June, 1959), pp. 201-15.

92. McCormick to Murray, February 23, 1955, WCA. It is unclear what were "the one little error" and "the mildest admonition" referred to by McCormick in this letter. Perhaps they refer to the missing "instructions" of the previous August from the superior general. Whether Murray had specifically asked permission to

reprint the *Thought* article is not clear from any of his correspondence. McCormick's letter could imply this but without any kind of certitude.

93. McCormick to Murray, March 4, 1955, WCA. This is the first and only mention of a possible Roman trip for Murray. The implication here is that Murray asked McCormick's advice on whether a trip to Rome might not help to clear the air. If such a letter exists it is not in the Archives.

94. The Industrial College of the Armed Forces, a sister institution of the Army Staff College, was publishing a symposium under the title: *America's Spiritual and Moral Resources in the Present Crisis*. Contributions were by members of different faiths. Murray had been asked to provide the Catholic viewpoint.

95. McCormick to Murray, July 9, 1955, WCA. Murray evidently passed a copy of this letter to the rector of Woodstock, Joseph Murphy, for on July 18, 1955, Murphy wrote to the provincial, Thomas E. Henneberry, enclosing a copy of the McCormick letter. Murphy expressed his own feeling about the way the matter was being handled. "In a rather peculiar way in which the affair of Father John Courtney Murray has been handled in Rome, information comes through odd channels. I do think that both the Fathers Provincial are well up-to-date on the whole matter. The latest chapter in the business is the enclosed letter from Father McCormick to Father Murray. . . . The more important section of Father McCormick's letter is, of course, the last paragraph. It refers to Father Murray's definitive statement of his position on *Church and State*. The writing of this became almost a small book, before he had finished. Unfortunately, he failed in his own mind to take a realistic view of things and had counted, I believe, on complete and public vindication by Rome. As a consequence, he is a bit depressed by the outcome."

Henneberry replied on July 22, 1955: "I had had some slight hope that the Roman examination of Fr. Murray's position would result in more than Fr. McCormick's advice to let the whole matter drop and be content with the expectation that someone in the future will profit from the work already done. The return of the books to the library is a practical way of following the advice given." (In his letter to Henneberry, Murphy had indicated that Murray had "cleaned all the books on Church and State out of his room and returned them to the library." It reflected his belief that he "was through.")

"I had first thought to ask you to let the article for the Army publication go since you have read it and find it unobjectionable. But Fr. McCormick takes such a serious view of the whole business that it will be better to avoid any possible recriminations falling on Woodstock. I do not expect to find any objection where you do not; but if something gets by both of us it will be more convenient to be able to inform Rome that the slip-up occurred here." Both of these letters are in the Archives of the New York Province of the Society of Jesus.

96. Murray to McCormick, July 15, 1955, Copy, WCA.

97. McCormick to Murray, July 21, 1955, WCA.

98. Murray to McCormick, August 3, 1955, Copy, WCA.

99. McCormick to Murray, December 14, 1955, WCA.

100. The address was given at the Founder's Day Commemoration of the 137th Anniversary of St. Louis University on November 15, 1955. The address appears in: *In Government, Business, Education and the Church: Eight Views of Responsibility* under the title: "The One River of Truth." It also appears in *The Catholic Mind*, LVII (May-June, 1959), pp. 253-60, as "The Catholic University in a Pluralist Society."

101. *The Catholic Mind*, LIII (October, 1955), pp. 590-97; reprinted from

Epistle, 115 East 57th St., New York.

102. *Life,* December 26, 1955; reprinted in *The Catholic Mind,* LVII (May-June, 1959), pp. 196-200.

103. "Catholic Polemic and Doctrinal Accuracy," *AER,* CXXXII (February, 1955), pp. 107-17. The article attacked James M. O'Neill's *Catholics in Controversy* (New York: McMullen Books, 1954) for the "serious confusion" in certain parts of the book, particularly the "completely inaccurate and objectionable statement about Cardinal Ottaviani's Lateran discourse and a seriously faulty description of the Church's power of jurisdiction." p. 107.

104. "The Holy Father's Statement on Relations between the Church and State," *AER,* CXXXIII (November, 1955), pp. 323-31. The discourse of Pius XII referred to here is: "Vous avez voulu," delivered to the Tenth International Congress of Historical Sciences on September 7, 1955. The official English translation of the allocution can be found in this same issue of *AER,* pp. 340-51. This was the Congress Ellis was to have attended. O'Boyle, as we have shown, persuaded him not to go.

105. Murray to McCormick, January 22, 1956, Copy, WCA. The text of the lecture given at Kent, Connecticut, is published in a symposium volume along with other lectures given by Jacques Maritain, Reinhold Niebuhr, *et al.* Published: Fuller, Edmund, ed. *The Christian Idea of Education:* Papers and Discussions by William G. Pollard and others (New Haven: Yale University Press, 1957). A cable from Rome dated February 2, 1956, sent approval to publish the text without the *"Thought* citations."

106. Murray to McCormick, January 22, 1956, Copy, WCA.

107. Murray to McCormick, February 3, 1956, Copy, WCA.

108. McCormick to Murray, February 3, 1956, WCA. On March 26, 1957, at Karlsruhe, Germany, the Constitutional Court of the Federal Republic upheld the validity of the Vatican Concordat of 1933. The treaty with the Holy See was concluded on June 20, 1933, shortly after the Nazis rose to power. While the original draft was drawn up by representatives of the Vatican and Germany, a dozen years before Hitler usurped the government, German Socialists and Free Democrats had been conducting a steady campaign against some of its provisions. The Christian Democratic government, however, always recognized the concordat as binding. For a text of the concordat, cf. "Inter Sanctam et Germanicam Reipublicam sollemnis conventio," July 20, 1933; Latin and German texts (parallel columns, *Acta Apostolicae Sedis,* XXV (September 10, 1933), pp. 389-413; see also, G. N. Shuster, "Germany under the Concordat; with editorial comment," *Commonweal,* XVIII (September 1, 1933), pp. 419-22.

109. Murray to McCormick, February 16, 1956, Copy, WCA. The article appeared in *Dokumente,* XII (February, 1956), pp. 9-16, under "Kirche und Demokratie."

110. Murray was obviously referring to Fenton's "Appraisal in Sacred Theology," *AER,* CXXXIV (January, 1956), pp. 24-36. In answering the question: "What actually constitutes achievement in Sacred Theology?" Fenton outlined some "objectively valid norms" used to rate the competency of a theologian. "The matter is particularly urgent in this country today. In some rather articulate but not too well-informed Catholic circles it has become fashionable to appeal to the authority of certain 'great theologians' in support of what can be most charitably described as highly questionable theses" (p. 24). Among the criteria Fenton lists to judge a theologian's competence are: (1) doctrinal accuracy: "Actually a man is a competent theologian only to the extent that his teaching . . . is an accurate statement of the truth contained ei-

ther formally or virtually in the deposit of public revelation" (p. 31); (2) Theological procedure: "The theologian is expected, not only to present accurate teaching, doctrine strictly in conformity with the statements of the Church's *magisterium*, but also to prove or to demonstrate the propositions he sets forth" (pp. 32-33); (3) Timeliness: The theologian is expected to express Catholic truth "effectively in terms of the problems and the questions of the time in which he is actually working. He should be able to use his own language well enough to teach in it accurately, clearly and effectively" (p. 34). Explicitation: "There is a definite contribution to the science of sacred theology when a man for the first time presents some aspect of a theological teaching explicitly" (p. 35).

111. Murray to McCormick, February 29, 1956, Copy, WCA.

112. Murray to Dr. Paul Botta, Editor of *Dokumente*, February 29, 1956, Copy, WCA. "Die Katholiken in der americanischen Gesellschaft," *Dokumente*, Vol. XII (August, 1956), is a summary of Murray's clarifications.

113. McCormick to Murray, August 18, 1956, WCA. The address: "Censorship in the Fields of Literature and Arts" had been given at the Thomas More Book Club Forum on the occasion of Murray's reception of the Thomas More Medal. It appeared under the title "Literature and Censorship" *Books on Trial* (June-July, 1956), and received wide publicity, being characterized by Bernard Theall as "the best modern contribution to the subject from the Catholic point of view." Considering America as a pluralist society, i.e., having many religious groups within its boundaries, Murray attempted to lay down principles on which minority groups within the larger whole may act as censor. They may do so for their own group, but not impose this censorship on others, though all groups have the right to work by persuasion and pacific argument toward the elevation of the standards of public morality. As a result of this article a debate ensued between Murray and John Fischer, editor of *Harper's Magazine*. Murray followed up his lead article with another in *America*, "The Bad Arguments Intelligent People Make" CXVI (November 3, 1956), pp. 120-23. Murray's indirect suggestion here as to the role of the National Organization for Decent Literature as formers of public moral views rather than as trigger men for police activity displeased the NODL people in Chicago and a number of bishops. In December, 1938, the American Catholic hierarchy had established the National Office for Decent Literature. The organization was established to safeguard the moral and spiritual ideals of youth through a program designed to remove objectionable literature from places of distribution accessible to youth. It also aimed at encouraging the publication and distribution of good literature and promoted plans to develop worthwhile reading habits during the formative years.

114. On two occasions Murray admitted to Thurston Davis, editor of *America*, that "morality seems at the moment to have hit a dead end" (Murray to Davis, May 16, 1956, WCA), and "the whole concept of public morality does not exist for some people." (Murray to Davis, November 20, 1956. WCA.) And in a lengthy private letter to John Fischer, Murray asserted that "the thing that gives strength to the NODL case is precisely the magnitude of the problem in public morality" (Murray to Fischer, November 23, 1956, WCA).

115. Murray to Donald Campion, S.J., August 1, 1957, Copy, WCA.

116. In his July 21, 1956, letter to Charles W. Lowry, President of the Foundation for Religious Action in the Social and Civil Order, Murray admitted: "The present moment of crisis does indeed call for whatever action we can take." Copy, WCA.

117. Murray sent a copy of the sermon to Robert M. Hutchins, President of the Fund for the Republic, saying: "I send it only that you may know that I am still

plugging away at the good task—the promotion of good public argument, and the definition of the next task for the liberal-minded American." Murray to Hutchins, October 18, 1956, Copy, WCA. And Hutchins to Murray, October 31, 1956, WCA: "I am lost in admiration. It is very seldom the truth is combined with a good literary style. You have stated the heart of our problem and done it so well that it must have some effect."

118. The lecture, given on October 18, 1956, is unpublished.

119. Murray to John S. Castelot, S.S., March 7, 1957, Copy, WCA. It would seem that Murray is referring here to "The Problem of State Religion, *TS*, XII (June, 1951), pp. 155-78. For he confessed his displeasure with this article in a letter to Father José M. Setien Alberro of Vitoria, Spain: "I am not at all pleased with the essay 'The Problem of State Religion.' It is not well written and there is some confusion of thought." Murray to Setien, December 11, 1956. In this same letter Murray admitted: "The essay in *Thought* ("The Problem of Pluralism in America") represents my most ambitious attempt to give an account of the American situation."

120. Murray to Fr. Murphy, March 23, 1957, Copy, WCA. Murphy cannot be identified other than last name. The manuscript referred to is entitled: "Leo XIII and Pius XII: Government and the Order of Religion," a copy of which can be found in the Murray Papers, WCA. It is in this letter to Murphy that Murray provides the background information, "altogether confidential," on why this last Leonine article never got beyond galley proof. "I don't quite know how to rank it among the 'secrets' that the moralists deal with: but it ranks as a secret." Explaining that the article was written in the spring of 1955, Murray outlined the reason for nonpublication: "After it had been approved by two censors over here, I sent it to our Roman curia for censorship, *ad cautelam*. One censor made no adverse criticism. The other, while he approved the substance of the argument, thought I had overemphasized the polemic intentions of Leo XIII. However, both censors independently agreed that it would be imprudent and inopportune to publish the article. This judgment was affirmed by my Father General. The reasons were related to the fact, which you know, that there is a difference within 'Rome' itself, not indeed with regard to Catholic doctrine but with regard to its *impostazione* (that glorious untranslateable word!). Moreover, it happens that I am *persona non grata* in certain powerful circles, quite apart from the question, whether I hold *doctrina non recta*. This is one of the repercussions of the famous 'controversy' over here. It is a story in itself, with which I shall not bore you."

121. In 1957 Murray published "The Christian Idea of Education" in *The Christian Idea of Education* (New Haven: Yale University Press, 1957) and "The Freedom of Man in the Freedom of the Church," *Modern Age: A Conservative Review*, I (Fall, 1957), pp. 134-45. In June, 1957, Murray delivered the commencement address at Manhattanville College of the Sacred Heart in New York, on "The Task of the Christian in the 'Post-Modern Age' " (unpublished).

122. Murray to Donald Wolf, S.J., July 20, 1958, Copy, WCA. The essay was written for a seminar on Church-State relations under the direction of Heinrich Rommen, professor of political science at Georgetown University. Murray's position on Church and State problems was Wolf's subject. Hoping to publish the paper, Wolf sent a copy to Murray for criticism and comments. In a letter to Charles J. Beirne, S.J., of Woodstock, who was collecting material for the Murray Papers, Wolf gave some of the background information on this incident (dated November 17, 1967). "While in graduate studies in government at Georgetown, I did a seminar paper on Fr. Murray's Church-State position. I sent a copy of this paper to Fr. Murray for his comments since I had hoped to publish the paper. The first page of the

enclosed letter (7/20-58) contains his suggested changes in my paper. . . . My paper was later published, "The Unitary Theory of Church-State Relations," *A Journal of Church and State*, IV (May, 1962), pp. 47-65, and I believe with Father Murray's suggestions incorporated. I think that Father Murray's letter to me is of some interest because of his own explanation of his 'silencing' and his attitude toward it. . . ." In the spring of 1968 Doubleday published Wolf's *Toward Consensus: Catholic-Protestant Interpretations of Church and State*, which contains a chapter on Murray's Church-State position, pp. 3-35, and a quotation from Murray's July, 1959, letter to Wolf in the Introduction.

123. Murray to Wolf, *ibid.*

124. Murray to McCormick, July 22, 1958, Copy, WCA. In this regard Murray explained that since "the question of a Catholic for President has begun to be a journalistic issue" and people here want to "do better than Al Smith," a statement must be made "on the perennially troublesome question: Can a Catholic support, in principle, the religion clauses of the Constitution? More recently Kennedy has decided not to make a statement unless he is forced by circumstances (it was Cardinal Spellman who told me this early in June)." Murray also reported Henry Luce asked him for advice about an article on the subject for *Life*. Finally, he reported that the bishops had also been considering the question and trying to formulate "a united opinion." Murray reported that the bishops had just turned down "as unsatisfactory" a position paper on the subject by Father F. J. Connell. In the context of papal approbation, Murray asserted that what was really at issue was "one of substantial truth and also of right methodology in argument."

125. This article in *Civiltà Cattolica* was referred to in Chap. I, p. 25, n. 41: Cavalli, "La Condizione dei Protestanti in Spagna," II (April, 1948), pp. 29-47.

126. Murray to McCormick, July 22, 1958, Copy, WCA.

127. McCormick to Murray, August 5, 1958, WCA.

3

Vindication: 1960-1967

The year 1959 was to be an historic year for the entire Church. On January 25 of that year, Pope John surprised the world by calling for a "Diocesan Synod for Rome" and an "Ecumenical Council for the Universal Church." World and Church leaders of all faiths responded positively and recognized this announcement as truly "momentous."[1] The seventeen cardinals present on that occasion, however, responded with stunned silence. During the next few months, the attitudes of the Pope's curial advisers toward the idea of a universal council grew increasingly negative, and suggestions were that it would take years for the necessary preparations.[2]

From the first years of Pope John's pontificate up to the opening of the Second Vatican Council in 1962, the Pope appeared almost helplessly at the mercy of his curial advisers. Decisions of the Holy Office in those early years showed the continuing strong influence of the curia and a clear intention to continue and strengthen some of the reactionary attitudes of the 1950s. On July 3, 1959, for instance, the Holy Office opted against the French worker-priests.[3] In June, 1961, the Holy Office issued a new warning against biblical scholars.[4] February 22, 1962, saw the imposition of Latin as the language for teaching seminary courses;[5] and in June of that same year came the *monitum* against the works of Pierre Teilhard de Chardin.[6]

Von Aretin has noted that "the first preparations and the *schemata* drawn for the Council also suggested a regressive tendency, almost a relapse into reactionary practices even beyond those of Pius XII."[7] Characterizing John XXIII as "anything but a revolutionary," he rightly viewed the Pope's greatest achievement as that of the Council, which "was to have given modern theology a fair chance against the curia."[8] Robert B. Kaiser, a commentator on the Second Vatican Council, quoted Murray as having said of the Pope: "John XXIII had created an atmosphere in which a lot of things came unstuck—old patterns of thought, behavior, feeling. They were not challenged or refuted, but rather just dropped."[9] According to Kaiser, in place of the dogmatic answer, John asked questions, and he encouraged others to join him in discovering whether old forms were still correct forms, and whether customary methods were effective methods. Kaiser again quoted Murray: "He raised some questions himself—notably the great, sprawling, ecumenical question—to which he returned no definitive answers. He encouraged the raising of other questions, both old and new, both theological and pastoral—and even political. The symbol of him might well be the question mark—surely a unique symbol for a pope."[10]

In spite of McCormick's rebuff of the July, 1958, initiative, Murray proceeded to assert more freedom. There is no evidence of any further correspondence between Murray and Vincent McCormick. As we have seen, after July, 1955, when Murray was rebuked, he decided no longer to pursue the publication of a collection of his articles. In May, 1959, however, Murray began negotiations for a publication of some of his writings by Sheed and Ward. A letter from Philip Scharper, editor of Sheed and Ward, referred to a discussion Murray had had with Frank Sheed on the subject. Scharper expressed delight at the prospect of his doing a book

> on the problem of American pluralism. More than any person I know you seem to have felt the situation on your pulses as well as to have grasped it conceptually. It is reassuring to think of your doing a book in this area; I have been fearful that a bad book might rush into the existing vacuum, and once there, be extremely difficult to dislodge.[11]

Murray's typed notes on the tentative outline of the book described how he envisioned it:

> The book should be, in effect, a primer of pluralism, paying special attention to the dilemmas posed to and by Catholics in a pluralistic society. The term "primer" is used . . . not to indicate that the book is projected for the unsophisticated, but merely to indicate that there is, despite decades of experience and discussion so much learned ignorance on the subject.[12]

In July Scharper indicated that Sheed shared Murray's view that the book should be confined "to an acceptance of a pluralist society as actually existed with an effort to take soundings about problems that a Catholic meets in such a society and the service he can render it."[13]

The book finally appeared in the late spring of 1960 under the title: *We Hold These Truths: Catholic Reflections on the American Proposition*. It received immediate and wide attention, becoming one of Sheed and Ward's best sellers. It thrust Murray further into the national limelight and by December of the same year *Time* magazine had chosen him for its cover story. Murray's portrait filled the cover of the December 12, 1960, issue and the yellow band across *Time*'s corner told the reader that this cover-story was concerned with "U.S. Catholics and the State." It was, in fact, a long discussion of Murray's book.

The book deliberately appeared a few months before the John Kennedy-Richard Nixon election and was most surely instrumental in helping to clear some of the popular confusion which played so great a role in the controversy that preceded the election. Murray had been called on to advise Kennedy in those crucial months before the election. Arthur Schlesinger, Jr., in his *A Thousand Days*, wrote that Kennedy's "basic attitude was wholly compatible with the sophisticated theology of Jesuits like Father John Courtney Murray, whom, he greatly admired."[14]

Perhaps the most important speech Kennedy gave on the issue of Catholicism was to the Houston Ministerial Association on September 12, 1960.[15] Theodore Sorensen, in his book *Kennedy*, noted: "I read the speech over the telephone to the Rev. John Courtney Murray, S.J., a leading and liberal exponent of the Catholic position on church and state."[16] Some years later, Murray was questioned on the matter and, while he did not remember all the details, he did confirm that Sorensen had read the speech to him over the telephone. According to Murray's recollection:

> It may be that I did suggest some changes but I cannot remember what they were. I told Sorensen at the time that it was unfair to ask me for an opinion just on hearing the speech on the phone, but he was standing by the side of a plane just about to take off for Houston. My impression is that Sorensen wrote the speech himself. Undoubtedly it had an effect on its immediate audience and on others and was of assistance to Kennedy.[17]

Sorensen characterized it as "the best speech" of Kennedy's campaign and "one of the most important in his life. Only his Inaugural Address could be said to surpass it in power and eloquence."[18] The Houston confrontation was widely applauded throughout the nation and according to Sorensen: "It made unnecessary any further full-scale answer from the candidate, and Kennedy, while continuing to answer questions, never raised the subject again."[19]

According to numerous reviewers, the publication of *We Hold These Truths* but a few months before the election did help to clear the air and it answered many questions about the still thorny Church-State issue. That Kennedy was elected must be considered a turning point in the history of American Catholicism. *Newsweek* magazine, in commenting on the two events, says: "Murray demonstrated in theory what John F. Kennedy demonstrated in practice: that Americanism and Roman Catholicism need no longer fear each other."[20] Prior to the election and to the performance in office of President Kennedy, a Catholic's ability to serve properly in that position was open to serious question in the minds of many non-Catholics. It was not altogether clear that an American Catholic was truly free in the area of politics.

While Murray's sound argumentation in *We Hold These Truths* succeeded in convincing many Americans of the validity of his assertions, he evidently had not convinced his greatest opponent in the United States that what he said was in keeping with good Catholic tradition. Fenton's review article of *We Hold These Truths* took issue with Murray on doctrinal grounds and characterized his position as an example of the "carelessness" and "sympathy for the liberalism of the day."[21] As we shall examine more closely in the last chapter, Fenton saw Murray's theory as running directly counter to papal doctrinal teaching, particularly *Longinqua oceani* and *Testem benevolentiae*, encyclicals directed to the American Church. Evidently Murray's days of controversy with Rome and its American spokesmen were not over.

John XXIII's dramatic announcement of January 25, 1959, allowed for many and varied opinions concerning the meaning and aims of the upcoming Council. Fenton's numerous articles on the Council eschewed all doctrinal speculation as a danger to the faith, and he worked at opposing any suggestions that serious change in Catholic theological thinking was possible.[22] For Fenton the Council would be expected to present "a clear and exact statement of God's supernatural revealed message." He saw this as an essential and urgent task of the Council if it was to check the contemporary onslaught of Modernism and liberal Catholicism.[23]

Murray, on the other hand, said and wrote nothing about his expectations with regard to the Council. Rather, his efforts focused on topics related to American public policy,[24] the religious issue as related to the Kennedy campaign,[25] and religious dialogue in America.[26] When the Council opened in October, 1962, Fenton was in Rome as Cardinal Ottaviani's personal adviser.[27] Murray was at Woodstock, Maryland, where the Holy Office wanted him, after having "disinvited" him from the first session.[28]

The American Bishops and the
First Session

At the opening of Vatican II it was said that the American episcopate was a perfect mirror of the thinking, aims, and prejudices of the Roman curia. Arriving in Rome in 1962, the large majority of American bishops were not prepared for new interpretations. Something had clearly taken place from the time of the American contribution at Vatican I by men like Peter Kenrick, John B. Purcell, Martin J. Spalding, and Augustin Verot to the beginning of Vatican II's first session.[29] Between the two councils the American Church had suffered the defeat of the Americanist heresy controversy. Leo XIII's *Testem benevolentiae* had had serious effects on American Catholicism. Combined with the condemnation of Modernism and the "heresy hunting" that followed throughout the world, the two condemnations had devastating results for the speculative and experimental qualities of the Church in America. *Testem benevolentiae*, in particular, brought effective silencing of discussions and debates. The condemnation also stifled the initiative, independence, and adventurous spirit which had been typical of the American Church until the turn of the century. The dominant attitude became one of caution and excessive prudence.

It was this kind of attitude that characterized the American bishops during the first session of Vatican II.

> Up to their arrival in Rome, U.S. bishops reacted individualistically. While in Rome, observing other national conferences meet as distinct groups, some U.S. bishops were at first scandalized. But soon it became evident that corporate identity, distinctively American, was imperative to the U.S. episcopate; and that Catholicism, in its American form, had a definite contribution to make. It was not that easy, though.[30]

Standing behind this attitude was "the fear of being labeled with the mark of 'Americanism,' the traumatic word which time had emptied of much of its original content but which still conveys the idea of cultural separation, paralyzes energies and stifles initiative."[31] Pope Paul VI, on the occasion of the first beatification of his pontificate, of Blessed John Nepomucene Neumann, is reported to have used the moment to show appreciation for Americans and his respect for the American way. The Pope appeared "to go out of his way to exorcise once and for all the ghost of pseudo-heresy known as 'Americanism.' " . . .[32]

Once the American bishops began to feel more sure of themselves their efforts began to match and even go beyond those of their predecessors at Vatican I. Defending the American prelates' position on the Church and State issue at Vatican I, James Hennesey wrote:

> European theorists might dismiss their effort as sheer pragmatism. It seems instead to have been prompted by a keen pastoral awareness and the desire to seek out the best way of carrying on their apostolic mission in the modern world. As such, it merited at least as much consideration as shopworn formulas which in many cases were themselves only the relics of practical adaptations which had been achieved in past centuries and in other political and cultural climates.[33]

Archbishop Paul J. Hallinan, in a splendid review of Hennesey's book, called his evaluation valid and termed the significance of the American contribution at Vatican I as "rooted in the word 'pragmatic' which with proper reservations can be translated, 'pastoral.' "[34] Initially the American contribution at Vatican II on the issue of Church and State would be similar in character. But Murray saw the need for more than a "pragmatic" solution to this complex problem.

In the months just preceding the opening of the Council, Archbishop Lawrence Shehan, of Baltimore, Maryland, sent Murray various drafts of the preparatory commission on the subject of religious freedom. In an August, 1962, personal memo to the Archbishop, Murray criticized the initial two drafts.

> Its main characteristic seems to be the desire that the Council should avoid all theoretical issues and simply say something "practical."
>
> I think this is a mistaken view of the problem as it exists, in the concrete. The practical question is, what is Catholic theory—theological, political, ethical—in the matter? This is what intelligent people want to know, inside and outside the Church.
>
> If the Council refuses this question, and is content simply to say that "in today's circumstances everybody ought to have a full right to religious liberty," we shall be exactly where we are at the moment, in the very predicament from which we want to escape.
>
> This is easy to see. Ottaviani's "two standard" theory (what I call the disjunctive theory) will remain on the books, untouched, as the essential and pure Catholic doctrine (he holds that it is proxima fidei, and Ruffini agrees). And the Council's "practical" statements will look like sheer concessions to "today's circumstances"— a matter of expediency, or, in a word, the thing called "hypothe-

sis," again affirmed, to the joy of the curial Right, who will have triumphed in what will have been in effect no more than an affirmation by the Council of their own doctrine.

Is this what the American bishops want?

For my part, I think that the only "practical" and "realistic" thing to do is to join frank issue with the curial Right on the issue of theory. This would not be difficult to do. Few seem to realize how dreadfully weak their position is—if it were exposed to free and full discussion. Presently it maintains itself only by the power of the Holy Office to shut up anyone who presumes to question it. . . .

I am inclined to think—I hope not unjustly—that many American bishops really believe in their own minds that the American constitutional situation is no more than "hypothesis" in the Ottaviani sense—a situation to be consented to only on the grounds of expediency, because in the practical order it works well, even though it cannot really be defined in principle. . . .

Not to be misunderstood, one point. I do not say that the American constitutional situation is "thesis." My point is that the whole disjunction, thesis-hypothesis, is invalid in sound and pure Catholic principles, and ought to be discarded. Like its supported concept, the "Catholic state," it is a time-conditioned disjunction, involved in the relativities of history.

All this is part of my first difficulty with the document—its unwillingness to face the issue in the full concreteness of its amplitude, which includes the vital practical importance of its theoretical aspects.

We have a heaven-sent opportunity to effect a genuine development of doctrine in this matter—an absolutely necessary development, and one that can quite readily be effected. The opportunity should not be missed by a too distant flight into the "practical," which is really a flight from the practical problem.[35]

Murray thus suggested to Shehan that an effort should be made to dismantle the curialist disjunctive theory of thesis-hypothesis, and to create the possibility of erecting a unitary theory, scil., a new "impostazione" of traditional principles. Such a theory would be limited to principles, with no admixture of the historically conditioned. It could then be applied in various circumstances with equal validity.

Shehan had prepared his own presentation for Rome and Murray reported to Leo Ward that he was displeased with it.

No, I have received no commission to do anything official for the American bps. Odd, however, that the report is around; I've heard it from several quarters. However, I did do a thing for Archbp. Shehan at his request—a critique of a letter and a memo to be sent to Rome, asking that the Church and state be restored to the conciliar agenda (did you know it had been taken off, as "too controversial"!), and submitting the draft of a capitulum. Again between us, his thing was bad. I'm afraid I fairly murdered it. Now maybe I'll get murdered![36]

On June 18, 1962, just prior to the Council opening, Augustin Cardinal Bea submitted a revised draft on religious liberty to the Central Commission. The Theological Commission under the leadership of Cardinal Ottaviani had submitted its own draft. By July, 1962, Pope John created an *ad hoc* commission to reconcile the two drafts. On July 15, the Secretariat for Christian Unity, under Bea's leadership, submitted a compromise draft to the *ad hoc* commission. But on August 2, 1962, negotiations between the Secretariat and the Theological Commission collapsed. It was just after this that Murray, still not a Council *peritus*, sent his memo to Archbishop Shehan and suggested how he might approach the problem.

By the end of the first session, the two opposing mentalities at the Council had clashed, and new commissions had been set up.[37] The old Ottaviani-Connell-Fenton position on Church and State, which had been the dominant "orthodox" view in the United States and throughout the Catholic world until the Council, was now seriously weakening and eventually would be in full retreat. The opposition made a last minute effort to win the day. Fenton came to Ottaviani's defense against attacks by the liberals at the Council and the world press.[38] Vagnozzi, as Apostolic Delegate in Washington, made every effort to slow the liberal drift here in the United States. At the urging of the Apostolic Delegate, Murray, Godfrey Diekmann, Gustave Weigel, and Hans Küng were forbidden to lecture at the Catholic University of America in the spring of 1963. The incident received national attention and further weakened the methods of suppression so characteristic of the 1950s.[39]

Once it became clear that the Council would chart new theological paths, the long-delayed invitation came. Murray went to Rome at the insistence of no less a traditionalist than Francis Cardinal Spellman. The official invitation came from Cardinal A. G. Cicognani, Secretary of State of the Holy Father, dated April 4, 1963: "Si è benignamente degnata di annoverare fra i 'Periti' del Concilio Ecumenico Vatican II il Reverendissimo Padre G. Courtney Murray, della Compagnia di Gesù. Tanto si partecipa al medesimo Padre Murray, per sua opportuna conoscenza e norma."[40]

In a letter to Leo Ward, Murray confirmed that he was in fact going at Spellman's request: "Between us, it was my Eminent friend of New York who pried me in. He said (and meant it, I think) that the Jesuits had got too slim a deal about *periti*, and that it was 'no more than right' that I in particular should be there. Which was nice of him."[41] From the day of his arrival in Rome for the second session, Murray was destined to play a central role in framing the eventual *Declaration on Religious Freedom*.

On November 22, 1963, Murray reported to his rector that he had prepared a four-page memo for the American bishops, stating the reasons why the religious liberty issue should be restored to the agenda and outlining the desired content of a conciliar statement. Although Cicognani cancelled discussion of the issue from the agenda Murray noted that his memo was accepted at a full meeting of the American bishops. A letter signed by Cardinal Spellman was then sent in their name to Cicognani, the Presidency of the Council, and to the four moderators. It demanded that the issue be discussed, and that the basis of discussion be the text prepared by the Secretariat for Christian Unity. Murray later learned from an important source that the issue would not have been restored to the agenda, had it not been for this strong American intervention.[42] According to another source the United States petition had also been passed to the Holy Father by Cardinal Spellman. The Pope is said to have ordered Cardinal Ottaviani to call a meeting of the Theological Commission to consider Chapter V of the Schema on Ecumenism which was the chapter on religious liberty.[43]

This was perhaps the most important meeting in the history of the religious liberty issue, and it came on November 11 and 12, 1963. Murray attended and reported his impressions to the rector at Woodstock.

A personal high moment was the meeting of the full Commission on Faith and Morals on November 11. They (i.e., Ottaviani) had claimed the right to review the Secretariat text. There was a big battle over this, but in the end the Secretariat had to give in. I was invited by Card. Léger, Card. Browne, Archb. Parente, and two others spoke strongly against our text. Bishop Charue of Namur, after speaking strongly for it, suggested that the periti be heard, beginning with me. Ottaviani, however, called first on Rahner, then on one or two others. Bishop Wright introduced my name again, amid other murmurs of approval and invitation, and I got to make my speech—face to face with Ottaviani, with Msgr. Fenton at the end of the periti table. The final vote was 18-5—a glorious victory for the Good Guys. The meeting lasted from 4:30 to 7:00. And it was pretty tense from the beginning to end. (We had a big party at the Hilton later in the week to celebrate the occasion.)[44]

A "feeling of euphoria" swept over the American bishops and the Council *periti*.[45]

A few days later in a letter to Spellman, Murray suggested that once the discussion of religious liberty began, the Cardinal should "make an intervention in defense of the American Constitutional system and its guarantee of 'the free exercise of religion.' " Murray advised the Cardinal to proceed in this way:

1) The practical value of the American constitutional law.

a) It guarantees to the Church what the Church wants, according to Pius XII: "A stable condition of right and of fact within society, and complete independence in the discharge of her spiritual mission" *(Ci riesce)*.

b) It guarantees to the Catholic faithful what they must have, according to Pius XI: "Ecclesiae, tamquam hominum societati, opus omnino esse ad vitae usuram atque incrementum justa agendi libertate, ipsosque fideles iure gaudere in societate civili vivendi ad rationes conscientiaeque praescripta" *(Firmissimum con stantiam)*.

c) It guarantees to all citizens freedom from governmental interference on the profession and practice of their religious faith and thus avoids all confusion between religion and politics—a confusion that has been disastrous in history.

2) The American constitutional system is not only a good practical arrangement: it also rests on sound moral and political doctrine:

a) All men are endowed by their Creator with certain inalienable rights, including the right to religious freedom in society (Declaration of Independence, and Pius XII, etc.).

b) The primary purpose of government and law is to protect the rights of the human person, including the right to religious freedom (Pius XII, John XXIII).

c) The functions of government and law are limited to the temporal and terrestrial affairs of men. In particular, the First Amendment declares government to be incompetent in the field of religion; government is not a judge of religious truth; it has no right to repress religious error; it has no share in the *cura animarum*; its sole function in the field of religion is the protection and promotion of *freedom* of the Church and of the churches and of all citizens.

3) The Catholic Church in America does not "tolerate" the U.S. constitutional system (this would be nonsense). The American bishops and the American faithful positively approve and support the First Amendment and its provision for the free exercise of

religion. They believe that it conforms to the judgment of their civic conscience and of their religious conscience too. They do not consider it to be "hypothesis" as opposed to "thesis."

In a word, the American people (here, both Catholic and non-Catholic) believe that there is harmony between their constitutional principles and the doctrine of *Pacem in terris*, as stated in Chapter V and explained in the *Relatio* of Bishop De Smedt.[46]

Murray reported to Maher that Spellman had accepted his suggestions and had asked him to write the speech "with which he was pleased."[47] Concerning the *Relatio* mentioned in his letter to Spellman, Murray admitted that he had written the initial draft for the Belgian Bishop Emile De Smedt.

You may have seen the story in the *Times* that I wrote the *Relatio*; if I say so myself, who shouldn't, it is substantially true, though De Smedt re-worked my thing to suit his own style. Actually, the thing was a bit of a *tour de force*. The essential problem—that of development both of the doctrine of the Church and of her pastoral solicitude for the freedom of the human person—could not possibly be treated in 22 pages. It was a matter of striking off a sort of story-line. It was also a matter of inviting the conciliar Fathers to improve the Secretariat text, which is not particularly good, by amending it in the sense of *Pacem in Terris*, which came out after the text had been composed.[48]

After four days of debate on the Ecumenism schema, November 18-21, a suggestion was made by Ermenegildo Cardinal Florit, Archbishop of Florence, that the discussion on religious freedom be postponed and discussed in connection with the schema on the Church in the Modern World (Schema 17).[49] The moderators called for a vote on the first three chapters as a basis for further discussion. Even the Secretariat for Christian Unity saw the advantage of discussing the more general first three chapters on Ecumenism independently of Chapter IV on Jewish-Christian relations, and Chapter V on religious liberty. But it was already too close to the end of the second session to hope for any worthwhile discussion on religious freedom. At the close of the second session on December 4, 1962, the chapter on religious freedom had not been formally discussed in the Council or given a preliminary vote. In a sense it was a victory for both sides. The curial opposition had managed to postpone discussion of the issue for two sessions, but the postponement would allow more time for the Secretariat to improve its text.

Between the second and third sessions, further efforts were made to prevent open discussion of the religious liberty issue. In a lengthy article appearing in *America* magazine just a few days before the conclusion of the second session, Murray termed religious liberty "*the* American issue at the Council." Praising the American episcopate for the strong support it gave to the issue, Murray criticized the "many efforts to block discussion of" religious liberty during the second session.[50]

On February 26, 1964, John J. McGinty, provincial of the New York Jesuit province, wrote to Michael F. Maher, rector of Woodstock College, informing him of a communication from the Apostolic Delegate in Washington, Archbishop Vagnozzi, on "the norms for the guidance of the *Periti* at the Council in their public statements." The Archbishop wanted these norms passed on to Murray. McGinty in turn sent the rector a letter for Murray along with the norms. Since Murray had suffered a severe cardiac arrest in early January, 1964, McGinty suggested:

> I am sending it to you to pass on to him in the event that you judge that it will not have an adverse effect on his health. In the event, however, you judge that this might occasion a relapse or even slow down his recovery, I would ask that you hold the letter and contact me. I hope Father Murray has continued to improve and that you will be able to give him the enclosed letter.[51]

McGinty's letter to Murray got immediately to the matter at issue:

> Recently I received a letter from the Apostolic Delegate in Washington, Archbishop Vagnozzi, in which taking the occasion of your article, "On Religious Liberty," in the November 22nd-30th issue of *America*, he asked me to bring to your attention, as is being done with all the Periti of the Council, the norms set down at a meeting held on December 28th, 1963.

His Excellency quotes the following:—

> "In the meeting of December 28, 1963 of the Coordinating Commission, the Cardinal President announced the following norms of the Holy Father, regarding the activities of the Periti:
>
> 1) According to the work assigned, the Reverend Periti should answer with knowledge, prudence and objectivity the questions which the Commissions have proposed to them.
>
> 2) They are forbidden to organize currents of opinions or ideas, to

hold interviews or to defend publicly their personal ideas about the Council.

3) They should not criticize the Council, nor communicate to outsiders news about the activities of the Commissions, observing always in this regard, the decree of the Holy Father about the secret to be observed concerning conciliar matters."[52]

On May 16, Murray informed his provincial that the rector had passed him the letter from the Apostolic Delegate. Reporting that he had already received a copy of the norms from the Secretariat for Christian Unity to which he was officially attached, Murray pointed out that it was sent out routinely to all official *periti*. While he called the document "sufficiently ambiguous," he raised the question: "What business is this of the Apostolic Delegate? He is in no sense an official of the Council. He has no jurisdiction whatever over the activities of the periti." Adding that the kind of article he did for *America* was done by all sorts of *periti*, he saw it as in no way out of order. Providing more details on the background of the article, he explained that the article was the original English version of an introductory statement that he had given, in German translation, to a press conference for the German-speaking press in Rome.

I gave the press conference, which went on for two hours, at the invitation of Bishop Kampe, the press secretary for the German episcopate. This sort of press conference was given in Rome by all sorts of periti, usually—as in my case—by official invitation of various national episcopates.[53]

Murray then suggested that if McGinty was to communicate with Vagnozzi he should simply inform him that "I have already received the *normae* and will give them due attention." He added the personal note that the Apostolic Delegate "has elected to be my personal enemy and has made statements about me throughout the country which are libelous. Friends of mine have urged me to take up the issue with him, but there is no sense in doing this." Murray concluded by assuring the provincial:

Finally, if there should be any trouble in my own case, which is hardly likely, I am sure that his Eminence of New York will stand behind me. He is one of the few American bishops who can be counted on to talk back to the Delegate. And he has—bless his heart—elected to be my patron. He mentioned to me in Rome that he had read the article in *America* and liked it. I also wrote an intervention for him, which he never gave because the debate was cut short. I might add that what I said reflected the general view of the American episcopate. I know, because I wrote the memorandum which gave the substance of their common intervention, asking that the issue of religious freedom be presented to the Council, over Italian and Spanish opposition.[54]

This kind of clash reflected the sort of atmosphere prevalent throughout the first two sessions of the Council. While Pope Paul VI made unmistakably clear his admiration and friendship for Council progressives he became, in many ways, more a prisoner of the Curia than John XXIII ever was. As Genoa's conservative Guiseppe Cardinal Siri put it: "The Pope and the bishops pass. The Curia remains."[55]

Here in America, Fenton was making a last strong attempt to win the day for the curial position. His article, "Cardinal Ottaviani and the Council," attacked those trying to discredit the president of the Theological Commission, and the "counter-reformation" theology which he represented. Calling Ottaviani the "most important figure of the first session," Fenton ended by asserting that Ottaviani:

> has not been "hoodwinked" into imagining that any good is going to come to the Church of God if it passes over some of its dogmas in silence so as to please those who dislike the unchanging continuity of Christ's teaching within His Church. He has insisted on the need for stating Catholic doctrine, even when that doctrine is opposed to the tenets of the Reformers and the Modernists.[56]

And in his article "The Roman Curia and the Council," Fenton assailed those lacking information about the position of the Curia in the true Church and called the "attack on the Curia" as a "veiled attack on the Pope."[57]

His final article to appear in *The American Ecclesiastical Review* came at the end of the second session and was an attack on Xavier Rynne's "Letters from Vatican City." He denounced him for his criticism of the Curia, its advisers, including Fenton himself, and for having left the impression that the curial procedure was one including "fear-inspired tactics" and "thought-control." He denied that the Curia had or would ever use such tactics; he compared Rynne to Paul Blanshard and termed him sympathetic to Modernism and those errors condemned in the Oath against the errors of Modernism.[58]

In the January, 1964, issue of *The American Ecclesiastical Review*, the following announcement was made:

> In December 1963, Msgr. Joseph Clifford Fenton, after twenty five years of outstanding service as Editor-in-chief of *The Ameri-*

can Ecclesiastical Review, resigned because of poor health. Made Prothonotary Apostolic by Pope Paul VI, Msgr. Fenton is now Pastor of St. Patrick's Church, Chicopee Falls, Massachusetts.[59]

Preparation for the Third Session

On May 16, 1964, in a letter to his provincial, John McGinty, concerning Vagnozzi's attempt to silence him, Murray explained the kind of work he was doing in preparation for the third session.

> At the moment I am under commission by the Secretariat to do an analysis of the comments sent in by the bishops on the issue of religious liberty. The job was to have been done in February, when I was ill. I intend to publish my work in one form, in the September issue of *Theological Studies*. I shall send it in another form to the Dutch documentation center in Rome, for translation and distribution to the conciliar Fathers.[60]

A letter from Archbishop Karl J. Alter, of Cincinnati, to Murray on July 22, 1964, revealed that the original essay was entitled "Right of the Human Person to Liberty on Matters of Religion." Alter, who was to become a close collaborator with Murray on the religious liberty issue at the Council, expressed extreme pleasure with the essay and judged that Murray's "presentation of the two contrasting viewpoints is fair, objective, and adequate for a right understanding of the issues involved." As consultor of the Secretariat, Murray had access to the exchange of views during the debate and to the comments and interventions submitted afterward. It placed him in an advantageous position to evaluate the differences. Alter expressed delight that Murray "made good use of this opportunity, and I am grateful to you for permitting me to share in part your experience and to profit by your clear and comprehensive analysis."

There was a double purpose to Murray's essay. First, he wanted to state with all possible objectivity the two existing Catholic views on religious freedom and second, he wanted to initiate a dialogue between them by presenting the objections that each had to the other. To avoid prejudicial characterization, he called his opponents' position the "First View" and his own the "Second View." He thus deliberately avoided any tendency to divide those who discussed the meaning of tradition into "liberal" and "conservative" groups. Murray recognized all too well that these terms, often inappropriate and misleading, caused people to ignore the fact that most individuals seriously involved in discussions of this kind have every intention of being fully orthodox and of standing squarely in the middle of their tradition. Ultimately the question that divided them was one of means.

Among the questions which Murray sought to answer were the following: How is one to approach his tradition in order to assess it rightly? What is tradition and how does it apply? Is it a body of material containing propositions, phrases, formulas, statements that are true literally and without qualification, standards forever fixed which are directly as well as universally applicable? Or is the expression of tradition historically conditioned, and does proper understanding require the tools of historical criticism? Can one depend on the inherited words themselves or must one look behind them for a dynamic but constant intent whose relevancy to changing circumstances demands periodically revised formulations?

It was this kind of analysis that Alter praised in Murray's essay:

> I agree with your criticism that the "first view" is too abstract, too theoretical, and proceeds from theological premises which divorce the question from actuality. It ignores the historical situation in which the doctrine is to be applied and treats the constitutional question in a sort of vacuum. I have always had difficulty in following the argument which starts with the proposition that "error has no rights." This is a rhetorical phrase, since rights and duties can be predicated only of persons, and not of abstract nouns. We are not talking, at least directly, of the relation of creature to the Creator, but of the relation of the citizen to the civil authority and of his immunity in human society from any form of coercion in his religious life.
>
> In my mind, a clear, precise, and comprehensive definition of what we mean by "Free Exercise of Religion" and "Freedom of Conscience" is absolutely necessary to avoid confusion and futile debate. Secondly, that our problem concerning "Religious Liberty" is primarily a pragmatic one; that it cannot be solved apart from the existing historical situation; and hence that the Church's doctrine on the subject admits legitimate development without contradiction of previous essential teaching.

With regard to the "second view," that held by Murray, Alter evaluated it in this way:

> The "second view" is explained in your treatise in such a way that, without the need to elaborate the argument, it carries conviction of its rightness. You have shown that the traditional position of the Church is embedded in history and that it has developed new aspects and grown more mature as political and social conditions changed. It has always remained consistent in its defense of

freedom of the Church to carry on her mission. Your exposition of the argument (in line with that of Monsignor Pavan) from the natural law, from the dignity of man due to his divine vocation, and from the limited power of civil authority, recognized widely in the present political and moral consciousness of mankind—all these build up into a powerful argument in favor of the "second view."

Alter concluded by encouraging Murray to give the essay "as wide attention as possible. This would have to be done immediately if it is to be effective; it would be too late if its distribution took place only after we return to Rome."[61] Murray's reply to Alter assured the archbishop that his essay had been sent "to all the American bishops at the insistence of Archbishop Shehan and Bishops Primeau and Helmsing, the three members of the Secretariat for Christian Unity." And he adds: "It has also been taken up by the DO-C (Documentazione olandese del Concilio) to be translated into four or five languages for distribution to the conciliar Fathers. I myself sent copies to some twenty bishops around the world whom I know personally."[62]

Murray's essay proved to be most influential at the third session, particularly in the drafting of the Secretariat's final text. But before that was to be accomplished a debate developed among those who wanted the Church to make a strong declaration in favor of religious liberty for all men.

The second session's draft on the subject had never been voted on. Some, even among those who agreed with its general purpose, objected to submitting it unchanged to the third session of the Council. The objection to Murray's thesis, which was reflected in the second session's draft of the Declaration, was that it was too "juridical." It seemed to rest its case for religious liberty too heavily on the Anglo-American constitutional tradition and, in particular, on American experience under the First Amendment to the United States Constitution. The objectors were seeking a more "theological" argument.

Murray's August 24, 1964, letter to Archbishop Alter expressed concern about this problem:

I have not yet had time and energy fully to study the new text to see what emendations it needs. One fault, however, was clear to me on first reading. It was also pointed out by Msgr. Pavan in a letter. The text was composed by theologians with a too exclusively theological mentality. From talking with the members of the Secretariat I had the impression that they are not inclined sufficiently to consider the political and legal aspects of the problem. At most, they give these aspects only a secondary importance. For my part, I agree with Pavan that the political-legal aspects are coordinate with, not subordinate to, the theological-ethical aspects.

Murray then suggested that this be the major point of Alter's intervention at the next session. In fact, Murray himself would write Alter's intervention. The real problem, as Murray saw it, and therefore the chief locus for conciliar clarification, did not concern the theological or ethical doctrines, such as the freedom of the act of faith, the immunity of conscience from coercion. "On these issues there is a Catholic consensus—indeed, an ecumenical consensus. The area of confusion and controversy, where a new clarification is needed, is political and legal—that is, in the question of the competence of the public powers *in re religiosa.*"

At issue here was a problem that had plagued Murray all his life, that of the Spanish situation. Though, by this time, the Spanish bishops were anxious to reach a Catholic consensus, they still wanted to retain their doctrine on the religious prerogative of government, and their theory that "the Catholic State" must be maintained as an ideal. According to this theory, government has far more extensive powers in religious matters than Americans were inclined to accept. In effect, the Spanish wanted to make government the servant of the nation's religious unity and the institution chiefly responsible for the common good of the people.

For Murray, the issue had to be resolved along pragmatic lines, and with due consideration of existent historical situations. At the same time, he felt strongly that the pragmatic solution must be so conceived and stated, and so undergirded by considerations of principle, that it would in effect disallow the contention that the Spanish system was "the Catholic ideal."

He was as convinced as always that if the notion of a Catholic "ideal" was not disallowed, things would be back where they always were, without any progress having been made. The thesis-hypothesis disjunction would still stand as Catholic doctrine. And the American system would be only hypothesis, a pragmatic solution reached for reasons of expediency, but at variance with the "ideal." The "ideal" would continue to be obligatory, wherever possible, namely, under conditions of a Catholic majority. And American Catholics would remain under the ancient suspicion.

In summary, as Murray hinted in his essay prepared for the third session, he was willing to let the Spaniards have their Spanish system, as suitable to their historical situation. But he was unwilling to let them qualify it as "the Catholic ideal," as the "thesis." The problem was to show the inadequacy of the Spanish theory without seeming to condemn the Spanish system as valid in its own circumstances.

With this in mind, one can appreciate why Murray insisted that an adequate doctrine of religious liberty could not be based on theological grounds alone. A political philosophy which carefully defined the limited functions of government was also needed. As he saw it, it was only when the body politic was seen as a society of citizens who, as citizens, are equal in their dignity and their civil rights, that religious liberty could be set on a solid foundation.

Juridical and constitutional principles were consequently essential to the discussion.

This was not, as some feared, a species of relativism that would permit the Church to espouse the cause of religious freedom at a time when it was useful to her, only to abandon it in the name of a higher truth at a later date. According to Murray, while freedom of religion was demanded by the personal and political consciousness of contemporary man, its foundations transcended this desire. With a deeper insight into the needs of the human person than possessed earlier generations, contemporary man has perceived the necessity for new dimensions of freedom. In his own words:

> The common consciousness of men today considers the demand for personal, social and political freedom to be an exigency that rises from the depths of the human person. It is the expression of a sense of right approved by reason. It is therefore a demand of natural law in the present moment of history.[63]

The idea of a developing natural law did not imply, according to Murray, that there were no fixed moral principles. Some actions will always be wrong because they are unnatural. By asserting, however, that man's rights spring from their basic needs and that what is required for the proper development of human nature changes in the course of time, he could insist that there is no difficulty in the notion that human rights evolve in history and emerge gradually into men's consciousness.

Murray's thesis, therefore, was an attempt to situate the right to religious liberty in the context of history. It was not a denial of natural law or of natural rights. He especially wanted to avoid any argument about the rights of the erroneous conscience considered in the abstract. In this he was right. There was a wisdom in his historico-philosophical approach to the problem of religious freedom that should have commended itself to the Council Fathers.

By the opening of the third session on September 14, 1964, Murray was expressing the hope that the principle of freedom would become more and more obvious. But he was also somewhat pessimistic about the Council's results. "Throughout the world expectations of the council have been built too high. People are expecting too much and there is not going to be that much coming out of the council. It is a very slow growth."[64] Beyond this he doubted whether change could ever become a reality for the "run of the mill American."[65]

In September, 1964, Murray worked at preparing a series of interventions to be made at the third session by a few American bishops. He noted that the premise of all the interventions should be "1) to vote, 'placet in genere'; 2) the desire to strengthen the Declaration *in senso suo* not to weaken it or cast any doubts on its general validity."⁶⁶

He proposed that Archbishop Shehan treat the topic of the remote biblical and theological foundations of religious freedom. Explaining that the Declaration had been criticized as too political and juridical in tone and therefore "too American," he argued that this was not a criticism of its substance but of its tone. He advised Shehan to speak on this aspect of the problem: In its essential content, he said,

> religious freedom is indeed formally a juridical notion, developed through historical experience, and presently affirmed by the rational consciousness of mankind, personal and political. However, it has its remote roots in certain scriptural texts, and, what is more important, in general scriptural doctrine (1) on the ways of God with men (God's free "descent" to man; His refusal to coerce, etc.), and (2) on the condition of man before God (man is free, but he stands under the judgment of God for the use of his freedom). The Church models her dealings with men on God's own way with men. A fortiori, all secular powers must respect the freedom of man, especially in matters of man's relation to God.⁶⁷

He advised Bishop Primeau to elaborate two particular points on the concept of religious freedom. First, that there is an inseparable connection between the internal freedom of religious decision, which is freedom of conscience; and external freedom of religious expression in worship, observance, witness, teaching, which is free exercise of religion. Secondly, there was a need to elucidate the distinction between the notion of "right" as an empowerment and as an immunity. He pointed out that in the Declaration religious freedom is called a right in the sense of an immunity from all coercion. On the ground of this distinction the charge of religious indifferentism is nullified, and the assertion can be made that the Church does not hold that all men are equally empowered by God, or conscience, to practice any religion they choose.

He suggested that Bishop Carberry treat the subject of the competence of government in religious affairs and thereby prepare Council fathers for the intervention by Archbishop O'Boyle. O'Boyle was to speak on the norm which should control governmental limitation of the free exercise of religion. His intervention should also distinguish between society and state, and then make the consequent distinction between the total common good of society and that limited sector of the common good which is committed to government to be protected and promoted but without coercive means. He proposed that the intervention call for an emendation in this sense:

The free exercise of religion in society is to be immune from governmental or legal inhibition, unless it results in serious disturbance of the public order, either by disturbance of the public peace,
or by violation of common standards of morality and health, or by
injury done to the rights of others.[68]

In a final note to Archbishop Shehan, Murray expressed the belief that
the Declaration would be greatly strengthened and made doctrinally more
sound if a special section were added, entitled, "De libertate Ecclesiae." The
point would be to make clear at the outset that the Church claims freedom
for herself *jure divino*, and that in today's world she claims only freedom. He
hoped to have explained that the principal American reason for supporting
the First Amendment was that it adequately guaranteed and protected the
freedom of the Church in the sense of Leo XIII, Pius XI, and Pius XII.
Therefore he urged that the above proposition be voiced by an American.
"The Declaration would then, with good consecution, go on to say that the
Church today claims for other churches and for every human person the
same freedom that she claims for herself and for her own members."[69]

On Monday, September 21, Murray addressed the American bishops
at the North American College to prepare them for the debate that would
begin a few days later. In spite of the objections of Monsignor George Shea
and Francis J. Connell, the bishops unanimously accepted the text of the
Declaration as a workable point of departure and agreed to have at least eight
United States bishops support it and suggest emendations.[70]

The debate began on September 23 with an introduction by Bishop
Emile De Smedt who described it as a great improvement over the original
text. He was immediately rebutted by Cardinal Ruffini, who criticized the
text for its tendency toward subjectivism and religious indifferentism.[71]
Meyer, Cushing, Ritter, and Alter defended the text.[72] On the second day of
debate, Father Joseph Buckley, superior general of the Marist order, and
Bishop Primeau came to its defense.[73] On the third day, Cardinal Suenens
called for a vote on whether to end the debate, and it passed overwhelmingly,
leaving a number of Americans without a chance to express themselves.

It was then left to the Secretariat to revise the text and De Smedt com-
missioned Murray as the "first scribe" to rewrite the Declaration. This was
done in collaboration with Monsignor Pavan, Willebrands, Hamer, and De
Smedt himself.[74] Murray later reported that this was his and Pavan's first en-
trance on the work of drafting.

Our joint influence has been recognized as "determinant" of the
new doctrinal line. But for the sake of accuracy it should be explicitly noted that it was a joint influence. The fact is that I should

have had little if any influence except for the fact that Pavan's views coincided with my own. Therefore he deserves "equal billing," as a matter of justice.[75]

The work was progressing well until October 9, when the Secretary General of the Council, Pericle Felici, wrote to Cardinal Bea announcing the appointment of a mixed commission to examine and revise the Declaration. Among those named to the commission were Cardinal Browne, Father A. Fernandez, master general of the Dominicans, Archbishop M. Lefebvre, Superior General of the Order of the Holy Spirit, Bishop C. Colombo, of Milan. The first three were noted for their opposition to the very idea of religious liberty.

A counter-offensive which included the Americans Ritter and Meyer and which was led by Cardinal Frings sent a letter to Pope Paul deploring the underhanded tactics and decisions reached contrary to Council rules.[76]

By October 13, the Pope had assured Cardinal Frings that the Declaration would remain under the Secretariat's jurisdiction and he provided for its examination by a joint committee composed of representatives of the Secretariat and the Theological Commission.[77] In the meantime the Secretariat, through Murray, continued its work of refining the text, and although De Smedt did not initially approve of Murray's political and legal approach to the issue, by October 24 the Secretariat unanimously approved Murray's draft and by October 27 had received the approval of four members of the Theological Commission. Although De Smedt attempted once again to reassert his own line of thinking, by October 29 De Smedt's abbreviated text was rejected and Murray and Father Hamer began writing the introductory report for the approved text.[78]

When the revised text was ready for printing and distribution on November 16, the closing date of the Council (November 21) was already upon the bishops. On November 17, the "textus emendatus" of the Declaration was distributed and on the 19th De Smedt made the introductory remarks on the text.[79]

By this time the text was a document on its own, no longer a chapter of the *Decree on Ecumenism*, and its argumentation developed along the Murray line. While the new text answered many of the questions which the opposition had raised to the first two texts, both supporters and opponents of religious liberty found difficulty with it. For some it was not theological enough; for others it lacked the strong support of Scriptural foundation, and was basically too legal and political in orientation, the approach Murray especially had suggested.[80]

Murray was himself not completely satisfied with the weakened version and felt the document was far from the best of the many forms through which the text had gone. Too many important concessions had been made in the attempt to please the minority.[81]

On November 19, Cardinal Tisserant, speaking for the Council Presidency, announced that a preliminary vote on the schema would be postponed until the fourth session. While the document had been ready some days, voting was deliberately delayed until time was so short that the Council Presidency could rule in this way. A strong reaction to this decision, led by Cardinal Meyer of Chicago, ensued on the Council floor and resulted in a petition to the Holy Father signed by over 800 Council Fathers requesting that a vote be taken. Meyer, himself a member of the Council Presidency, had never been consulted by Tisserant. Meyer, Léger, and Ritter went immediately to the Vatican to present the petition to the Pope. But Pope Paul, following the Council rules, upheld the decision announced by Tisserant. The events of this day have been referred to as "Black Thursday" while Murray called it the "Day of Wrath."[82] Many of the Council Fathers returned to their dioceses disappointed that not even a preliminary vote could be reached. It was another day of defeat for religious liberty.

Soon after the closing of the third session Murray made certain to reject the idea that blame for the delay should fall completely on the curial opposition. Rather, as he honestly explained, "a series of interrelated factors was at work." First, there was still a strong minority insisting that the Declaration uphold the classical theory of tolerance. "They oppose not so much the institution of religious freedom as such, but rather the affirmation of progress in doctrine that an affirmation of religious freedom necessarily entails."[83]

A second factor was of greater significance. The advocates of religious freedom were themselves divided on the methodology to be employed. The one, represented particularly by the French-speaking theologians and bishops, supported an ethical and theological approach which led to a juridical notion of religious freedom. The second, represented by the English- and Italian-speaking theorists, with Murray as their spokesman, approached religious freedom from the legal and political point of view, and then sought to support it by theological and ethical principles.

The third factor involved a fear on the part of some that religious liberty would undermine authority in the Church. Finally, since free discussion on the subject had not been permitted over the years, the Council was not prepared to reach a consensus. Calling the debate "a distraction from the real issues" Murray concluded by lamenting the fact that the Church had still not come to grips with the principle of religious liberty, when it had long been accepted on principle by the "common consciousness of men and civilized nations." And he urged that the debate be concluded so as to "get to the deeper issue of the effective presence of the Church in the world today."[84]

On December 29, 1964, Cardinal Ritter sent a letter to all the American bishops asking them to stand in support of the third text.

As you are well aware, the Holy Father has assured us that the schema on Religious Liberty will be on the agenda for the Fourth and final Session of the Council. However, since there has never been even a preliminary vote on the subject, no text can be said to be "in possession." It is on this account that a number of Bishops have urged me to write to solicit the support of the American hierarchy to maintain the text distributed just prior to the conclusion of the Third Session as the basis for discussion.

If you are in accord with this proposal, I would suggest that you write to the Secretariat for Promoting Christian Unity . . . in this vein, adding any suggestions you may have for the further improvement of the declaration.[85]

From the end of the third session until mid-February, written interventions on the *textus emendatus* were sent to the office of the Secretariat. Members of the Secretariat met at Monte Mario, outside Rome, from the eighteenth to the twenty-eighth of February to prepare a revision of the Declaration.[86] From February 28 to March 6, 1965, a plenary session of the Secretariat met in Aricia, Italy, and finalized the *textus re-emendatus*. By May 11, 1965, the revised text was complete and was sent along with an introductory report to the Council Fathers by June.[87]

During the summer months of 1965 Guy de Broglie, S.J., who was more or less the spokesman for the French bishops' "theological approach" to religious liberty, prepared a critique of the revised text and sent a copy to Murray who in turn prepared a detailed reply. Before the opening of the final session there was clearly a need to work out some compromise between the "French" and "American" approaches. This was accomplished through the persuasive urging of Bishop J. Sauvage, an influential French bishop from Annecy who had been generally favorable to the revised text, now considered the fourth text, and Murray's explanation of it. Father Yves Congar's sympathy with the fourth text and with the Murray-Pavan approach was also influential in getting the necessary support from the French bishops.[88] On September 20, 1965, at a news conference sponsored by the American bishops at which Murray explained the "pragmatic approach" to newsmen, he reported that "he had been in touch with French correspondents during the course of the summer and came to an agreement with them about this particular issue."[89]

In the final months before the last session Murray made every effort to persuade even the most unlikely supporters to accept the text. For instance, in an August 20 letter to Michael Cardinal Browne, one of the Council's staunch conservatives and long-time opponent of religious liberty, Murray expressed gratitude that he had been allowed to write a memorandum explaining the schema. "My only function as a peritus is to explain, as best I

can, the document of the Secretariat." And he added in all seriousness but
with a note of humor:

> There is an old folk-ballad among us about a boy who was treed
> by a bear (it is of Negro origin, as many are). The refrain runs
> thus: "O Lord, if you can't help me, for heaven's sake don't help
> the bear." It comes to mind as an expression of my hope in this
> matter: if your Eminence does not find it possible, in conscience, to
> come out in favor of the schema, I hope that you will not find it
> necessary, in conscience, to come out against it![90]

The Council's fourth session opened on September 14, 1965, and the
following day Religious Freedom was the first matter on the agenda. After
the introductory remarks by Bishop De Smedt, the debate began once again.
Spellman led with a strong approval of the revised text followed by Cushing
and Ritter. Further support for the text was given through the interventions
of American bishops: Lawrence Shehan, Albert Meyer, Ernest Primeau,
John Mussio, Robert E. Tracy, John Whealon, Paul Hallinan, and Philip
Hannan. One bishop is reported to have said at this moment: "The voices
are the voices of United States bishops; but the thoughts are the thoughts of
John Courtney Murray!"[91] However, the opposition began to muster forces
to oppose voting on the Declaration which they understood to be a "mere
American political document aimed at easing pressures from a pluralistic
community back home, no matter the cost to Catholics in other countries."[92]

On September 21, an historic vote was taken to close debate on the
schema and it passed with 1,997 voting *placet*, 224 *non placet*, and 1 spoiled
vote. This meant the text was now "in possession" and could no longer be
debated in the Council or its text essentially changed.[93] It was now left to the
Secretariat for Christian Unity, and not a mixed commission, to rework the
final draft. But Murray was not able to participate in the final revision. On
October 5, he suffered a lung collapse and was hospitalized indefinitely. In a
letter to Richard Regan, he admitted:

> The high probability is that I would have had little influence, even
> if I were there; by that time the currents were being set by the
> bishops, as usually happened in the latter stages of a conciliar doc-
> ument. Not even Pavan had much influence.

Among those working on the final draft were, according to Murray, Bishops
De Smedt, Willebrands, A. Ancel, and Carlo Colombo, together with
"Pavan, Hamer, Congar, Benoit and several other periti, including
Medina."[94]

In addition to the collapsed lung in October, Murray had suffered two heart attacks in January and December, 1964. Bishop Marcos McGrath of Panama, in a letter to the rector of Woodstock College on September 23, 1967, reflected on Murray's illness during the last months of the Council:

> During the Council years we very frequently discussed at length the underlying issues and whenever possible during his illness during the last session, I visited him at the hospital where I found his mind alert and he unwilling to space himself when so much was in the balance at the Council. I remember very well during the last two hectic weeks of our work on "Gaudium et Spes," when some of us who were working on the text began to despair at the pressure of time and the few rumors began that perhaps we would have to suppress parts of the text or leave it as a post-conciliar document, that Father John, from his hospital bed, made the very serious observation to me. "The most important thing is that it exists." This has been amply proven in the aftermath, since it is the method of "Gaudium et Spes" more than anything else which marks a turning point and this Father saw very clearly.[95]

On October 25, 1965, following Pope Paul's historic visit to the United Nations, the *textus recognitus* was introduced to the Council. On the following day, the Council fathers approved the text by a greater majority than the two-thirds required. Despite a number of suggested revisions only a small number of changes were made in the final text, and very few of these were significant.[96] The changes came at the suggestion of the conservatives who succeeded in introducing a number of altogether unnecessary phrases into the text.[97] These changes, however, weakened the Declaration and left it somewhat ambiguous. In all likelihood many of the last-minute changes would never have been made had Murray not been ill.

More than anyone else, Murray was responsible for the best parts of the final Declaration. One of its finest paragraphs is clearly representative of Murray's manner and approach:

> This Vatican Synod declares that the human person has a right to religious freedom. This freedom means that all men are to be immune from coercion on the part of individuals or of social groups and of any human power, in such wise that in matters religious no one is to be forced to act in a manner contrary to his own beliefs. Nor is anyone to be restrained from acting in accordance with his own beliefs, whether privately or publicly, whether alone or in association with others, within due limits. The Synod further de-

clares that the right to religious freedom has its foundation in the very dignity of the human person, as this dignity is known through the revealed word of God and by reason itself. This right of the human person to religious freedom is to be recognized in the constitutional law whereby society is governed. Thus it is to become a civil right.[98]

On November 9, the Secretariat had completed the final text, and on the 19th, the Council overwhelmingly approved it. The final vote took place on December 7, 1965, with 2,308 for, 70 against, and 8 invalid votes. Promulgation of the Declaration by Pope Paul followed immediately in Saint Peter's Basilica.[99]

The happiest day of Murray's life came on November 18, when, while still convalescing, he was invited to join a number of other theologians for a concelebration with Pope Paul. Some time later, Murray is reported to have said that this was one of the most wonderful masses he had ever celebrated.[100] A close friend of Murray said of the event:

In public, the happy ending of the long struggle was symbolically celebrated by his invitation to take part in Pope Paul's concelebration of the Mass in St. Peter's. In private, the event was celebrated with champagne, friends, smiles—and toasts that were really prayers for the future of a beloved Church in a kind of turmoil that its servant could only wish to prove holy.[101]

Murray's own appraisal of the victory was realistically restrained: "Its [the Declaration's] achievement was simply to bring the Church abreast of the developments that have occurred in the secular world. The fact is the right to religious freedom has already been accepted and affirmed by the common consciousness of mankind."[102]

Along with many of Europe's noted theologians, with whom he so greatly contributed to the renewal of theology, Murray had been called to taste misunderstanding, formidable opposition, and a period of temporary defeat. Christian fortitude and confidence, however, and a balanced appreciation of the theologian's function in the Christian community and in the world, brought him vindication and acceptance. Few theologians received the tribute voiced by the German bishop Walter Kampe, who applauded Murray's "concern about civil rights and specifically, religious liberty," as the "American contribution to the Council."[103]

Although many other important members of the commission helped to pen the final text of the Declaration—and their work has often been underestimated—no one would deny that Murray's contribution was decisive. The very acceptance of Murray's basic thrust, only ten years after his admonition from the Jesuit curia in Rome, was itself a singular recognition.

Recognition of this achievement came from many non-Catholics including Paul Blanshard, so long a foe of the Church and an opponent of Murray. Blanshard praised him for having written "the best parts of the final declaration," and for having built "verbal bridges to the modern world."[104] Another saw Murray's work as an historical occasion of singular significance in that through him "in its doctrinal development the Roman Catholic Church has gone far beyond the toleration of error, to the position that even error has civil rights."[105] Throughout the Council years the "toleration school" was never able to transcend the thinking of the last century. They were not opposed to the institution of religious liberty as such but rather, as Murray pointed out, to "the affirmation of progress in doctrine that an affirmation of religious freedom necessarily entails."[106]

Following the Council's conclusion Murray returned to Woodstock, Maryland, to devote himself to topics of greater personal interest. The religious liberty issue had taken up most of his time and he had not been able to pursue related topics such as freedom within the Church, the development of doctrine, or the problem of contemporary atheism. In his final years, these would become his major interests. In a letter to Paul Weber, S.J., who was seeking information on the subject of religious liberty, Murray referred him to Richard Regan, who "spent the summer here working on my council papers." "I myself," he added, "have given up the idea of writing a history of the Declaration on Religious Freedom. I have done six articles on various theoretical aspects of the declaration and I am frankly tired of the whole subject."[107]

Murray had been deeply affected by his experience at the Council and saw a whole area of theological concerns that needed investigation of the kind he could carry out. Had he lived to do it, his contribution in this field might have been as fruitful as his early work on religious liberty.

In the spring of 1966, Murray was appointed director of the John LaFarge Institute. Founded in 1964 by the editors of *America*, the institute gathered leaders from many sectors of society and from the full spectrum of religious belief for off-the-record discussions of almost any and all subjects. Included were religious liberty, racial discrimination, censorship, abortion, the population explosion, business and political ethics, religion and the arts, war and the antiwar movement.

Through this institute, Murray was able to dedicate the last years of his life to ecumenical and racial problems. He applied his theological principle of freedom to the critical social, political, and moral issues of the late 1960s. In every discussion, he always brought with him the conviction that freedom was "the first truth about man, a positive value, both personal and social, to be respected even when it involves man in error and evil."[108]

The deeply troubled area of interracial relations is an example of Murray's deep personal concern. For Murray, this problem raised a larger issue, that of this nation's integrity as "one nation indivisible." "The interracial issue vitally concerns the whole American enterprise, which was, in paramount, 'to form a more perfect union.' " He felt summoned to respond to the question of how the "civil unity of negro and white, who have been declared equal before the law of the land—how are they to be one in the civic oneness of the one American community?" For Murray it was clear that the achievement of this "national objective, which is to form a more perfect union, can only be a work of freedom."[109]

His deep conviction concerning the value of freedom influenced his attitude and position when he served on the presidential advisory commission on policies that could affect millions of youth. The final report to President Lyndon Johnson on conscientious objection was studded with his precise distinctions. In this area, Murray made valiant efforts to represent the importance of honoring the selective conscientious objector. When the commission of twenty-four was polled for its final vote on the matter, only Kingman Brewster, President of Yale University, and Murray voted in favor of selective conscientious objection. Convinced that this was a freedom to be respected, Murray asserted that "strictly on the grounds of moral argument, the right conscientiously to object to participation in a particular war is incontestable." Murray went on to advocate a revised draft law which could include not only the absolute pacifist but also the relative pacifist. He made it clear, however, that he advocated selective conscientious objection in the name of the traditional doctrine on war and in the name of American political doctrine which safeguards the rights of conscience.[110]

War and racism were not the only moral problems to which Murray applied his theological understanding of freedom. But a few months before his death he addressed himself to the burning issue of birth control. He asserted that the minority report of the papal commission on birth control, by upholding the traditional ban against contraceptives, revealed a mentality of "classicism." In this context he discussed the conflicting views of "classicism" and "historical consciousness" in the Church. For Murray, "The Church reached for too much certainty too soon, went too far."[111]

He supported the approach of the commission's majority, searching for a new understanding which would be in continuity with the past but which would also represent progress. Murray felt that for the minority the issue was no longer birth control but certitude and the related issue of authority.

Before his death, Murray was able to pursue the dialogue between himself and those who held different views. In December, 1966, he was deeply involved in the growing Christian-Marxist dialogue. "It is a very tricky, but necessary thing," he said. "We have to listen to the Marxist critique of religion. We can learn much about our faith. You don't inquire at the outset how it will turn out. Rather, you commit yourself to a learning process with the knowledge that you may wind up against a wall. Dialogue is a contemporary way of presenting the Gospel."[112] He evaluated the "Christian-Communist Dialogue" as "a helpful beginning"; adding, "There exists a potential for mutual understanding and perhaps co-operation. . . . There is a need for a methodology of dialogue, a methodology that will permit us to deal with our own histories, Christian and Communist, without descending to polemics."[113]

Just prior to his death, his interest in dialogue also involved him in the Lutheran-Catholic dialogue. In February, 1966, he was chairman of a section of the first Institute on Judaism and Christianity held at Woodstock College in cooperation with the American Jewish Committee.

In a July, 1967, letter to Murray, the Superior General of the Jesuits, Pedro Arrupe, expressed interest in a lecture Murray had delivered at Fordham in late June on "The Ecclesial Dimensions of Unbelief." "I am very much interested in this question because it is becoming a greater problem from day to day. . . . I would be very grateful if in addition to your lecture you would jot down any of your thoughts concerning this problem and send it along with the text of your lecture."[114]

In response, Murray reported that the lecture, still only in the form of a "little sheath of scribbled notes," had been given in the early spring at Fordham University as one of a series on contemporary atheism sponsored by the Cardinal Bea Institute. It was his intention to present a version of it at the Episcopal Seminar on Doctrinal, Pastoral, and Canonical Questions scheduled at Fordham from June 25th to July 1st.

As it happened, Murray explained he could not appear at the Episcopal Seminar "owing to some congestive heart failure in the beginning of June which obliged me to cancel all obligations for the rest of the summer. I am better now but the thing was potentially serious. I hope to begin writing the lecture sometime late in August when I also hope to be permitted to resume serious work."

In conclusion he described for the Superior General the thrust of that address:

The lecture was a speculative attempt to situate contemporary unbelief in a theological view of reality. I took as the basic systematic concept the notion of the Church as *sacramentum Christi*—the "sign" which at once reveals and also somewhat conceals the mystery of Christ, the mystery of the divine salvific action in the world. From this basic concept I think it might be possible to go on to do justice to the theories about the belief of the unbeliever and the unbelief of the believer which are being written about today. I am inclined to think that these theories of themselves lack an adequate basis which I was hoping to supply. I should add, that the whole structure of my thought is highly tentative, as are many things today.[115]

In the last few months of his life Murray's letters were filled with feelings of tentativeness, doubt, uncertainty, and even some pessimism. He was "saddened" by Charles Davis's break with the Church,[116] and expressed to another friend that these were "difficult times" for the Church.[117] He refused to endorse James Kavanaugh's *A Modern Priest Looks at his Outdated Church*.

I attempted to read the book ... but I had to give up. I confess that I do not like angry men or angry books, chiefly because I am not convinced that they do any good. Surely at the moment what we chiefly need is not passionate outpourings but calm and reasonable discourse, suited to a time of troubles.[118]

To another, he wrote, "Instead of getting simpler, life seems to get more complicated all the time and I have gone back to my earlier theological pursuits."[119] In May, he wrote to Roberto Tucci, S.J., editor of *Civiltà Cattolica*, and spoke "with 'spirito giovanile' of the interesting era we are living in," and he added: "There is no doubt that we are all in trouble, but I courageously hope that it is a good kind of trouble."[120] To another friend in Rome Murray expressed some pessimism about the upcoming first Synod of Bishops scheduled to convene in Rome on September 29, 1967. The conciliar fathers had envisioned the Synod as a specific implementation of the doctrine of episcopal collegiality. "From where we sit over here, it does not look as if the Synod is going to be particularly interesting. I myself expect it to be no more than a ballet. At that, I hope I am wrong."[121]

In the final months of his life everyone knew Murray was not in good health. On more than one occasion he talked about death with his friends, a subject which he discussed as coolly as he would any other "problematic," using one of his favorite words. According to his friend, John Cogley, he was convinced that he would not reach old age and accepted the fate stoically. "He had no overriding ambition to finish any particular work before his hour struck, he said."[122] In another place, Cogley recalled one particular conversation about death. " 'It's the only real thing to look forward to,' Father Murray said in one of his typically understated affirmations of his Faith. . . ."[123]

In mid-June Murray suffered a new and serious heart attack and was ordered to cancel all engagements and to spend the summer in complete rest. Writing to his close friend, Thomas Watson, Jr., Murray said of this: "I ran into some cardiac trouble owing to having taken on a little too much during the past year. I am grounded here [at Woodstock] until July 4, when I must have another check-up. At that, I feel much better already. The lazy life seems to agree with me."[124] In early August he spent a week at the Watson's summer home on the coast of Maine. His death came in a taxi-cab on August 16, while traveling from the home of his sister in Queens, New York, to the John LaFarge Institute in Manhattan.

World and religious leaders immediately bemoaned his passing. "I consider his departure a great loss to us in this essentially transitional period in which we find ourselves in the Church throughout the world, since he had such a short life for the daring conditions affecting the transition in the Church," said one bishop-friend.[125] President Lyndon Johnson characterized his life as one that "transcended the barriers of nation, race and creed,[126] while from Vatican City, Archbishop Giovanni Benelli expressed the Pope's regret by describing Murray as one "who never stinted in his service of God, Church, and the Society of Jesus. His humble yet precious theological contributions will be his monument and a guide to others."[127]

In an eloquent eulogy of Murray given by his close friend and confidant, Walter J. Burghardt, Murray's name was made synonymous with "the freedom of man."

> Unborn millions will never know how much their freedom is tied to this man whose pen was a powerful protest, a dramatic march, against injustice and equality, whose research sparked and terminated in the ringing affirmation of an ecumenical council. "The right to religious freedom has its foundations" not in the Church, not in society or state, not even in objective truth, but "in the dignity of the human person."[128]

It is only in his very last years that Murray ventured to give a definition of freedom, and then it came after many years of work and reflection, after having himself undergone a long process of liberation. "In order to be free," he said, "a man or a society must undergo a process of liberation. The process is never complete, and it is always precarious, subject to deflection or defeat. Man is never more than an apprentice in the uses of freedom. Their mastery eludes him." And he added "the possession of freedom, like the possession of truth, is the term, always only proximate, of an arduous education." And where does this education come from? From secular experience, and those who have not learned it have only themselves to blame because "they have been absent from class, truants from the school of history."[129]

Murray, himself a "master in the school of history," had not feared to lay some of the blame where it belonged. He clearly pointed out in his writings that while man was continuing to move on his pilgrimage toward his rightful freedom, religious and civil, while society moved "toward its rightful autonomy—that is its proper secularity," the Church was not willing to join man on his human pilgrimage. "On the contrary, it has opposed man's historical movement toward freedom."[130]

Murray's life work was to change this course in the Church's self-understanding. And thus it was only near the very end that he would define what he had himself experienced and what his life had described, namely, that freedom

> is inwardness, spontaneity, the capacity of a man to find within himself the reasons and the motives of his own right decisions and action, apart from external coercion. Freedom therefore is authenticity, truthfulness, fidelity to the pursuit of the truth and to the truth when found. . . . Freedom is experienced as duty, as responsibility—as a response to the claims of justice, to the demands of rightful law, to the governance and guidance of legitimate authority. In its intimately Christian sense, however, freedom has a higher meaning than all this. Freedom, in the deepest experience of it, is love. To be free is to be-for-the-others. The Christian call to freedom is inherently a call to community, a summons out of isolation, an invitation to be-with-the-others, an impulse to service of the others.[131]

His work as a theologian was an attempt to develop a Christian understanding of man, of the world, and of government. Its point of departure was his Christian faith and his American experience. His theological work was in a real sense a task of bringing the Church and the world to greater consciousness of that freedom which Murray himself rightly called "the forgotten truth."[132] Through his revision of the Church's understanding of her relationship to the world he contributed to her liberation from an outdated sociological and political concept of Christendom and led her to a more contemporary understanding of presence. For Murray, such progress was essential if the Church was once again to perform her mission of serving man's humanization, a goal equivalent to that genuine freedom which promotes growth and reconciliation. Murray's lifelong effort led the Church to a greater consciousness of herself as the public witness to the freedom of Jesus and as the living bearer of its dangerous remembrance.

Notes

1. Vincent A. Yzermans. *A New Pentecost: Vatican Council II, Session I* (Westminster: Newman Press, 1963), p. 9.
2. Xavier Rynne. *Vatican Council II* (New York: Farrar, Straus, Giroux, 1968), p. 4.
3. "End of the Worker-priests," *Commonweal*, LXX (September 25, 1959), p. 532; Cardinal G. Pizzardo, "Priest-workers," *Tablet*, CCXII (September 26, 1959), pp. 819-20.
4. The Holy Office text is dated June 20, 1961, and can be found in *Acta Apostolicae Sedis*, LIII (July 15, 1961), p. 507; see also: Joseph A. Fitzmyer, "Recent Roman Scriptural Controversy," *TS*, XXII (September, 1961), pp. 426-44.
5. *Acta Apostolicae Sedis*, LIV (March 31, 1962), pp. 139-49. For an English translation: "The Apostolic Constitution 'Veterum Sapientia,' " *AER*, CXLVI (April, 1962), pp. 272-79.
6. The Holy Office text is dated June 30, 1962, *Acta Apostolicae Sedis*, LIV (August 6, 1962), p. 526.
7. von Aretin, *The Papacy and the Modern World*, p. 230.
8. *Ibid.*
9. Robert B. Kaiser. *Pope, Council and World: The Story of Vatican II* (New York: Macmillan, 1963), p. vii.
10. *Ibid.*, p. viii.
11. Philip Scharper to Murray, May 8, 1959, WCA.
12. Murray Papers, WCA.
13. Scharper to Murray, July 20, 1959, WCA.
14. Arthur M. Schlesinger, Jr. *A Thousand Days: John F. Kennedy in the White House* (Boston: Houghton Mifflin Co., 1965), p. 108. Though compatible, there was considerable difference between John Kennedy and Murray. Murray in a letter to Mrs. J. M. DeWine, May 19, 1967, says of their positions: "I should say that Kennedy was far more of a 'separationist' than I am. In this connection you might look up William Buckley's review of a book by a man named Fuchs in a recent *New York Times* Sunday Book Review Section. He compares my views with Kennedy's on the school question." And Thomas Watson, Jr., a close friend of Murray, a friendship which developed when both served on Kennedy's Advisory Committee to the Secretary of Defense on Non-Military Instruction in 1962 says: "Politically, Father Murray and I were somewhat apart. He tended toward the conservative side of things and, although I had him at a number of functions in honor of various members of the Kennedy family, I could never get him to whole-heartedly accept the liberal view of the Kennedys or of myself. At the same time, he was able to address to them, very profound questions which I'm sure stimulated their thinking, as well as my own." Watson Notes, Murray Papers, WCA.
15. John F. Kennedy, "Remarks on Church and State," in *Church and State in American History*, ed. John Wilson (Boston: D. C. Heath and Company, 1965), pp. 188-90. A transcript of Kennedy's statement along with the questions and answers which followed its delivery may be found in the *New York Times*, September 13, 1960, p. 22.
16. Theodore C. Sorensen, *Kennedy* (New York: Harper and Row, Publishers, 1965), p. 190.
17. Murray to DeWine, May 19, 1967, Copy, WCA.
18. Sorensen, *Kennedy*, p. 190.

19. *Ibid.*, p. 193.

20. "The Voice of Reason," *Newsweek*, August 28, 1967.

21. Fenton, "Doctrine and Tactic in Catholic Pronouncements on Church and State," *AER*, CXLV (October, 1961), p. 274.

22. "Technical Excellence in the Teaching of Catholic Doctrine," *AER*, CXL (May, 1959), pp. 333-42, is an attack on George Tavard's *The Church, the Laymen and the Modern World*. Fenton criticized Tavard for failing to understand what the technique of explaining the body of Christian revelation really is. Accusing Tavard of Modernism and the errors condemned in *Testem benevolentiae*, particularly the tendency to leave out what is offensive to non-Catholics, Fenton called for an exposition of "an accurate, complete and clear statement of the Catholic message," p. 338. A similar message can be found in "Doctrinal Function of the Ecumenical Council," *AER*, CXLI (August, 1959), pp. 117-28. In "The Ecumenical Council and Christian Reunion," *AER*, Vol. CXLI (July, 1959), Fenton described the function of the Council as a "Conversion of all dissident Christians to the true Church," p. 55. In "The Council and Father Küng," *AER*, CXLVII (September, 1962), pp. 178-200, Fenton criticized Küng for his suggestion that the Church must (1) "renew her forms and structures tirelessly in every age"; (2) for his minimizing of doctrine; (3) for his belief that dogma is subject to development.

23. "*Sacrorum Antistitum* and the Background of the Oath against Modernism," *AER*, CLXIII (October, 1960), pp. 239-60; "Revolutions in Catholic Attitudes," *AER*, CXLV (August, 1961), pp. 120-29. In "Modernism and the Teachings of Schleiermacher, Part II," *AER*, CXLV (July, 1961), p. 38, John L. Murphy reminded the review's readers that "the spirit of liberalism and modernism is far from dead."

24. "Morality and Foreign Policy," *America*, CII (March 19, 1960), pp. 729-32; Part II, CII (March 26, 1960), pp. 764-67; "The American Proposition," *Commonweal*, LXXIII (January 20, 1961), pp. 433-35; "The Return to Tribalism," *The Catholic Mind*, LX (January, 1962), pp. 5-12; "Federal Aid to Church-Related Schools," *Yale Political: A Journal of Divergent Views on National Issues*, I (Summer, 1962), pp. 16, 29-31.

25. "On Raising the Religious Issue," *America*, CIII (September 24, 1960), p. 702.

26. "What Hopes and What Misgiving Do You Entertain Regarding the Currently Emerging Religious Dialogue in America?" An Exchange of Views Among Christian Writers, *America*, CIV (January 14, 1961), pp. 459-60.

27. *AER*, CXLVII (November, 1962), p. 351, announced the presence of Fenton in Rome for the Council. "He is a member of a group of experts *(periti)* who are available for special consultation by any of the Fathers of the Council. In his position as a pontifical theologian he has the privilege, not extended to private theologians at the Council, to attend general congregations where the real work of the Council is being done"; see also Vincent A. Yzermans, *A New Pentecost: Vatican II: Session I* (Westminster: Newman, 1963), p. 134. At the beginning of the Council there were ten original American experts, Yzermans reports. Besides Fenton there were: Msgr. Francis J. Brennan, William J. Doheny, John Steinmueller, Rudolph Bandas, George Higgins, John Quinn, Frederick McManus, Ulric Beste, and Edward Heston.

28. A number of commentators on Vatican II speak of Murray's being "disinvited" from the first session. Xavier Rynne, *Vatican Council II*, reported the following as excluded or invited late to the preparatory meetings: Murray, John L. McKenzie, Henri DeLubac, M.D. Chenu, J. Daniélou, Hugo and Karl Rahner, p. 33. Robert B. Kaiser, *Pope, Council and World* (New York: Macmillan, 1963), reported that Car-

dinal Tardini kept complete control over the preparations of the Council making sure that the members of most commissions followed the curial mind-set, excluding such theologians as Rahner, Congar, and Murray. At the insistence of the German bishops, Rahner was finally invited to join a preparatory commission in March, 1961, but not the important theological commission of Ottaviani. He said: "Jesuit John Courtney Murray, a man whose ideas on Church-state relations were too 'American' to suit the theocratic notions of an Ottaviani, was never asked to come to Rome in any capacity. He was, as a matter of fact, *dis*invited and warned by Ottaviani, through his Jesuit superiors, not even to write on Church-State relations," p. 65. Michael Novak, *The Open Church: Vatican II, Act II* (New York: Macmillan Co., 1964), claimed that Murray had been invited to attend the first session of the Council but "the invitation was suddenly and embarrassingly withdrawn," p. 257. The only reference Murray made to this incident is found in a letter to Richard J. Regan, February 23, 1967. "It was not Ottaviani who 'disinvited' me to the first session; it was the Apostolic Delegate (Vagnozzi) (and I know this only on confidential information)." John Cogley, reflecting on this incident in Murray's life after his death, says: "I recalled that evening when word came the other day about his death. Our dinner took place during the first session of the Vatican Council, the session from which, as he put it, he had been abruptly un-invited. 'Do you feel bad about it?' I asked. 'I do," he said, 'A man doesn't live long, and if something this big is going on, a man feels that he ought to be there.' The statement was as impersonally worded as a proposition from *We Hold These Truths*. There was no note of having been abused in it, no self-pity, no plea for sympathy—simply the unadorned expression of how a 'man' under certain circumstances truly feels"; *America*, CXVII (September 2, 1967), p. 221.

29. It is interesting to compare the participation of the American bishops at Vatican I and the participation of the United States bishops at Vatican II. James Hennesey, S.J., *The First Council of the Vatican: The American Experience* (New York: Herder and Herder, 1963), provides an attractive and scholarly analysis of the American prelates' "first serious contact with the Universal Church." Because the Council concentrated almost exclusively on the definition of papal infallibility, the Americans never had occasion to contribute to the important topics of Church-State relations, freedom of conscience, and ecumenism, based on their experience of living in a pluralistic society. They were a strong minority at Vatican I and aided in the refinement of the decree of infallibility till it expressed "the limit, conditions, and objects of infallible papal pronouncements." Although they did not play a major role in what came to be a "European Council," they did make their contribution—which was both pastoral and pragmatic. Because of the Council they became aware of Europe's problems and Europe became aware of the American Church. Hennesey writes: "If those bishops of 1870 seemed out of the mainstream of thought at the council a century ago, they would be very much at home in Vatican Council II." See Hennesey, "The American Experience of the Roman Catholic Church," *Catholic Mind*, LXIII (November, 1965), p. 34. For perhaps the best study of Vatican I from a European's point of view: Dom Cuthbert Butler, *The Vatican Council 1869-1870* (2 vols.; London, Longmans, 1930).

30. Rock Caporale, *Vatican II: Last of the Councils* (Baltimore: Helicon, 1964), p. 64.

31. *Ibid.*, p. 65; Novak, *The Open Church*, says: "The lack of intellectual boldness and creativity among the American bishops over the past generation was no doubt responsible for their initial lack of preparation at the Council. On the other hand, the openness, modesty, and piety of the Americans made them docile once the leadership of the Church insisted on renewal and reform"; p. 336.

32. Rynne, *Vatican Council II*, p. 201.

33. Hennesey, *The First Council of the Vatican*, pp. 141-42.

34. Paul J. Hallinan, "The American Bishops at the Vatican Councils," *The Catholic Historical Review*, LI (October, 1965), p. 381.

35. Murray to Archbishop Lawrence J. Shehan, August, 1962, Copy, WCA. For a complete study and analysis of the development of the religious liberty issue at Vatican II, see: Richard J. Regan, S.J., *Conflict and Consensus: Religious Freedom and the Second Vatican Council* (New York: Macmillan Company, 1967). Regan used Murray's Council notes to do this study. Murray to Regan, January 31, 1967, Copy, WCA. The letter was accompanied by a detailed memo to Regan: "*Comments on the MS about the Declaration on Religious Freedom.*"

36. Murray to Leo Ward, June 20, 1963, Copy, WCA.

37. Rynne, *Vatican Council II*, pp. 52-56.

38. Fenton, "Cardinal Ottaviani and the Council," *AER*, CXLVIII (January, 1963), pp. 44-53. For a rebuttal to Fenton's defense of Ottaviani, see editorial "Excess of Zeal," *America*, CVIII (February 23, 1963), p. 251.

39. Leonard Swidler. *Freedom in the Church* (Dayton, Ohio: Pflaum Press, 1969), pp. 39-41; Novak, *The Open Church*, p. 15.

40. A. Cardinal Cicognani to Murray, April 4, 1963, WCA.

41. Murray to Ward, June 20, 1963, Copy, WCA.

42. Murray to Michael F. Maher, Rector of Woodstock College, November 22, 1963, Copy, WCA.

43. Rynne, *Vatican Council II*, pp. 191-92.

44. Murray to Maher, November 22, 1963. *America*, CIX (November 30, 1963), p. 701, is more specific in its description of this scene. "The president of the commission, Cardinal Ottaviani, is almost blind. He did not recognize or distinguish the tall figure of Father Murray when he spoke . . . before the commission's members and consultants. Cardinal Ottaviani, one hears, leaned over to his neighbor, Cardinal Léger, to ask who was speaking. The Canadian cardinal perhaps to spare Father Murray any unwelcome publicity at that point, replied simply: 'peritus quidam' (one of the experts)." In his tribute to Murray on the occasion of his death, Wright referred to this incident: "Deeply regret diocesan commitment prevents presence to pay tribute to great scholar, good friend, exemplary priest. However, consoled by thought he once was present at my invitation at a meeting where his presence meant more for him than would mine in New York this morning." Wright telegram to Robert Mitchell, Provincial of the New York Jesuit Province, August 21, 1967, WCA. Wright implied that he himself had invited Murray to attend the November 11 meeting. Novak, *The Open Church*, also reports it was Wright who offered the invitation, p. 257. Murray claims it was Léger. Those voting against release of the text at the November 12 meeting were Cardinals Ottaviani, Michael Browne, Rufino Santos of Manila, E. Florit of Florence, and Pietro Parente of the Curia.

45. Michael Serafian, *The Pilgrim* (New York: Farrar, Straus and Company, 1964), p. 198.

46. Murray to Francis Cardinal Spellman, November 18, 1963, Copy, WCA. For an analysis of the text of De Smedt's *relatio*, see Regan, *Conflict and Consensus*, pp. 36-37.

47. Murray to Maher, November 22, 1963. Murray was also responsible for the writing of similar speeches on the subject for Albert Cardinal Meyer; for P. Veuillot, the auxiliary bishop of Paris; for S. Mendez Arceo, Bishop of Cuernavaca, Mexico; and for R. Cardinal Silva Henriquez of Chile.

48. *Ibid.*

49. Rynne, *Vatican Council II*, pp. 248-49.
50. Murray, "On Religious Liberty," *America*, CIX (November 30, 1963), p. 704.
51. John J. McGinty to Michael F. Maher, February 26, 1964, WCA.
52. John J. McGinty to Murray, February 26, 1964, WCA.
53. Murray to McGinty, May 16, 1964, Copy, WCA.
54. *Ibid.*
55. *Time*, December 6, 1963, p. 57.
56. *AER*, CXLVIII (January, 1963), p. 53.
57. *AER*, CXLVIII (March, 1963), p. 189.
58. "A Letter From Rome," *AER*, CXLIX (December, 1963), p. 418.
59. *AER*, CL (January, 1964), p. 1.
60. Murray to McGinty, May 16, 1964, Copy, WCA. The article appeared as "The Problem of Religious Freedom, *TS*, XXV (December, 1964), pp. 503-75; also, *The Problem of Religious Freedom*, Woodstock Papers, No. 7 (Newman Press, 1965); "Le problème de la liberté religieuse au concile," in *La liberté religieuse exigence spirituelle et problème politique* (Editions du Centurion: Paris, 1965), pp. 9-112. This text was also translated and published into Dutch, Portuguese, German, and Spanish.
61. Alter to Murray, July 22, 1964, WCA.
62. Murray to Alter, August 24, 1964, Copy, WCA.
63. *The Problem of Religious Freedom*, Woodstock Papers, 7 (Westminster: Newman, 1965), pp. 18-19.
64. "Conversation at the Council," *American Benedictine Review*, XV (September, 1964), with Hans Küng, Godfrey Diekmann, Gustave Weigel, Vincent Yzermans, p. 349.
65. *Ibid.*, p. 351.
66. Unpublished notes, WCA.
67. Murray Memo to Archbishop Shehan, September, 1964, Copy, WCA.
68. Unpublished notes, WCA.
69. Murray to Shehan, September, 1964, WCA.
70. Rynne, *Vatican Council II*, p. 301.
71. *Ibid.*, pp. 298-99.
72. *Ibid.*, pp. 299-300.
73. *Ibid.*, p. 301.
74. Regan, *Conflict and Consensus*, p. 95.
75. Murray to Regan, January 31, 1967, WCA.
76. Rynne, *Vatican Council II*, pp. 318-19; Regan, *Conflict and Consensus*, p. 97.
77. Regan, *Conflict and Consensus*, p. 98.
78. *Ibid.*, p. 99.
79. *Ibid.*, p. 100.
80. *Ibid.*, pp. 109-10.
81. Murray, "This Matter of Religious Freedom," *America*, CXII (January 9, 1965), pp. 40-43.
82. *Ibid.*, p. 40; also: Rynne, *Vatican Council II*, p. 417; Robert E. Tracy, *American Bishop at the Vatican Council* (New York: McGraw-Hill, 1960), p. 170; Vincent A. Yzermans, ed. *American Participation at the Second Vatican Council* (New York: Sheed and Ward, 1967), pp. 618-21.
83. Murray, "This Matter of Religious Freedom," p. 42.
84. *Ibid.*, p. 43.

85. Joseph Cardinal Ritter, Archbishop of Saint Louis, to American bishops, December 29, 1964, Copy, WCA.

86. For a discussion of the emendations sent to the Secretariat, see Regan, *Conflict and Consensus*, pp. 117-21.

87. For an analysis of the revised text see *ibid.*, pp. 121-27.

88. *Ibid.*, pp. 127-29.

89. Rynne, *Vatican Council II*, p. 458.

90. Murray to Browne, August 20, 1965, Copy, WCA.

91. Tracy, *American Bishop at the Vatican Council*, p. 172.

92. *Ibid.*, p. 173.

93. *Ibid.*, pp. 174-75.

94. Murray to Regan, January 31, 1967, WCA.

95. McGrath, Santiago de Varaguas, to Rector of Woodstock College, September 23, 1967, WCA.

96. Regan, *Conflict and Consensus*, p. 164.

97. "Vatican Council: The Uses of Ambiguity," *Time*, November 5, 1965, reports that "Italian Bishop Luigi Carli of Segni, one of the council's most outspoken conservatives, has submitted a host of amendments seeking to emphasize the truth of Catholic thinking and the error of other views," p. 52.

98. "Declaration on Religious Freedom," No. 2; the translation is that of Murray, from *The Documents of Vatican II*, eds. Walter M. Abbot, S.J. and Joseph Gallagher (New York: America, 1966), pp. 678-79.

99. Regan, *Conflict and Consensus*, p. 167.

100. Dominic Totaro, S.J., to Murray Papers, September 13, 1967, WCA.

101. Emmet John Hughes, "A Man For Our Season," *The Priest*, XXV (July-August, 1969), p. 392.

102. Murray, "The Declaration on Religious Freedom," in *Vatican II: An Interfaith Appraisal*, ed. John H. Miller, C.S.C. (Notre Dame: University of Notre Dame Press, 1966), p. 565. A more detailed analysis of the Declaration's achievement will appear in Chap. IV.

103. "John Courtney Murray," *National Catholic Reporter*, August 23, 1967, p. 10.

104. Paul Blanshard, "Religious Liberty, Limited: A Report From Vatican II," *The Register Leader*, February, 1966, p. 4; also: Blanshard. *Paul Blanshard on Vatican II* (Boston: Beacon Press, 1966), pp. 76, 87-96.

105. Thomas T. Love, quoted in Stanley I. Stuber and Claud D. Nelson, *Implementing Vatican II in Your Community* (New York: Guild Press, 1967), p. 162.

106. Rynne, *Vatican Council II*, p. 460.

107. Murray to Weber, October 18, 1966, Copy, WCA.

108. Murray, "Freedom in the Age of Renewal," *American Benedictine Review*, XVIII (September, 1967), p. 323.

109. Murray, "Make the News Good News!" *Interracial Review*, XXXVI (July, 1963), p. 130. This is taken from an address given at the Annual Dinner of the New York Catholic Interracial Council on May 20, 1963.

110. From an unpublished commencement address given at Western Maryland College on June 9, 1967.

111. From unpublished notes of Murray's address to a group of diocesan priests in Toledo, Ohio on May 5, 1967, WCA.

112. *New York Times*, Saturday, August 19, 1967, p. 23.

113. "Christian-Communist Dialogue," *America*, CXV (December 17, 1966), p. 805.

114. Arrupe to Murray, July 6, 1967, WCA.

115. Murray to Arrupe, July 14, 1967, Copy, WCA. There are two un-published manuscripts in the Murray Papers but neither seems to be the one referred to here. The first is entitled "Death of God" and was an address given on January 10, 1967, at the University of Connecticut, Storrs, Connecticut. The second is entitled "Religious Freedom and the Atheist." The manuscript is undated and there is no in-dication on what occasion it was written. However, remarks in the text would in-dicate that it was written within the last year of Murray's life.

116. Murray to Edward Duff, S.J., December 28, 1966, Copy, WCA.

117. Murray to Nicholas Predovich, S.J., February 10, 1967, Copy, WCA.

118. Murray to Eugene J. Prakapas, Vice President and Senior Editor of Tri-dent Press, April 21, 1967, Copy, WCA.

119. Murray to Robert Hutchins, February 14, 1967, Copy, WCA.

120. Roberto Tucci, S.J., to Felix Cardegna, Rector of Woodstock College, August 18, 1967, WCA. A copy of the letter Tucci quotes is also in the WCA dated May 16, 1967.

121. Murray to Francis J. McCool, S.J., July 5, 1967, Copy, WCA. In re-trospect Murray's fears about the Synod proved correct. The first Synod had been called to discuss the following issues: (1) The dangers of faith in the world today; (2) The reform of Canon law; (3) Seminaries; (4) Mixed marriages; (5) Liturgical reform. The Synod was not much of a success. Not one deliberative vote from the beginning to the end was taken, "not a single 'act of collegiality.'" See: David Slow, "End of a Beginning," *America*, CXVII (November 11, 1967), pp. 564-65; also: "Dossier of the Month: What Is the Synod of Bishops?" *The Month*, XXXVIII (July-August, 1967), pp. 7-25; Robert Trisco, "The Synod of Bishops and the Sec-ond Vatican Council," *AER*, CLVII (September, 1967), pp. 145-60.

122. John Cogley, "Fr. Murray's Death, Great Loss to American Catholicism," *The Catholic Messenger*, August 23, 1967, p. 4.

123. Cogley, "John Courtney Murray," *America*, CXVII (September 2, 1967), p. 221.

124. Murray to Thomas J. Watson, Jr., June 21, 1967, Copy, WCA.

125. Marcos G. McGrath to Felix Cardegna, September 23, 1967, WCA.

126. Lyndon B. Johnson to Robert A. Mitchell, Provincial of the New York Jes-uit Province, August 19, 1967, WCA.

127. Archbishop Benelli, Vatican City to Felix Cardegna, August 19, 1967.

128. Walter J. Burghardt, S.J., "A Eulogy," *Woodstock Letters*, XCVI (Fall, 1967), p. 417. The tribute was also published in *America*, CXVII (September 9, 1967), pp. 248-49. In a letter to Miss Rosemary Kenah from Robert Kennedy, Unit-ed States Senator, September 27, 1967, WCA, Kennedy praised the tribute. "I found Father Burghardt's tribute most moving and agreed with you that it should be placed in the Record. It appeared in the Record for September 21st, and I have enclosed a copy of the tribute for you." The introduction to the publication of the tribute in the *Congressional Record* reads as follows: "Mr. Kennedy of New York, Mr. President: 'Each man's death diminishes me,' John Dunne once wrote. With the death of John Courtney Murray, we are all diminished. Father Murray was a scholar—who was passionately involved with life. He was a man of God—who committed himself to the world of men. He was an advocate—whose mind was never shut to opposing views. A moving tribute to this extraordinary man was offered by Walter J. Burghardt, S.J.,

of Woodstock College. The sermon preached by Father Burghardt at Father Murray's funeral touches on the features which make John Courtney Murray's death a diminution of us all. I ask unanimous consent that the sermon be printed in the Record."

129. Murray, "Freedom in the Age of Renewal," p. 320.
130. *Ibid.*, p. 321.
131. *Ibid.*, p. 324.
132. *Ibid.*, p. 323.

4

Murray's American Political Philosophy

Perhaps the most significant of the methodological changes to bring about a greater awareness of the role of the sciences in theology was the shift from a classicist worldview to a more historically conscious worldview.[1] Using a classicist method, Catholic theology could not avoid a somewhat *a priori* deductive approach to reality. This was accentuated by an overly exaggerated argument from authority and tradition.[2]

The more historically conscious approach, on the other hand, provided theoretical justification for an understanding of change and development in the doctrinal teaching of the Church. Changing empirical data indicated a change in the norms and values of a particular historical time. As we have already briefly seen in the historical study of the Church-State debate, Murray appealed to historical consciousness for an explanation of change in the teaching of the Church-State doctrine. While affirming that the older teaching was true in its nineteenth-century historical setting, he also insisted that the Church's teaching on religious liberty was situated in a "given historical-social-political context."[3]

Murray understood the crucial development of this debate in the following terms:

The link between religious freedom and limited constitutional government, and the link between the freedom of the Church and the freedom of the people—these were not nineteenth-century theological-political insights. They became available only within twentieth-century perspectives, created by the "signs of the times." The two links were not forged by abstract deductive logic but by history, by the historical advance of totalitarian government, and by the corresponding new appreciation of man's dignity in society.[4]

Those who disagreed with Murray could not be accused of rejecting the idea of religious freedom as such. This applies to Ottaviani, to members of the Roman curia and, in this country, to Fenton. Their opposition was to the doctrinal progress implied by Murray's affirmation of religious freedom. In brief, the dispute represented mainly a clash of methodologies.

This chapter presents Murray's thought and reflection on the question of religious freedom as it emerged from his experience of the American proposition and Catholic tradition. In order to situate his position, it is necessary to discuss the various factors which contributed to the "traditional" concept of freedom of religion, a concept which Murray more accurately described as the "received opinion."[5]

We shall then examine how Murray saw his own theological task when confronted with the new historical situation represented by American constitutional democracy. The roots of Murray's political philosophy lay in this experience and in the teachings of Gelasius I and of John of Paris. Murray brought his political philosophy to the Second Vatican Council. Demonstrating through the historical method that his position was in continuity with authentic tradition he wielded a significant influence on the final drafting of *The Declaration on Religious Freedom*. The chapter will conclude with an analysis of Murray's fully developed position on religious freedom.

The Context of Murray's Position

The Confessional State

The conservative position to which Murray responded was rooted in the relation between Church and State which characterized the medieval Christian state and later Catholic nation states.[6] In both of these Catholicism was institutionalized as the state religion. The "Catholic state" was, therefore, not only a political community in which Catholics constituted the majority of the population, but also one in which the Catholic Church was given *constitutional* recognition and preferential treatment. Such a union of Church and State resulted in the legal repression of all "heresy." Its understanding and practice of religious freedom was thus extremely limited. Its basis was a theory of the Church's "direct power" in the temporal realm.[7]

This theory asserted the primacy of the spiritual power of the Church and did so in such a way that the power of the state was included in it and derived from it. As such, it was bound not only by the natural law, but also by the positive, divine law. Faith and Church law constituted the foundations of civil law, and their preservation became identified with the common good of the society. What this meant in practice was that the prince's political power could be employed directly for the accomplishment of the Church's spiritual purposes. The rule of *cuius regio ejus religio* dictated a subject's religious persuasion. In this political axiom religious freedom became the prerogative only of the prince, not of the people.[8] Chief among the prince's prerogatives was the defense of the faith against heretics, which in fact, was a political duty and a means of promoting the common good of society. This was possible precisely because the community of faith and society were coextensive. The preservation of Church unity was essential to political unity and to the welfare of society. In describing the theoretical justification of Catholic government's "right" to repress heresy, Murray said:

> If . . . the prince is within the one body of the Church as *minister sacerdotii*, whose temporal power the spiritual power is free directly to use for its own spiritual ends, he may be charged with vindicating violations of the supernatural unity of the Church. His power is none other than hers, simply brought into execution by him. In a word, in this theory, the prince has a direct religious power, as the Church has a direct temporal power.[9]

Furthermore, since Catholicism was thought to be of divine origin, it was viewed as the one "true religion," and the only religion with the *right* to public existence and expression. Rights are grounded in truth. Error, and heretics, since they are in error, have no rights and are subject to legal repression by the state. In other words, a religion which has not been established by divine law has no right to exist and to function in the public sector of society. Further, since it is destructive of the common good (of the Catholic majority), it may and ought to be repressed by the state.[10]

It is clear that religious freedom was understood as grounded in religious truth. Those not sharing this truth could not publicly express, manifest, or disseminate their beliefs. They were, however, free to believe and practice what they wished as private individuals. The state could not violate an individual's internal personal freedom of conscience in matters of belief and practice by any form of coercion. No one could be forced to abandon his convictions or to adopt what was regarded by others to be the one true religion. This freedom of conscience also applied to the individual's family in matters of religious upbringing, education, and practice.

Only the Catholic believer, therefore, enjoyed public religious freedom and had a right to it because he alone possessed the truth. As Murray explained:

This conscience, which is the Catholic conscience, possesses the fullness of religious freedom, because religious freedom is rooted in objective truth. It is a positive concept. It is the social faculty of professing and practicing what is true and good, as the true and good are objectively proposed by the eternal law of God (both natural and positive) subjectively manifested by a rightly and truly formed conscience, and authentically declared by the Church.[11]

The above religio-political situation is what was called in traditional thought the "thesis" or ideal relationship of Church and State in which Catholic principles could be applied without qualification. Where this was not possible, that is, where Catholics were a minority of the population, a "hypothesis" situation existed. Murray explained,

The Church foregoes her right to legal establishment as the one religion of the state, with its juridical consequence, legal intolerance. The Church, however, gives no positive approval to the resultant constitutional situation. *Per se* the situation is an evil, but it may be regarded as the lesser evil than the evils which would result from application of the thesis. Therefore it may be tolerated, *per accidens* and in practice.[12]

In terms of religious freedom what the "thesis-hypothesis" position meant was tolerance whenever necessary and intolerance whenever possible. Necessity and possibility were determined by whatever was more conducive to public peace. Finally, it should be noted that the "ideal" situation of the Church-State relationship and of religious freedom arose from a methodology that transformed concrete, historical facts into immutable and transhistorical theoretical principles. Little or no recognition was given to historical determination. This contrasted considerably with Murray's method of solving the problems of religious freedom and Church-State relations.

Continental Liberalism

Another historical factor in traditional thinking was nineteenth-century European Liberalism and its correlate, totalitarian democracy. Liberalist teaching contained two major tenets. The first was the absolute autonomy of individual reason. Every individual was a law unto himself and the sole judge of truth. He was subject to no external authority. His individual free will was sovereign in private life. With regard to freedom of religion this meant that the individual had the right to worship or not worship God as he pleased, and to do so in the way he pleased. In a sense, he was the creator of his own religion. This was obviously saying far more than that the individual has the right to worship God according to his conscience without state interference. Furthermore, as Murray explained:

> Every man could privately be as religious as he pleased, if indeed he pleased. But let him not attempt to make his religion a force in shaping the structure, the institutions, the spirit and tendency of society. Blocking such an attempt was the mighty power of the only divine majesty which Liberalism acknowledged—the state.[13]

The juridical omnipotence of the state constituted the essential tenet of Liberalism. Quite simply, the state was considered to be subject to no sovereignty higher than itself. Its supremacy was political as well as spiritual and moral, since it recognized neither God nor a natural law of divine origin. The state was itself the source of its unlimited authority, of the order of justice and of all laws and rights. Such was the root of totalitarian democracy and of a secularist monism. Murray beautifully summarized and described continental Liberalism:

> Its cardinal assertion is a thorough-going monism, political, social, juridical, religious: there is only one Sovereign, one society, one law, one faith. And the cardinal denial is of the Christian dualism of powers, societies, and laws—spiritual and temporal, divine and human. Upon this denial follows the absorption of the Church in the community, the absorption of the community in the state, the absorption of the state in the party, and the assertion that the party-state is the supreme spiritual and moral, as well as political authority and reality. It has its own absolutely autonomous ideological substance and its own absolutely independent purpose: it is the ultimate bearer of human destiny. Outside of this One Sovereign there is nothing. Or rather, what presumes to stand outside is "the enemy."[14]

It was upon the claim of absolute sovereignty and monism that the state tried to effect a "freedom from religion" and a separation of the Church from the state. The Church, which not only claimed the right to exist as a sociological entity, but also as a spiritual supremacy within the state, independent of and superior to it, was an intolerable threat to the nature of the state. There was no room in the totalitarian framework for divided interests. The Church, therefore, had somehow to be eliminated or made to be noneffective. If she were left to exist, it was due not to any inherent right, but only to the concession of the state. The state, in other words, itself determined what the Church was to be and what role it was to play in society. According to the liberalist doctrine, it was to play no role in society and to be limited therefore to the private lives of the members. Liberalism, by its "separation," destroyed the distinction between Church and State and most surely eliminated from the public realm any notion of the primacy of the spiritual. This separation from the Church was only a means to the complete secularization of society and the demise of religious influence in all areas of political, social, and economic life. Secularism itself gradually took on the fervor and characteristics of a religious faith.

As a result of nineteenth-century totalitarian democracy, the terms "freedom of religion" and separation of Church and State took on an extremely pejorative connotation. In the minds of those who held the traditional position, both were associated with the destruction of faith and of the Church. Murray had to cope with these fears as well as with the statements of Leo XIII and Pius XII on the question of Liberalism and totalitarian democracy. Traditional thinkers such as Fenton often interpreted these documents as immutable Catholic doctrine in all respects, whereas much of what was said was historically conditioned and, hence, relative, as we shall later show.

The problem of religious freedom confronted by Murray was thus rooted in two abstract principles. Of these the first was that error has no rights, and second, its correlate, was that government should repress error whenever possible and tolerate it only when necessary. Both principles were related to a historically conditioned form of government and to what was taken to be the "ideal" relationship between Church and State. The problem was further complicated by the notions of "separation of Church and State" and "freedom of religion" which arose out of continental Liberalism. Murray's contribution was to distinguish the immutable principles from the historical concretization of these principles. In doing so, he propounded a political theory that gave full recognition both to the spiritual supremacy of the Church and to the autonomy of the state. He thereby dissolved one of the previously accepted bases of religious intolerance. Finally, his own experience and reflection within the American democratic tradition were brought to bear on the problem, and he developed a concept of religious freedom in Catholic doctrine. What follows aims to show how Murray did this.

The Theologian's Role

Murray's Theological Task[15]

Murray envisioned his theological task first as an examination of the data of history and of the present historical situation in order to determine what is permanent and what is relative in the Church's encounter with the state and with religious liberty, and secondly to show how this applied to the present moment. In this process, which involved a method of historical consciousness, the theologian was also to show the organic development of Catholic doctrine and to "vindicate its internal consistency." Said Murray:

> In a matter in which the relativities of history have played such a large part it is not the theologian's task to defend as necessarily permanent and of divine origin every right that the Church or the state has asserted or exercised in particular periods of history. His task is the formulation of principles in such terms that they may be asserted as constantly valid, and their organization into a coherent system that will cover all contingencies because it is dependent on none.[16]

If a doctrine was to be truly absolute and to represent immutable truths applicable to all historical contingencies, it could not have its origins in any of these.[17] Nor could any particular form of spiritual and temporal relationships be considered as an ideal realization. The Church's transcendence required that she remain above all political forms, identifying with none. Her immanence required that she adapt her thought and conduct to any rational political exigency.

Murray was of the conviction that the traditional position had confused permanent principles with historical relativities. He felt that this was the case even in papal utterances where historical facts were often elevated to theory. This position had consequently not been able adequately to respond to the political developments which had created a new situation of social fact and political right, namely, democracy. With the development of democracy the juridical autonomy of the Church and of the state had also evolved both in theory and in fact. This development included the constitutional guarantee of freedom of religion as one of the *libertas civilis*.[18] These developments were rooted in the very definition of democracy:

> For the theologian, the basic question concerns that constitutional situation itself—is it or is it not the theologically necessary, permanently valid, unalterably ideal realization of Catholic principles on Church-state relationships, in such wise that any constitutional situation which deviates from it can be the object only of "toleration," not of approval in principle—a concession to the exigencies of an "hypothesis," prompted by expediency, and not the embodiment of a "thesis," warranted by theological and political doctrine. In other words, the question is whether the concept of *libertas ecclesiastica* by intrinsic exigence requires political embodiment in the concept of "the religion of the state," with the "logical and

juridical consequences" that have historically followed from that concept.

Surely the answer must be no.[19]

Expressed differently, Murray saw his task as an exploration into the possibilities of a genuine adaptation of Church-State doctrine to "the constitutional structure, the political institutions, and the ethos of freedom characteristic of the democratic state."[20] He believed that the Church's principles could be applied to this political reality and could be justified by traditional Catholic political and theological thought.

The American Democratic Reality

Murray considered the American Constitution and the American political system as the best exemplification of the modern political development of the lay democratic state. Within this system, religious liberty and the distinction of Church and State, in their origin and ends, are political and juridical realities. Two factors were chiefly responsible for this situation: first, the existence of religious pluralism and, secondly, the emergence of " 'the people' into active self-consciousness, into a spiritual autonomy that extends to a rejection of governmental determination or even tutelage of their religion; with this fact is allied the concept of 'the state' as the instrument of the people for limited purposes sanctioned by the people."[21]

The concept of "the people" is crucial. It implied an important distinction between society and the state. It also gave the latter a limited function within the former, refusing that society be completely encompassed by the state.[22] It is the citizen who constitutes the basis and the end of social life and "who as free citizen is the responsible agent for the public processes, the participant by right of human dignity in the public power whereby his temporal destiny is ruled—in a power too whose exercise is limited by a constitution that is the common act of 'We, the People.' . . ."[23] He is also the subject of inviolable rights and duties—civil liberties—among which is religious freedom. Thus religious freedom is part of a whole complex of democratic freedoms that form an organic whole. All the particular freedoms rest "on the same general judgment—that the system as such is rational, necessary for the common good, related to the political realization of personal dignity. . . ."[24]

The fact of religious pluralism in America also necessitated the formulation of a political policy that would best serve the common good of all while maintaining respect for the dignity of each. The formulation of this policy is expressed in the First Amendment. There are two bases for this Amendment, one political and one ethical. The political basis is social unity which could not have been achieved through religious coercion. Murray explained:

Consequently, there was put into the First Amendment a prohibition against the use of government authority to create an official American faith and enforce adherence to it as the bond of national unity. The national political community was to achieve its own proper unity, on a political level; in order to do so, it was to remain "separate" from the religious community with all its inner divisions. In turn, the religious community so far as government was concerned, was to be free to be divided; but to this end, it had to remain "separate" from the united political community, and not let its own divisions disrupt the sphere of civic life. In the circumstances, this separation was the only way to social peace.

It was, therefore, initially in the name of the state's own end that the First Amendment uttered its prohibition against a State Church and against state interference with the rights of conscience. Religious liberty was rightly regarded as functional to a particular order and its unity. In this sense, therefore, the so-called "principle of separation of Church and State" appears as a political prescript; for it is related to a political end.[25]

The ethical basis is the dualism inherent in the nature of man. Man is both citizen and creature of God. He is engaged in the temporal realm and in the spiritual realm. In one he is subject to the authority of government and ordained to this-worldly goals. In the other, he is subject to the authority of conscience and ordained toward a transcendental goal. Since this dualism is inherent in man's nature, it must be respected.

As citizens of a state, therefore, all men, whatever their religion, have the right to be equal in their civic liberties and in the freedom of their access to all the benefits of organized society. As religious men, all citizens have equal right, as against the state, to follow in every rational way the will of God as it is known to them through conscience.[26]

The First Amendment gives the two factors concrete expression by limiting the powers of the state to the temporal order and guaranteeing the individual religious conscience immunity from all coercion by any part of government. In the first instance, religious freedom is a civil liberty and in the latter it is social. The content of this liberty is freedom of conscience, a free exercise of religion, and a freedom of religious assembly. The First Amendment forbids the establishment of religion precisely to allow the free exercise of religion and to assure civic equality regardless of religious belief. Religious pluralism in America ultimately requires that the state regard all religions as equal in order to preserve the equality of its citizens. In this sense, America is a "lay" state; it is separate from the Church and has no competence or authority in religious matters.[27]

This is the modern political development as Murray understood and experienced it. His theological endeavor was to show the validity of traditional Catholic principles as applied to this reality and thereby to reformulate a doctrine of religious freedom. We now turn our attention to Murray's political theory which made possible this reformulation.

Murray's Political Philosophy

Murray's political thought is grounded in Western Catholic tradition and provides the basis not only for developing Church doctrine on the Church-State question but also for affirming the validity of the present understanding and practice of religious freedom. This political theory provides some of the principles which Murray proceeded to enunciate.

As will be seen, the doctrine of Gelasius I is fundamental to Murray's thought. It asserts the existence of two distinct societies—the spiritual and the temporal.[28] John of Paris later took up this theory, developed it, and formulated a theory of the Church's indirect power in temporal affairs.[29] He greatly influenced Murray with regard to both the two societies and the indirect power, and these in turn are crucial in the question of religious freedom.

The Two Societies

Like John of Paris, Murray maintained the existence of two autonomous societies, distinct in their origin and ends. The temporal originates not in the spiritual but in nature, and ultimately in God. Man is by nature a civil animal and possesses a natural instinct to live in society. The state evolves as a necessary and useful institution for furthering the justice, peace, and well-being of that society. Its ends, which include the promotion of the temporal welfare of the society and the animation and protection of justice, are also determined by nature. The state receives its power to promote these ends from God and from the consent and choice of the people. In the exercise of that power it is limited by its origin and finality, both of which remain in the temporal realm.

By its origin and end, the temporal power is clearly distinguished from the spiritual. It is thus a "lay" state. While it acknowledges that it and its mission are from God, it neither identifies with nor promotes any particular religious group. It no longer performs a religious function as the "arm" of the spiritual power, but is autonomous and the sole immediate authority in the realm of human affairs.

On the other hand, there is the spiritual power whose character, stated Murray, is absolutely spiritual. It is directed solely to man's highest end, his supernatural end. Because of the primacy of this end, the spiritual power enjoys a primacy in *dignity*, but extends to nothing that is not necessarily related to Christ's redemptive work. The means by which the Church pursues her end are also spiritual, and have no *direct* bearing on the temporal order. From none of her powers can she derive any earthly power or jurisdiction.

Murray's thought clearly indicated the presence of two distinct orders of reality in contrast with the earlier theory of two functions within the one society. Obviously, such a distinction required principles of collaboration between the two powers. Again, Murray drew from the basic theory and formulation of John of Paris in clarifying the issue.

Indirect Power

Given the distinction and independence of the two societies, Murray stated that there could no longer be direct involvement of one in the sphere of the other, working directly toward the realization of the other's ends. This the state had formerly done in promoting the spiritual unity of the Church. More specifically, the spiritual power is limited to spiritual matters and terminates at the conscience of the individual believer. However, its activity does produce "after effects" in the temporal order, and this, through the citizen. It is through the conscience of the individual who is both citizen and Christian that the spiritual power has a reach into human affairs. Said Murray:

> The action of the Church on him terminates at conscience, forming it to a sense of its Christian duties in all their range and implications for temporal life. The Christian then as citizen, in the full panoply of his democratic rights, prolongs, as it were, this action of the Church into the temporal order, in all matters in which Christian doctrine and law has implications for life and law and government of society.[30]

According to Murray's theory, the Church confronts not the government or state (understood legally and constitutionally) as in the one society theory, but rather the citizen to whom government is responsible and who is himself responsible for the right functioning of government and the order of the state.[31] In this theory, the state is clearly freed of subservience to the Church as an instrument in maintaining her unity and in repressing in the public domain those not of the faith. Religious intolerance is no longer considered essential to the common good of society.

Murray also clarified the relationship of the state to a spiritual power which is based on the distinction of both. Since the state is limited in its action by its origin and finality, it can only assist the Church indirectly by supplying the temporal conditions and occasions for the Church's realization of her ends. This it does by actualizing its own ends.[12] The Church cannot demand or expect anything more than this from the state. It can only require that the state act according to the necessities of its own nature.

More precisely, with regard to state assistance to the spiritual power in carrying out its proper spiritual mission, it is necessary only that the state guarantee the Church the freedom to pursue her ends in her own way. This is essentially a recognition of the Church's dignity and as a result of that dignity the granting of a place in the juridical order of society. In the words of Murray:

> As the human person is free in society when his intrinsic dignity as the image of God is recognized and all his inalienable rights are juridically guaranteed immunity from inhibition and provided with the due conditions for their exercise, so also the Church is free in society when her intrinsic dignity, her unique juridical personality as the visible and only Church of Christ is recognized, and her independently sovereign powers to lead, rule, and sanctify are guaranteed immunity from inhibition and provided with the due conditions of her exercise.[13]

This aspect of the temporal power's relationship to the Church is a necessity of its very nature, asserted Murray. The state must organize what it did not create, what it finds already there in society. Through the citizen, who holds membership in religious groups, the state finds not only Catholics but a plurality of sects. In accepting and recognizing what is there, the state can neither define the nature of the Church or her juridical status in society nor impose the definition of the Church on those who do not wish to accept it. It follows that repression of religious sects is not within the power of the state:

> . . . government has neither right nor duty to "exterminate" them; for they are composed of citizens, who have their own loyalties to what is beyond government. These loyalties may be illusory in themselves, but they are related to government inasmuch as they are the loyalties of citizens, to which government is obliged to give place in the public order; for the order of the state is by definition the order of all that is "there" in society, immune from governmental creation or destruction.[14]

The state cannot repress heresy or attempt to maintain or establish religious unity in society because such action is beyond its finality.

This, in brief, is the main line of Murray's political philosophy as it applied to the relation of Church and State, and in particular to religious freedom. In Murray's thought, the basic theories of Gelasius and of John of Paris have undergone considerable development. As he noted, they have received greater clarification in the long process of development of political fact and theory. From his own experience, Murray could say that both theories had become political reality. No longer was the state under the tutelage of the Church, or was the spiritual a part of the definition of the temporal. Religious unity was no longer seen as belonging to the finality of the state or even as necessary to the welfare of the state as state. Citizenship and rights are grounded in a political reality and not in religious belief.

Moreover, Murray maintained that this was a full and legitimate development of the traditional Catholic doctrine of the two societies and of their proper collaboration for the best interests of each. Such a development was based on political experience and theological reflection. No other doctrine is applicable to the present historical reality and consequently no other has the characteristics of genuine doctrine. This is the Catholic "thesis" in its application to democratic society. Murray went to great lengths to show the development of political philosophy and Church doctrine in the more recent thought of Leo XIII, Pius XII, and John XXIII, giving further support to his claim that religious liberty was a valid political and doctrinal development. We now turn our attention to a study of this development.

The Development

As we have already seen in the first part of this study, Murray's greatest source of frustration came from the difficulty of explaining to Rome and its American spokesmen the difference between the antireligious spirit that permeated the European drive toward the separation of Church and State in the late eighteenth century and the very different significance of this doctrine seen as an expression of the intention of the First Amendment of the United States Constitution. While Murray used every occasion to repudiate the secularism of continental democracy, he urged Fenton and his associates to avoid their irrelevant attacks on European separatism and consider the American phenomenon seriously.[35]

Murray was right in recognizing that a completely different sense of the issues, a totally new mentality was needed for a contemporary Catholic theology of Church-State relations; and that method itself was profoundly involved, emerging from openness to the data of contemporaneous social, political, and personal life. As early as 1947, Fenton clearly took issue with Murray's approach to the problem by stating:

Sacred Theology seeks only to bring out a clear, certain, and unequivocal expression of the meaning of that message which we know as divine public revelation. This particular section of Sacred Theology strives to grasp and to present God's own teaching on how the Church and State are meant to live together.[36]

Such an understanding of the theological task excluded at the outset any cognizance of historical reality and stood in opposition to Murray's analysis of the theologian's task. What was ultimately of concern was an understanding of the development of doctrine.

From the very beginning of the debate on religious liberty in the 1940s through the 1950s and into the Council years Murray was clearly aware that this was the crucial issue. It was this issue that Murray tackled head on in the famous *relatio* of November 17, 1963, which he had prepared for Bishop De Smedt.[37] The ultimate success of *The Problem of Religious Freedom* was that it was able to provide for the bishops a clear and attractive analysis of the historical method and its application to the religious liberty issue. It was necessary to explain how the Church moved from the nineteenth-century position as epitomized in the *Syllabus of Errors* to the position set forth in *Pacem in Terris* and clarified in the Council's *Declaration on Religious Freedom.*

Two Essential Doctrinal Components

As Murray saw it, the final draft of *The Declaration on Religious Freedom* had two essential doctrinal components, one juridical, the other political.

> The juridical affirmation is that every man has a right to religious freedom—a right that is based on the dignity of the human person, and is therefore to be formally recognized as a civil right and protected by an armature of constitutional law. The political affirmation is that the powers of government are to be employed in the safeguard of this right and are not to be used to limit its free exercise, except in cases of proved necessity.[38]

But what was the conception embodied in this affirmation? "The Declaration presents the content or object of the right to religious freedom as simply negative, namely, immunity from coercion in religious matters."[39] Religious freedom as immunity is conceived as a two-fold immunity. In the first place, no one is to be coerced into belief or action contrary to his own convictions. Secondly, no one is to be "coercively restrained from action—that is, from public witness, worship, observance and practice—according to his own convictions."[40]

In the Liberal Tradition of the West

Murray saw this position as resting on the solid ground of the constitutional tradition of the West, whose development in matters of religious freedom was first affected by the Constitution of the United States in 1789 and by the First Amendment in 1791. "The fundamental freedoms of the First Amendment, including the 'free exercise of religion,' were concerned to be not claims upon government or society, but assurances against government and society."[41] They were what the Fourteenth Amendment would later come to call them: certain specified "immunities of the citizens of the United States."

Thus the political tradition affirmed is the tradition within which the American commonwealth came into being and it is the essence of the liberal tradition of the West.

> It is a tradition of a freeman in a free society. It is the theory of what we call "constitutional government" that is to say, a regime composed of organs and offices whose powers are defined and limited by a written constitution, a fundamental law that somehow incorporates a bill of rights and directs and controls the processes of government.[42]

Theological Significance of the Declaration

Besides the political and juridical significance of the Declaration, Murray saw the document as having theological significance. He saw it as being narrow in scope in that it sought only to distinguish sharply the issue of religious freedom in the juridico-social order from the larger issue of Christian freedom. The Council merely suggested that the two kinds of freedom were related without undertaking to specify their precise relationship more closely. However, with this step made, Murray felt that dialogue on the meaning of Christian freedom would be more successful. The Declaration had settled the lesser issue of the free exercise of religion in civil society.[43] But if the document is considered in the light of the two great historical movements of the nineteenth century, Murray claimed we can begin to see the theological significance of the Declaration.

Movement Toward Secularity of Society and State

The first movement was from the sacral conception of society and State to the secular conception. This sacral conception is the heritage of medieval Christendom. Characteristic of this conception was first the view that the Christian world—or at least the Catholic nation—was considered to be somehow enclosed within the Church, which was herself the Great society. Second, the religious prerogative of the prince extended to a care of the religion of his subjects and a care of their religious unity as essential to their political unity.[44]

With the breakup of the sacrality of society and state the nineteenth century saw a movement toward secularity. The Church, through Rome, opposed this movement because the term of the historical movement was not a proper secularity of state and society. "What emerged was the laicized State of rationalist or atheist inspiration, whose function was the laicization of society."[45]

Though the Church could not accept this movement, she failed to discern the signs of the times and to discover the true and valid dynamism that was at work beneath the transitory historical forms assumed by the new movement. Murray saw the true underlying direction of the new movement toward a proper and legitimate secularity of society and state. "In the depths, where the hidden factors of historical change were operative, what was really going on was a work of differentiation from the religious community, the Church."[46]

For Murray, Leo XIII had first begun to discern where the deep currents of history were setting. Leo was able to restore its proper centrality and also develop the traditional truth that Gelasius I had sought to enforce upon the Emperor Anastasius in A.D. 494. "Two there are, august Emperor, whereby this world is ruled by sovereign right (*principaliter*), and sacred authority of priesthood and the royal power." Said Murray:

> In a series of eight splendid texts from *Arcanum* (1880) to *Pervenuti* (1902), Leo XIII made it clear that there are two distinct societies, two distinct orders of law, as well as two distinct powers. This was the ancient affirmation in a new mode of understanding, an authentic development of doctrine.[47]

On this basis, Pope Leo was also able to accomplish a second development by reiterating that the essential claim which the Church makes on civil societies and their governments is stated in the ancient formula "the freedom of the Church." Because of Leo XIII's thrust, further progress could be achieved by Vatican II. The sacrality of society and state is now transcended and archaic. Its duties and rights do not include the *cura religionis*. The government's function is secular, that is, "It is confined to a care of the free exercise of religion within society, a care therefore of the freedom of the Church and of the freedom of the human person in religious affairs."[48]

The Declaration adds to *Pacem in Terris* a true Christian understanding of society and state in their genuine secularity by insisting, according to Murray,

> that the highest value that both State and society are called upon to protect and foster is the personal and social value of the free exercise of religion. The value of religion itself for men and society are to be protected and fostered by the Church and by other religious communities availing themselves of their freedom. Thus the Declaration assumes its primary theological significance.[49]

Movement toward Historical Consciousness

The second great trend of the nineteenth century was the movement from classicism to historical consciousness. For Murray classicism designated a view of truth which holds to objective truth, precisely because it exists objectively "already out there now. . . ." This makes truth exist apart from its possession by someone. It also exists apart from history, formulated in propositions that are verbally immutable. If there is to be any such thing as development of doctrine, it can only mean that the truth, remaining itself unchanged in its formulation, can find different applications in the contingent world of historical change.

In contrast to the above, historical consciousness, while still holding to the nature of truth as objective, is especially concerned with the possession of truth, with man's affirmation of truth, with the understanding that is contained in these affirmations, with the conditions, both circumstantial and subjective, of understanding and affirmation, and therefore with the historicity of truth and with progress in the grasp and penetration of what is true.[50]

Murray showed how this movement, especially as it emerged in modernism, was also opposed by the Church. The work of discerning had to be done. It was first achieved at Vatican II. As the Council went on, it was clear that classicism was giving way to historical consciousness. The pastoral effort of the Council became a concern to seek out the progress in the understanding of truth which was demanded both by the historical moment and by the subject who must live it. "In a word," said Murray, "the fundamental concern of the Council is with the development of doctrine" and this was the second theological significance of the Declaration.

Religious Freedom: Murray's Developed Position

Before concluding it would be helpful to summarize Murray's thinking on religious freedom as it was at its fully developed stage. As Murray saw it, freedom of religion is a fact of the contemporary lay democratic state as exemplified in the American situation. The concept and its practice have undergone such development, said Murray, primarily because of a growth in man's consciousness of his personal dignity and a concomitant awareness that this dignity ought to be protected by constitutional law.

> The common consciousness of men today considers the demand for personal, social, and political freedoms to be an exigency that rises from the depths of the human person. It is the expression of a sense of right approved by reason. It is therefore a demand of natural law in the present moment of history. This demand for freedom is made especially in regard to the goods of the human spirit. . . . In a particular way, freedom is felt to be man's right in the order of his most profound concern, which is the order of religion.[51]

In view of this social and political reality, Murray asserted that the problematic with regard to religious freedom had changed. It is simply religious freedom, and no longer the exclusive rights of truth and its correlate, legal tolerance and intolerance. Since the problematic has changed, it must be confronted as it presents itself in the contemporary historical situation. The first question to be dealt with is the meaning of religious liberty in the present reality as Murray understood it.

Murray saw religious freedom as located in the social and civil orders, that is, as a constitutional guarantee to "the people," taken individually, collectively and in assembly, of immunity from all external coercion in religious matters. As we noted earlier, this liberty, as it is found in a constitutional democracy, is essentially comprised of "freedom of conscience" and "the free exercise of religion."

Freedom of conscience refers to the individual's human and civil right to be unhindered by any external restraining or constraining force in matters religious. "It is the freedom of personal religious decision."[52] And no individual or group within society has the right to exert coercion in any form whatsoever to influence such religious decisions.

The validity of this freedom is established by the convergence of theological, ethical, political, and legal arguments, in spite of the fact that religious liberty is primarily a juridical notion. Theologically, freedom of conscience is supported by an unbroken tradition of the necessity of freedom in the act of faith. The ethical argument lies in the immunity of conscience from any coercion in the question of religious decisions, while the political-legal argument consists in the immunity of conscience from restraint or constraint by powers of state or society in matters of belief or unbelief independently of whether conscience is true or erroneous. It is not within the competence of the state to make that judgment. Obviously, the political-legal argument is based on the distinction of the two societies and the conviction of the sacredness of conscience.[53]

The free exercise of conscience means that an individual cannot be coerced to act against his conscience nor be restrained from acting in accord with it. We are here on the level of action rather than decision. There are three aspects to this free exercise. First, it implies corporate freedom, the internal autonomy of religious communities and organizations. These may, in other words, define and organize themselves and function as they see fit. This freedom is also based on the autonomy of the two powers, and the consequent "freedom of the Church," and the limited competence of the state that were discussed earlier.[54]

Secondly, there is the freedom of religious association, meaning the right to immunity from force in assuming or terminating membership in a religious group, or in establishing such a group. The personal freedom of conscience and its immunity from coercion in religious matters is the primary support of this freedom. Religious affiliation or nonaffiliation is ultimately related to religious belief or nonbelief and, therefore, belongs to a special sphere.[55]

Thirdly, the free exercise of religion involves free expression in religious matters, whether that expression be in the form of worship, practice, preaching, or witness in the public sector of society. This freedom derives from freedom of conscience and freedom of the Church, and the social-historical existence of both the individual and the Church. This dimension of existence cannot be denied to either nor can it be separated from their internal-personal lives. Hence, in granting internal freedom, freedom of external expression must also be granted. "Both freedoms are given in the same instance; they are coequal and coordinate, inseparable, equally constitutive of the dignity and integrity of man."[56] Furthermore, from the political-legal point of view, it is simply not within the competence of the state (in the constitutional tradition) to inquire into or pass judgment on the truth of any religious belief and its expression. "It is not within the competence of the public powers to consign churches to the sacristy, or to exterminate religious opinions from the public domain."[57] They have no power to coerce the social expression of the religious conscience. To bring any force upon the former is to bring force upon and to violate the latter freedom.

Those aspects of religious liberty, argued Murray, that deal with man's relationship with God either individually or collectively are freedoms *sui generis* because of their transcendent end. They are unique freedoms. When they pertain to relationship with men, however, they belong to the realm of civil rights and are therefore subject to regulation by public powers as are all social freedoms. The first limitation of religious freedom ought to be a sense of personal responsibility toward the common good of society, the state with its laws and authority, and one's fellow-men. When this limitation fails, restraint by the state may be necessary in order to maintain public order. However,

> the public powers are authorized to intervene and to inhibit forms of religious expression . . . only when such forms . . . seriously violate either the public peace or commonly accepted standards of morality, or the rights of other citizens. The public powers are competent to make judgments only with regard to the essential exigencies of the public order and with regard to the necessity of legal or police intervention in order to protect the public order.[58]

This juridical criterion, said Murray, is the same which limits the state's control over other civil liberties. In its exercise, however, recognition must be given to the privileged character of religious freedom.[59]

Religious Freedom and Limited Government

A further consideration bears on the problem of religious freedom in a constitutional government. This is in fact the political correlate of the juridical notion of religious freedom. A government of limited power is based on four principles.[60] The first is the distinction between the sacred and the secular spheres of life. This distinction is rooted in the Western Christian tradition, although it was blurred by the medieval Christian state and later the nation-state. The theory of the two societies simply asserts the autonomy of both Church and state in their particular spheres because of the unique origin and finality of each. A corollary of this theory is that neither has direct power in the sphere of the other. The state is limited in its power and activity to the temporal sphere by its origin and finality, and can in no way be directly employed in furthering the spiritual purposes of the Church. The state has no right to reach into the religious area of man's life.

Secondly, a distinction between society and state must be maintained. The latter functions in a limited way within the former as law and administration.

> The public powers, which are invested with the power of the state, are charged with the performance of certain limited functions for the benefit of society—such functions as can and must be performed by the coercive discipline of law and political power. The functions are defined by constitutional law in accord with the consent of the people.[61]

The third principle is the distinction between the common good and public order. It follows upon the previous distinction. "The common good includes all the social goods, spiritual and moral as well as material, which man pursues here on earth in accord with the demands of his personal and social nature."[62] The common good is the responsibility of the entire society. Public order on the other hand is a more limited concept and is the responsibility of the state. It involves the maintenance of public peace, morality, and justice through the coercion of law. This is the limitation of the state's power.

The final principle is both a political truth and a primary method of political procedure. As political truth it is simply "freedom under law." Murray explained:

> The freedom of the people is a political end, prescribed by the personal consciousness among the people. The freedom of the people is also the higher purpose of the juridical order, which is not an end in itself. Furthermore, freedom is the political method *per excellentiam*, prescribed by the political consciousness among the people.[63]

As a rule of jurisprudence, this principle affirms the right to as much freedom as possible with only as much constraint as is necessary. Such a principle obviously limits the power of government.[64]

In summary, we may say that John Courtney Murray affirmed the validity of religious freedom as "a legal institution, a juridical notion, a civil and human right." Contemporary man's demand for this liberty is an exigency of reason and therefore merits affirmation. He also affirmed the validity of constitutional government "within whose structure religious freedom . . . finds its necessary place."[65] Murray did not, however, regard religious liberty as either thesis or hypothesis because he did not accept as his premise the principle that error has no rights. Rights for him are located in persons and not in abstract principles. His starting point was the exigency of the present political reality.

Furthermore, he rejected the position that the public care of religion necessarily entails the principle that error has no rights and that all religious dissension be repressed. Rather, Murray said:

> The public care of religion is provided in both necessary and sufficient measure when the order of the constitutional law recognizes, guarantees, and protects the freedom of the Church, both as religious community and as a spiritual authority, at the same time that it gives similar recognition, guarantee and protection to the

general religious freedom—personal, ecclesial, associational, and practical—of the whole body politic. Within the new perspectives of today, the Church does not demand, per se and in principle, a stature of legal privilege for herself. The Church demands, in principle and in all situations, religious freedom for herself and religious freedom for all men.[66]

In brief, what Murray did was to advance the theory of the two distinct powers and the indirect power of the Church. For Murray, the two societies and the freedom of the Church are transtemporal principles. He thereby removed the grounds for legal intolerance and the traditional position on religious liberty. He was then able to give recognition and emphasis to religious liberty as inherent in the dignity of man. Since it has essentially to do with man's relation to God, it is a unique freedom. Its expression may be constrained or restrained only if it violates the public order. Otherwise, the duty of the state with regard to religious freedom is to give it full protection.

Notes

1. Bernard J. F. Lonergan. *Insight: A Study of Human Understanding* (New York: Philosophical Library, 1957); also Lonergan, "The Transition from a Classicist World-View to Historical Mindedness," a paper presented to the seminar on the Role of Law in the Church sponsored by the Canon Law Society of America, now published in *Law for Liberty: The Role of Law in the Church Today*, ed. J. A. Biechler (Baltimore: Helicon, 1967), pp. 126-33.

2. Fenton's approach to the problem of religious liberty is a clear example of this kind of method. See Fenton, "The Doctrinal Authority of Papal Encyclicals (1)," *AER*, CXXI (August, 1949), pp. 136-150; Part 2 (September, 1949), pp. 210-20; "*Magisterium* and Jurisdiction in the Catholic Church," *AER*, CXXX (March, 1954), pp. 194-201; "Infallibility in the Encyclicals," *AER*, CXXVIII (March, 1953), pp. 177-98; "Catholic Polemic and Doctrinal Excellence," *AER*, CXXXII (February, 1955), pp. 107-17; "The Holy Father's Statement on Relations between Church and State," *AER*, CXXXIII (November, 1955), pp. 323-31; "The Doctrinal Authority of Papal Allocutions," *AER*, CXXXIV (February, 1956), pp. 109-17.

3. Murray, *The Problem of Religious Freedom*, p. 85.

4. *Ibid.*, p. 100.

5. *Ibid.*, p. 84. Murray refers to the thesis-hypothesis theory of Church and State as the "opinio recepta." In a lengthy unpublished paper for Franz Cardinal König written in late 1965 and explaining the conciliar history of the *Declaration on Religious Freedom*, Murray again speaks of the older view on Church and State as the "received opinion." "There have been indeed instances in history of men who were forced to profess the Catholic faith against their own will and belief: but there never was a received opinion within the Church that justified this practice. On the

other hand, there has been within the Church a received opinion which gave theoretical justification for the practice of legal intolerance by Catholic governments." Murray saw John XXIII as "quietly bidding good-bye" to this theory in *Pacem in Terris*, "The Conciliar History of the Declaration," unpublished paper for Franz Cardinal König, WCA.

6. The majority of the material for this section has been taken from works by Murray: "The Problem of State Religion," *TS*, XII (June, 1951), pp. 155-78. It was the first part of this article by Murray in *AER*, CXXIV, "The Problem of 'Religion of the State' " (May, 1951), pp. 327-52 that Fenton took issue with (see p. 35). See Fenton, "The Status of the Controversy," *AER*, CXXIV (June, 1951), pp. 451-58, and "Principles Underlying Traditional Church-State Doctrine," *AER*, CXXVI (June, 1952), pp. 452-62. See also Murray's book *The Problem of Religious Freedom*, and his article "The Governmental Repression of Heresy," *Proceedings of the Catholic Theological Society of America*, III (Chicago, 1948), pp. 26-98.

7. "The legal institution known as the state-church, and the later embodiment in the written constitutional law of territorial states of the concept of Catholicism as 'the religion of the state,' represent an application of Catholic principles (and of the medieval tradition, itself an adaptation) to the complex political, social, religious, and cultural conditions prevailing in the modern state, as it appeared on the dissolution of medieval Christendom, took form in the era of political absolutism, flourished in the era of 'confessional absolutism' . . . under the royal governments in the 'Catholic nations' of post-Reformation Europe, and sought reinstatement in the monarchic restorations of the nineteenth century. As a necessary adaptation of principle this legal institution was at first tolerated by the Church; later, in the circumstances of fixed religious divisions, it became the object of more positive acquiescence; still later, in the circumstances created by the French Revolution, it was defended against the laicizing monism of Continental Liberalism, which destroyed the institution of the state-church in consequence of its denial of the Catholic thesis of juridical and social dualism under the primacy of the spiritual, of which the institution was, however defectively, an expression. In the course of this defense the application of the thesis was identified with the thesis itself—an identification that was never canonized by the Church." "The Problem of State Religion," p. 161.

8. Murray, *The Problem of Religious Freedom*, p. 36.

9. "Governmental Repression of Heresy," p. 40. A qualification must be made here with regard to those who were and are in this line of thought. Although they hold that the *cura religionis* belongs to the state, i.e., that it is the state's obligation to promote the one true faith, they do not accept all the implications of this, such as were present in former times. In Murray's words, the position "recognizes that the modern Catholic nation is not the medieval Christian commonwealth; hence it denies that the religious prerogative of the emperor is to be transferred without alteration to the public powers in the Catholic state today. It denies that public care of religion may be prolonged into a *ius in sacra* or a *ius circa sacra*. It also denies the *ius reformandi* of the prince and its pendant, the *beneficium emigrationis*. It denies that the prince, by reason of his political sovereignty, is a judge of religious truth and *custos utriusque tabulae*. It rejects the notion that the prince, although he has no right to compel or impose religious faith, has nonetheless the duty and right to compel his subjects to hear the true word of God and to enforce outward conformity with the official faith. It admits, therefore, in principle, that certain kinds of external constraint are incompatible with personal freedom of conscience" (*The Problem of Religious Freedom*, p. 16).

10. Error should be repressed because it is *per se* contrary to the rational and moral nature of man and to the common good of society, is injurious to other's rights, and is *per se* a scandal. *Ibid.*, p. 11.

11. *Ibid.*, p. 7.

12. *Ibid.*, p. 12.

13. "How Liberal Is Liberalism," *America*, LXXV (April 6, 1946), p. 7.

14. "The Church and Totalitarian Democracy," *TS*, XII (December, 1952), p. 531.

15. The principal sources used in this section are: "Governmental Repression of Heresy," pp. 33-38; "Contemporary Orientations of Catholic Thought on Church and State in the Light of History," *TS*, X (June, 1949), pp. 177-234.

16. "Governmental Repression of Heresy," p. 34.

17. A clarification should be made here of the nature of Murray's historical consciousness. He, like those using the classical methodology, is operating in the natural law tradition, and hence, is employing absolutes, etc. The classical methodology, however, was absolutizing the relative and Murray was trying to distinguish between the two and to show the influence of concrete historical circumstances on what was thought to be absolute. See "Contemporary Orientations," p. 214.

18. For the change of the problematic in this whole question (ultimately a conflict between Roman and common law traditions), see *ibid.*, pp. 186-97 and "The Problem of State Religion," pp. 163-64.

19. "Contemporary Orientations," p. 229.

20. "The Problem of State Religion," p. 163.

21. *Ibid.*, p. 166.

22. Murray made crucial distinctions between "civil society," "political society," "state," and "government." I will indicate here only the essence of these distinctions. *Civil society* "designates the total complex of organized human relationships on the temporal plane, which arise either by necessity of nature or by free choice of will in view of the cooperative achievement of partial human goods by particular associations or institutions." *Political society* is civil society politically organized for the common good. The *State* is "that particular functional organization of the body politic, whose special function regards the good of the whole. . . . It is a set of institutions combined into a complex agency of social control and public service." See "The Problem of State Religion," pp. 158-69, n. 6.

23. "Contemporary Orientations," p. 192.

24. *Ibid.*, p. 183.

25. "Separation of Church and State," *America*, LXXVI (December 7, 1946), p. 262.

26. *Ibid.*

27. *Ibid.*, pp. 262-63. The term "lay" is not meant to convey in this case anything like agnosticism or atheism. It simply describes the state's position of not acknowledging, as state, any particular religion. It is not a refusal to acknowledge God.

28. Gelasius I was Pope from 492-496. Just less than a century after St. Augustine battled the Donatists, Pope Gelasius attempted to define more precisely the relationship between the Church and the State. Where St. Augustine emphasized the need for Church and State to work together, Gelasius stressed their separate spheres. His was not a full-fledged theory of Church and State. But he succeeded in making clear that Church and State are not one but two distinct spheres, each with its own ruler and authority. His famous text on the "two powers" written in A.D. 496 to Emperor Anastasius I can be found in the letter "Famuli Vestrae pietatis." See

Andreas Thiel, ed., *Epistolae Romanorum pontificum a S. Hilario usque ad S. Hormisdam* (Brunsbergae: in aedibus E. Peter, 1868), I, pp. 349-358. "Duo quippe sunt, imperator auguste, quibus principaliter mundus hic regitur: auctoritas sacra pontificum et regalis potestas—There are indeed, your Majesty, two [powers] by which this world is mainly ruled: the sacred authority of pontiffs and the royal power." For a study of basic importance see: Aloysius K. Ziegler. "Pope Gelasius I and His Teachings on the Relation of Church and State," *The Catholic Historical Review*, XXVII (January, 1942), pp. 412-437; also Murray, "Contemporary Orientations," pp. 195ff.; "Leo XIII: Separation of Church and State," pp. 187ff.; "The Freedom of Man in the Freedom of the Church," pp. 137ff.

29. John of Paris, *De postestate regia et papali* (1302), discusses the distinctions and limitations of civil and papal authority. John's position on "indirect power" is the logical outcome of the idea of the origins of the state in natural law, Gelasian dualism, and medieval constitutionalism. He provided the basis for a truly indirect power of the Pope. See: Jean Leclerq. *Jean de Paris et l'ecclésiologie du XIIIe siècle* (Paris: J. Vrin, 1942). Murray makes special reference to Leclerq's work in "Contemporary Orientations," p. 177. Besides this article see also the following articles where Murray examines the teaching of John of Paris: "For the Freedom and Transcendance of the Church," p. 28, and "Governmental Repression of Heresy," pp. 52-62. For a brief study of John of Paris and Murray's understanding of John's "indirect power," see: E. A. Goerner. *Peter and Caesar: Political Authority and the Catholic Church* (New York: Herder and Herder, 1965), pp. 94-126. Goerner's book also contains a chapter on Murray, pp. 173-191. After appreciative analysis, Goerner criticizes Murray primarily for historicism and a tendency to precipitate church thought into pure situationalism. Such a critique recalls the more stable element in Murray's own thought, natural law theory.

30. "Contemporary Orientations," p. 223.

31. *Ibid.*

32. "Governmental Repression of Heresy," pp. 70-72.

33. *Ibid.*, pp. 76-77.

34. *Ibid.*, pp. 83-84.

35. Fenton, "The Theology of the Church and State," *Proceedings of the Second Annual Meeting of the Catholic Theological Society of America* (Boston, 1947), pp. 15-46.

36. *Ibid.*, p. 16. If one compares Fenton's analysis of the theological task to Murray's as enunciated earlier in the chapter, a clear clash of methodology is apparent. This clash will become more evident in the final chapter.

37. See Chap. III, p. 84.

38. Murray, "The Declaration on Religious Freedom," in *Vatican II: An Interfaith Appraisal*, ed. John H. Miller (Notre Dame: University of Notre Dame Press, 1966), pp. 567-68.

39. *Ibid.*

40. *Ibid.*, p. 569.

41. *Ibid.*, p. 568.

42. "Religious Liberty and the Development of Doctrine," *The Catholic World*, CCIV (February, 1967), p. 281.

43. "Religious Freedom," in *The Documents of Vatican II*, ed. Walter M. Abbott (New York: America Press, 1966), p. 674.

44. "The Declaration on Religious Freedom," *War, Poverty, Freedom: The Christian Response, Concilium*, XV (New York: Paulist Press, 1966), p. 6.

45. *Ibid.*, p. 7.
46. *Ibid.*
47. *Ibid.*, p. 8.
48. *Ibid.*, p. 9.
49. *Ibid.*
50. *Ibid.*, p. 11.
51. *The Problem of Religious Freedom*, pp. 18-19.
52. *Ibid.*, p. 24.
53. *Ibid.*, p. 34.
54. *Ibid.*, pp. 34-35.
55. *Ibid.*, pp. 35-36.
56. *Ibid.*, p. 38.
57. *Ibid.*, p. 39, also pp. 36-37.
58. *Ibid.*, p. 43.
59. *Ibid.*, pp. 40-45.
60. *Ibid.*, pp. 29-31.
61. *Ibid.*, p. 29.
62. *Ibid.*
63. *Ibid.*, p. 30.

64. The principles enunciated above are an essential part of the English-American legal experience. Murray's Church-State reformulation emerged out of this common law tradition and not the Roman law tradition. Common law is the law which not only governs the nations joined in the British Commonwealth but also forms the basis of the legal order of the United States. Its history is part of the medieval and modern tradition of Christian society. Medieval canon law has contributed not a little to its historical development. Denis O'Connell, one of the Americanist bishops whom we shall discuss in the final chapter, likewise appealed to the English-American legal experience to argue for the compatibility of Catholicism and Republicanism. See O'Connell's August 20, 1897, address to the Fourth International Congress of Catholic Savants in Fribourg, Switzerland. The text of the address can be found in Félix Klein. *Americanism: A Phantom Heresy* (Atchison: Aquin Book Shop, 1951), pp. 70-76. Some years earlier another prominent American Catholic bishop, John England, had also defended the common law tradition as applicable to the Church-State issue in the United States. Having apostrophized religious prejudice as a disease of the Republic, England strongly affirmed the compatibility of Catholicism with the spirit of republicanism by declaring: "The principles of the common law, that mighty fabric in which English liberty is said to reside, have been traced back to the Catholic Church. In this, then, is the germ of liberty to be found. . . . Let us be a band of brothers as to our common rights—as to our religious differences, let us bury them" in *The Works of the Right Reverend John England, First Bishop of Charleston*, Sebastian Messmer, ed. (7 vols.; Cleveland, 1908), VII, pp. 66-75. For more recent material on common law see: Ladislas M. Örsy, "The Dynamic Spirit of Common Law and the Renewal of Canon Law," in *Law for Liberty: The Role of Law in the Church Today*, James E. Biechler, ed. (Baltimore: Helicon, 1967), pp. 172-80; Stephan Kuttner, "The Code of Canon Law in Historical Perspective," *The Jurist*, XXVIII (January-October, 1968), pp. 129-48; Bernard F. Deutsch, "Common Law," *The Jurist*, XXVII (January-October, 1967), pp. 37-57.

65. *The Problem of Religious Freedom*, p. 31.
66. *Ibid.*, p. 32.

5

In the "Americanist Tradition"

The preceding chapter dealt with Murray's political philosophy. As we have seen, he derived his political philosophy from the American experience and produced America's first significant contribution to the Church's doctrinal life. Through Murray's persevering and persuasive efforts, the classicist approach to religious freedom gave way to the more historically conscious approach and provided the way for a new development in the Church's teaching.

This final chapter deals with a more specific aspect of this clash in methodologies. Working with a different methodology Murray's different understanding of the theologian's approach to the interpretation of previous papal teaching placed him in outright opposition to Fenton and his associates. In Fenton's eyes, Murray's theological position on religious freedom represented a re-emergence of the late nineteenth-century heresy called Americanism.

In order to situate Murray in this context, a brief examination of a few of the nineteenth-century Americanists is required. This is followed by a more detailed examination of Americanism itself. The major part of the chapter provides an examination of the interpretations of Fenton and Murray concerning the important papal teaching related to this subject.

More than a century and a half before Murray tackled the problem of the relationship of American democracy to traditional teaching on the Church-State question and religious liberty, John Carroll, the future first bishop of the United States, had already publicly confirmed the compatibility of democracy and the Church. From the very beginning, Catholicism in

America was faced with the separation of Church and State, with religious pluralism, and with the freedom of religion. These questions were a political reality rooted in a particular constitutional structure. They were accepted as altogether compatible with Catholic doctrine. After Carroll, a whole line of American bishops reiterated his affirmation, perhaps the most outstanding being the great promoters of democracy—the Americanists. Even a brief survey of their thought reveals ardent support of the democratic system with its constitutional separation of Church and State and its constitutional guarantee of human dignity, civil liberties, and religious freedom. Above all, these elements of our political system were seen to be in harmony with the Church's teaching.

In his famous Roman address of 1887, James Cardinal Gibbons not only praised American democracy, but emphatically noted the government's protection of the freedom of the Church in her spiritual mission. Underlying this, at least implicitly, is the theory of the two societies and of the indirect power of the Church. He said:

> For myself, as a citizen of the United States, without closing my eyes to our defects as a nation, I proclaim, with a deep sense of pride and gratitude, and in this great capital of Christendom that I belong to a country where the civil government holds over us the aegis of its protection without interfering in the legitimate exercise of our sublime mission as ministers of the Gospel of Jesus Christ.[1]

As he praised freedom of the Church in America, he also praised the freedom of conscience and of religion. The latter he considered to be the "true right of every man, because it corresponds with a most certain duty which God has put upon him."[2] It is enjoyed when the individual "possesses the free right of worshipping God according to the dictates of a right conscience, and of practicing a form of religion most in accordance with his duties to God."[3] Gibbons praised an Act of the General Assembly of Maryland proclaimed in April, 1649, which forbade that anyone be menaced for his choice or free exercise of religion, or that he be compelled to believe or practice any other religion against his will.[4] The Church, said Gibbons, is contending everywhere for the principle of freedom of conscience.[5] In America, this freedom of conscience is protected as is the freedom of the Church. Repeating a similar thought echoed in the Roman Sermon, he said of America:

> But, thank God, we live in a country where liberty of conscience is respected, and where the civil constitution holds over us the aegis of her protection without intermeddling with ecclesiastical affairs. From my heart, I say: America, with all thy faults, I love thee still.

Perhaps at this moment there is no nation on the face of the earth where the Church is less trammelled, and where she has more liberty to carry out her sublime destiny, than in these United States.[6]

Similar concepts and sentiments resound in the writings of another of America's great leaders, Archbishop John Ireland. In his essay entitled "The Catholic Church and Civil Society," he clearly made a distinction between the two powers and their competencies.

The distinction between the temporal and spiritual realms was marked, in clearest terms, by the Incarnate God: "Render to Caesar the things that are Caesar's, and to God the things that are God's." The government of the temporal had been committed to Caesar. When the time came to establish on earth a spiritual society, God took nothing back from Caesar: He had kept to himself the things of the soul, "the things of God"; and over these only He claimed immediate power during His tabernacling among men, and over these only He gave immediate authority to His Church. The Church has never departed from the principle laid down by Christ.

The Church reserves to her own jurisdiction faith and morals. Beyond these she does not go; over these the state should claim no control. The State is sovereign in the administration of temporal affairs, and in the practical methods of government: in these the Church has no voice. The limitations of jurisdiction in both Church and State are well defined, and, each one confining itself to its own sphere, no conflict can arise between them.[7]

In another address, he pointed out that both Church and State are supreme in their own respective spheres. The former is in charge of faith and morals, and the latter of temporal and political interests.[8] Government has a divine origin and its purpose is to secure society's most sacred rights, life, liberty, and the pursuit of happiness.[9] If civil power is from God, it is to be used for the purposes intended by God—the preservation of society, the defense of the rights of individuals and families. Beyond these purposes, rulers have no jurisdiction. . . ."[10] Furthermore, although civil power is from God, the rulers receive their authority from the people with certain conditions and limitations placed upon it. "Rulers govern by the will of the people, and derive their just powers from the consent of the governed in the sense that the consent, the choice of the governed is the condition upon which heaven conveys authority."[11]

Ireland was no less democratic in his concept of liberty. He frequently reiterated the fact of the Church's struggle to preserve and protect personal liberty and the rights of man.[12] "The Church has encouraged the fullest development of personal freedom and personal rights, and that so far as political liberty is compatible with civil liberty, and avoids anarchy no less than despotism, she rejoices in its widest expansion."[13] All men are civilly and politically equal and have the same rights which are grounded in their "manhood."[14] The citizen is left as much freedom as is consistent with the safety of the commonwealth. Among these is that of religion.

> We are not all of one mind upon religion and social questions: indeed, upon many matters, we are at variance. But we know one another and we love liberty—and we take as our rule to grant to others what we wish to have for ourselves. We never use the law to enforce our own personal ideas. We respect others because we wish ourselves to be respected.[15]
> . . . .
> In America there is no established church. All religious confessions . . . are absolutely equal before the law; all have common rights; none enjoy particular privileges. . . . While we adhere very firmly to our own faith, we live in peace with those of other beliefs. We have our rights, and we freely concede the rights of others.[16]

In sum, Ireland was convinced that the Church had no reason to fear democracy because in it her own principles of equality, fraternity, and liberty of all men flourished.[17] In no way did it contradict her teaching.[18] In fact, within democracy, the Church found complete freedom to pursue her spiritual mission with guaranteed protection from the state.[19] "I say that the government of the people, by the people, and for the people, is, more than any other, the polity under which the Catholic Church, the Church of the people, breathes air most congenial to her mind and heart."[20]

Another significant prelate deserves to be mentioned, Denis O'Connell. In his address to the Fourth International Congress of Catholic Savants at Fribourg in 1897 he clearly outlined the meaning of political and ecclesiastical Americanism. Political Americanism, O'Connell affirmed, could be seen in the principles of the Declaration of Independence which proclaim the equality of all men and the guarantee of their individual rights by the solicitude of a government that received its authority immediately from the people and ultimately from God.[21] He saw no conflict between these principles and Catholic doctrine. With regard to ecclesiastical Americanism, he cited the First Amendment, the free exercise of religious belief, and the freedom of the Church that resulted from it. He concluded his address with these words:

This, then, is Americanism; and from what has been said in the foregoing it must appear evident to every candid inquirer that it involves no conflict with either Catholic faith or morals, that in spite of repeated statements to the contrary, it is no new form of heresy or liberalism or separation, and that fairly considered "Americanism" is nothing else than the loyal devotion that Catholics in America bear to the principles on which their government is founded, and their conscientious conviction that these principles afford Catholics favorable opportunities for promoting the glory of God, the growth of the Church, and the salvation of souls in America.[22]

This brief glance at the thought of three "Americanists" indicates that even in the nineteenth century and earlier a sound tradition was developing in American Catholicism. This tradition recognized in the American political and social reality an expression of authentic principles—the autonomy of the state and the primacy of the spiritual, the freedom of the Church, the freedom of the individual conscience, the freedom and dignity of man, and the freedom of religion. Although the adaptation of the Church's transtemporal principles to concrete situations may not have been extensively elaborated or developed in scholarly fashion, it nevertheless was expressed implicitly in its basic elements, and was surely practiced.

That Gibbons, Ireland, and O'Connell were able to speak as they did was due largely to the development in Leo XIII's thinking on Church and State. While Leo himself had not elaborated a new theoretical basis for Church-State relations, he had provided a new approach to modern political problems. In *Au milieu des sollicitudes* he had tried to detach French Catholics from their loyalty to monarchical government. In *Longinqua oceani* he had praised the religious situation in the United States. In *Libertas* he had emphasized the God-given gift of liberty of the human person, and in *Diuturnum* he had declared that the people had the right to choose their rulers freely, but not the right to confer the power to rule.

It took a man of Murray's stature to take up the scholarly task begun by the Americanists. As we have seen, he was himself familiar with their thinking, particularly through the influence of his friend John Tracy Ellis.[23] Like the Americanists Murray saw the possibility for further development because of Leo XIII's pronouncements. Through his scholarly analysis of the Pope's teaching he worked out a restatement of the Gelasian formula. As will be shown, Murray was indeed rooted in the American Catholic tradition reflected by the Americanists. His great contribution to the American Church's self-understanding and to the universal Church's doctrine was a highly systematic and scholarly articulation of traditional doctrine in relation to the

American experience. More particularly, Murray significantly furthered the understanding of religious liberty, bringing it from the narrow concept that had arisen out of the medieval Christian state and continental Liberalism to one in which it was a fundamental right of man, guaranteed by constitutional law. Murray played no little role in bringing the Church to recognize that the American proposition is compatible with Catholic doctrine and that freedom of religion is inherent in human dignity.

If Murray is to be considered one of the major spokesmen of the Americanist tradition, his life-long difficulty at getting official Church approval for his position must be considered in the context of the Americanist heresy controversy. The effects of that controversy had plagued American Catholics since the turn of the century. A case can be made showing that Murray's difficulties with churchmen, both in America and in Rome, stemmed from these very same issues which divided American Catholics at the turn of the century and resulted in the condemnation of "Americanism" in 1899. In fact, J. C. Fenton, Francis Connell, and George Shea of *The American Ecclesiastical Review* clearly and publicly accused Murray of the errors reproved in the condemnation of Americanism. In order to properly situate this debate, a brief examination of the Americanist controversy will be necessary. This will be followed by an analysis of Murray's position within this context and his opponents' reaction to it.

Americanism

Since the turn of the century "Americanism" has been a touchy topic in Catholic Church history circles. When the *Catholic Encyclopedia* began to be issued volume by volume, consideration of "Americanism" was postponed by the following note: "See *Testem Benevolentiae*."[24] When the editors reached Volume XIV, a simple résumé of the text of the papal encyclical was all that they published. The placing of this controversy in its proper perspective is extremely important.

"What is Americanism? Is it a state of mind? Is it a doctrine?" asked the Abbé Paul Naudet, editor of *Justice sociale*, in the issue of March 11, 1899. Historians have been trying to answer that for the last sixty years. Félix Klein, a participant in the movement, called it a phantom heresy. Thomas T. McAvoy's *Great Crisis in American Catholic History 1895-1900* (1957) is by far the best-known treatment of this phenomenon and its meaning. The work of Robert D. Cross, *The Emergence of Liberal Catholicism in America*, published the year after McAvoy's work, is also valuable. Margaret Reher's unpublished dissertation, "The Church and the Kingdom of God in America: The Ecclesiology of the Americanists," provides the most recent appraisal of the controversy.[25]

Americanism grew out of the first genuine attempt to come to grips with the whole gamut of important American values: democracy, pluralism, cooperation between religions, state neutrality toward the churches, and the problem of the relationship of religion and culture. The Americanist crisis involved the question of the extent to which the Church should enter the mainstream of American political, economic, and social life. She could do either of two things: accept wholeheartedly "Americanization," the assimilation of immigrants into the American culture, embrace the American life and its institutions, or remain aloof and adopt an attitude of cultural separation and protectionism.

For a number of American bishops, particularly John Ireland, James Gibbons, John Keane, and Denis O'Connell, the first choice was the only hope for the viability of the Church in America. "She must become American," said John Ireland, but of course, the Church in America should also be as Catholic as in Jerusalem and Rome, "so far as her garments be colored to suit environment."[26]

Strongly opposed to this "liberal" attitude were Bishops Bernard McQuaid of Rochester, Michael Corrigan of New York, and in particular the midwestern German-American bishops. These men also saw culture and religion inextricably bound together. But the German bishops, for instance, could not see how the Catholic faith would survive apart from the cultural framework which had kept it alive in Germany. They therefore feared rapid assimilation into the American way.

This discussion developed into very serious disputes among members of the American hierarchy. As early as 1895, Pope Leo XIII had to address himself to the subject of the feuds among the bishops in America. *Longinqua oceani*, the first papal letter to the Church in the United States, dated January 6, 1895, dealt specifically with the serious division among the American bishops. The encyclical analyzed the strengths and weaknesses of American society and explained at length the recently established Apostolic delegation, which had been a source of much of the quarreling. While it expressed the admiration and affection of the Pope for the faithful of this country, there was one passage in the encyclical which was not well received by Archbishop Ireland and his friends. The Pope warned them not to say that the conditions under which they had made so much progress were ideal.

> For the Church amongst you, unopposed by the Constitution and government of your nation, fettered by no hostile legislation, protected against violence by the common laws and the impartiality of the tribunals, is free to live and act without hindrance. Yet, though all this is true, it would be very erroneous to draw the conclusion that in America is to be sought the type of the most desirable status of the Church, or that it would be universally lawful or expedient

for State and Church to be, as in America, dissevered and divorced. The fact that Catholicity with you is in good condition, nay, is even enjoying a prosperous growth, is by all means to be attributed to the fecundity with which God has endowed His Church, in virtue of which unless men or circumstances interfere, she spontaneously expands and propagates itself; but she would bring forth more abundant fruits if, in addition to liberty, she enjoyed the favor of the laws and the patronage of the public authority.[27]

That this period was a time of general progress for American Catholicism is undeniable. American Catholics numbered more than twelve million. Europeans were notably impressed with the continual numerical growth, increasing prosperity and the complete freedom of Catholics in the United States. A number of progressive thinkers hoped that the Church in their own countries might be modeled according to the American pattern. Unfortunately in their overenthusiasm they frequently used careless language about the situation here and often gave false interpretations of the American experience. This ultimately aroused the distrust of conservative Churchmen both here and abroad. What began as a strictly American controversy developed into an international problem for Pope Leo because of the effects it was having in Europe, particularly in France.

Conservative churchmen were all the more disturbed by the participation of Catholic churchmen in the World Parliament of Religion at Chicago in 1893. Pope Leo, consistent in his attitude of "accommodation," had permitted Cardinal Gibbons to take part in the organization of this exhibition. Here was a further example of the "Americanist" prelates tendency to encourage Catholics to mix with Protestants. The idea of the parliament, says E.E.Y. Hales, was

> to show the basic unity of man's religious beliefs by inviting representatives of all the great world religions to share for ten days in a public affirmation of basic religious truths—God, immortality, the soul—and to explain their own peculiar tenets without attacking those of others.[28]

The conservatives had very strong feelings against Catholic participation at the World Parliament. They felt that by appearing on the same platform with other churchmen, Catholic prelates were encouraging indifferentism. This error had been condemned by Pius IX in the *Syllabus of Errors*. It was heretical to deny the unique and divine nature of the Church.

A controversy over this issue became all the more serious when the French, in hope of imitating the American event, sought permission to stage a similar Congress of Religions at the Paris Fair in 1900. The conservative French churchmen were so enraged by this that Pope Leo felt compelled to prohibit any further Catholic participation in similar gatherings. Only nine months after the issuance of *Longinqua oceani*, the Apostolic Delegate to the United States, Archbishop Francis Satolli, requested Pope Leo to send a letter condemning parliaments of religion like the one held in Chicago and the one planned for Paris. The letter sent to Archbishop Satolli was issued on September 18, 1895. While it was meant primarily for the French who were planning the Congress of 1900, it contained an implicit expression of disapproval with regard to the actions of the progressives who had participated in the Congress of 1893. The first hopeful signs of Catholic participation in interfaith activities were extinguished.[29] As we shall see later Francis Connell would use this against Murray in the early 1940s.

By this time the "American approach" had become so popular in France that a group of enthusiastic followers there had begun to call themselves "Americanists." From this point on, the Americanist controversy became international. The incident which sparked the confrontation was a careless French translation and adaptation of Walter Elliott's *Life of Father Hecker*, which appeared in 1897. The introduction to the English edition had been written by Archbishop John Ireland who by now had become very popular in France. He had already given numerous lectures there on the subject of republicanism. Because of these talks, Ireland had become the object of much hatred by the ultramontane school which wanted a restoration of the monarchy. Abbé Félix Klein's translation into French included an enthusiastic preface in which he praised Hecker as "the priest of the future,"[30] and extolled the American Catholic way of life. The incident brought about an angry outburst from Catholic journals in France.[31] The controversy became so serious that the Pope finally appointed a commission to study the entire question and report to him. At the same time Pope Leo refused to have Hecker's biography placed on the Index. With the commission reporting adversely on the doctrines called "Americanism," Leo XIII issued his papal letter, *Testem benevolentiae*, on January 22, 1899. Although Cardinal Gibbons sent a cable to Rome to prevent the condemnation and John Ireland quickly left for the Vatican, both arrived too late to stop the publication of the encyclical.

The papal letter was addressed to Cardinal Gibbons and the American Church. The Pope was careful to say that the erring doctrines had been imputed to American Catholics by a foreign source. He stated clearly that the issue had nothing to do with the legitimate patriotism of the Americans and that he was not accusing Catholics of the United States of holding these views. He merely warned that if such doctrines were being taught, they were erroneous.

In measured and temperate language he spoke of these errors "called by some Americanism." The basic principle of the censurable Americanism was that the Church should adapt her doctrines to modern civilization, express them in a manner appealing to those not of the Church by passing over some less attractive doctrines and adapting Church teachings to popular theories and methods. In the words of Pope Leo:

> The principles on which the new opinions We have mentioned are based may be reduced to this: that, in order the more easily to bring over to Catholic doctrine those who dissent from it, the Church ought to adapt herself somewhat to our advanced civilization, and, relaxing her ancient rigor, show some indulgence to modern popular theories and methods. Many think that this is to be understood not only with regard to the rule of life, but also to the doctrines in which the *deposit of faith* is contained. For they contend that it is opportune, in order to work in a more attractive way upon the wills of those who are not in accord with us, to pass over certain heads of doctrines, as if of lesser moment, or to so soften them that they may not have the same meaning which the Church has invariably held.[12]

Leo saw several specific errors emerging from adaptation to modern society. Religious vows were deemphasized as incompatible with religious liberty. Natural virtues tended to be given preeminence over the supernatural. The action of the Holy Spirit on the individual soul was exaggerated. Less importance was given to external spiritual direction. The Pope saw this preference for modern trends and methods as leading to a restriction of the Church's right to determine questions of a moral and doctrinal nature. If this is what "Americanism" meant, said Leo, it stood condemned, but he was careful to add:

> If, indeed, by the name be designated the characteristic qualities which reflect honor on the people of America, just as other nations have what is special to them; or if it implies the condition of your commonwealths, or the laws and customs which prevail in them, there is surely no reason why We should deem that it ought to be discarded.[13]

In effect, the condemnatory part of the letter stated that in an effort to make Catholic teaching attractive to Americans some churchmen had so accommodated themselves to American society that they were unaware of minimizing the importance of true doctrine.

In his work, McAvoy studied whether Americanism really existed and whether it was particularly American. It is especially in this area that his treatment of Americanism is most helpful, for he makes some important distinctions regarding different kinds of Americanism.

The first kind of Americanism he called "political Americanism" "which is a byword in the United States for patriotism and devotion to the political and social ideals of this country under the Constitution."[34] As we have already indicated, Leo expressly exempted this kind of Americanism from his condemnation.

The second kind is that Americanism which was condemned by Leo. The Pope never said that this Americanism did in fact exist in the United States. This gave rise to the charge that the condemned heresy was an "imaginary or phantom heresy."[35] But he did say that its false views and principles were expressed in the preface of the French translation of the *Life of Father Hecker*.

The third kind of Americanism was that which was advocated by the liberal Catholics in the United States and "was the source of those doctrines condemned in the papal letter,"[36] insofar as it was misinterpreted by certain French writers with liberal views of a much more radical type.

When the Holy Father condemned the second or the French version of Americanism, the "Americanist" bishops here gave their unqualified acceptance to the encyclical letter and declared that they knew of no intelligent Catholic in the country, instructed in his religion, who held the condemned doctrines.

Cardinal Gibbons, spokesman for the hierarchy in this country, immediately answered the Holy Father by saying: "This doctrine I deliberately call extravagant and absurd, this Americanism as it is called has nothing in common with the views, aspirations, doctrine and conduct of Americans."[37] At the same time, however, the more conservative prelates expressed gratitude to the Pope for saving the Church from heresy.[38] Among the so-called Americanists who did write letters of submission to Rome, McAvoy indicated that there was "not one word . . . that would imply that they felt any inclination to defend the propositions reprobated by the Holy Father."[39] Did the Pope then condemn an imaginary heresy? McAvoy feels that the answer depends upon what is implied by "the imaginary or phantom heresy." What the Pope really believed will only be determined when his papers are opened to historians. But even had Leo XIII felt that these errors did not really exist, McAvoy feels his actions would be justified on the score of "stopping a controversy which had gotten out of hand. . . . In that sense the heresy was not a phantom heresy."[40]

Margaret Reher's dissertation, "The Church and the Kingdom of God in America: The Ecclesiology of the Americanists," provided an "alternate

interpretation" to the thesis that the conflict of Americanism was "devoid of
any theological content," and therefore a censure of a "phantom heresy."
Rather she rightly asserts that it was "an incipient ecclesiology of a distinc-
tively American cast which precipitated the Americanist controversy." Her
general conclusion was that "the ecclesiology of the Americanists, reflective of
the contemporary Protestant interpretation of America as God's chosen
Kingdom, was strongly colored by their own experience of American republicanism." She explained that the Americanists believed that the political situation in the United States was the most desirable one for the Church, and that
it afforded the Church full freedom to exercise its spiritual mission. They considered democracy to be the form of government most congenial to Christianity. They also "transferred their appreciation of the balance between authority and freedom in the republic to the Church"; and "emphasized
individual initiative, under the impulse of the Holy Spirit, and deemphasized
external authority." They were anxious to present the Americanism of the
Catholic Church to their Protestant countrymen, and insisted that the
Church be purged of all foreign, nationalistic traits. As a result, "they distinguished between the essentials and the accidentals of the Church and advocated that the contingent elements be changed in order that the Church be
brought into closer contact with the people and with the progress of civilization." Further, "they accepted as fact America's 'manifest destiny,' extended
it to include the Catholic Church in America, and envisioned the American
model as paradigmatic for the Church Universal." *Testem benevolentiae* was
thus in fact a censure of "some of the authentic tenets of the Americanists,
despite their own claims to the contrary."[41]

In this matter, Reher concurred with Fenton, who firmly believed that
while *Testem benevolentiae* never used the term "heretical," it did call attention to "certain things to be avoided and corrected." It was, in fact, a condemnation of "errors" or "inaccurate propositions." "The errors with which
it was concerned, however, were far from being 'phantoms.'"[42]

This is a crucial point for understanding Murray's position within the
Americanist tradition. While Murray, like the Americanists, never saw himself as being in error for holding theological opinions contrary to the teaching
of *Testem benevolentiae*, his opponents, in fact, believed him responsible for
errors "called by some Americanism," and for contradicting the teaching of
Longinqua oceani. And like the Americanist controversy, the Church-State
controversy of the 1950s represented a clash of methods and ecclesiologies.

One important similarity between the two controversies was the fear of
the conservatives over Catholic association with non-Catholics. Like their
predecessors of the 1890s who objected to participation at the World Parliament of Religion in 1893, the conservatives of the 1940s strongly discouraged
American Catholic participation in the National Conference of Christians

and Jews and any interest in intercredal cooperation. It was partly in reply to Murray's call for intercredal cooperation in 1942-43 that in October, 1943, Francis Connell published his "Pope Leo XIII's Message to America."

While admitting that Pius XII had relaxed the restrictions against cooperation previously established in Leo XIII's letter to Archbishop Satolli, Connell warned Americans of "the care they must exercise lest this faith suffer from the spirit of religious indifferentism that is so prevalent in our land today."[43] In noting the sources of the danger, Connell referred, in particular, to the contemporary emphasis on freedom of religious worship. Though he supported this freedom he insisted that a Catholic may not defend it "to the extent of denying that a Catholic government has the right, absolutely speaking, to restrict the activities of non-Catholic denominations, in order to protect the Catholic citizens from spiritual harm."[44]

That there were risks involved in a cooperative adventure, Murray was ready to admit. But he asserted that "co-operation of itself, and in the long run, can just as well be the destruction of indifferentism." In addition, he also expressed regret at the "traditional defensive mentality of Catholics in the United States."[45] Soon after, Fenton and Paul Furfey, also a contributor to *The American Ecclesiastical Review*, joined the debate by warning that intercredal cooperation and "interfaith movements" implied an indifferentist attitude and risked the danger of interconfessionalism.[46]

Murray responded to these objections by providing an analysis of previous papal teaching condemning indifferentism, particularly Pius X's *Singulari quadam*. To Murray it was clear that some development had taken place. ". . . While Pius XII has gone way beyond Pius X, and even beyond Pius XI, in his thought on intercredal co-operation, the progress has been Catholic—*eodem scilicet dogmate, eodem sensu, eademque sententia*."[47]

Admitting that the former condemnations were justified, Murray worked at showing that they in no way applied to this new and different kind of situation and criticized the "relative absence from our midst of what must be the dynamic of the whole idea—a profoundly felt and widely operative concern over the spiritual crisis that confronts us today, perhaps more starkly in America than elsewhere, because its depth and menace are so inadequately realized."[48]

While Murray continued to urge quick and cooperative action by the churches in resolving the world's crises, Fenton continued to support the "state of siege" mentality and pressed for a continued defensive attitude toward the world. For the Church "has always been correct in judging the mass of mankind outside the fold as hostile to her and to her interests."[49]

The above statement contains an evident clash between an understanding of the Church's nature and the method employed in examining the Church's doctrinal teaching. It was inevitable that in this peculiarly American problem the teachings of *Longinqua oceani* and *Testem benevolentiae* would be introduced into the debate.

Longinqua oceani and
Testem benevolentiae

The first mention of *Longinqua oceani* is found in Fenton's "*Time* and Pope Leo," which appeared in the May, 1946, issue of his *Review*. Fenton was responding to the following assertion:

> Vatican and other European clerics had also frowned deeply at the U.S. principle of separation of Church and State, which had been condemned by Leo XIII. But U.S. Catholics, uneasily aware that they were a minority, were early convinced that such a separation was their own strongest safeguard. Though Leo's views are still repeated by a few academic theologians, they are largely ignored by the U.S. hierarchy.[50]

To Fenton this was seriously misleading. Quoting the pertinent passage from *Longinqua oceani* to which we have already referred, he explained that Leo had in no way condemned the position of the United States government toward the Church. Rather, "because there was need for him to do so, he insisted also upon the fact that the position of the Church in this country did not represent the absolute ideal," nor could it be "duplicated laudably in every country on earth." "Pope Leo taught that it would not be universally expedient or licit to have the Church and the State dissociated *more Americano* everywhere."[51] According to Fenton, for a Catholic country to hold the contrary would involve a hostile act against "the principles of the Church," and "a kind of apostasy." He concluded by reasserting the Church's unchanging teaching "that all men should be Catholics, since ours is the true Church and the true religion."[52]

Murray approached the problem somewhat differently. He began by insisting that the problem of religious liberty in America was primarily a "political problem" and one "of the first magnitude." But because of the nature of the problem, "one's conception of it and one's solution to it must be framed in terms of some kind of an ecclesiology. . . ." As far as he was concerned, it would be impossible to propose a political solution to the problem "except in the perspectives of one's theological solution."[53] In response to Protestant attacks on Catholicism and suggestions that the Church is "not interested in freedom," Murray called for a "pacific and full exposition of our own theory of religious liberty." In doing so he suggested that this anti-Catholic attack could "not be successfully met simply by the strenuous defense of the position that the Catholic Church is the one true Church." While admitting that the position "must be guarded at every point," he maintained that what was at issue in the minds of many Catholics and Protestants was rather "the political implications of our position in the present world situation."[54]

Unpersuaded by Murray's argumentation, Fenton persisted in his strenuous defense of the Church as the one true Church[55] and insisted that the fundamental error on the part of those contributing toward the tendency to minimize a Catholic's loyalty to his Church lay in "their belief that the doctrine of the Church, or at least its policy, with reference to association with non-Catholics has changed during the past few years."[56]

Soon afterwards, Murray began his own theological reformulation of the problem, one which would raise serious disagreements with his opponents. His first task at reformulation he saw as "undertaking to begin a statement of Catholic principles in the matter, with a view to showing how they organize themselves into a complete theory." For a reformulation to be valid, he said, judgments on a particular theory must be "based on a sane appreciation of the relativities of history and on a just allowance for the inevitable gap that always separates theory from practice; but it is even more important that they should rest on principles that have been antecedently formulated and supported by orderly argument."[57]

Even in this early stage of his reformulation, Murray argued for use of new formulas. He began his critical "historical" analysis of Leo XIII's thought and isolated the human rights of the individual to religious freedom as essential to this reformulation.[58] In a series of brief articles for *America* magazine he began to examine the religious liberty issue in the context of the First Amendment of the United States Constitution.[59] Noteworthy in these was his dissatisfaction with the "ambiguous" and "deceptive" phrase "separation of Church and State." "The confused polemist can . . . make use of the formula to great effect: 'Catholics support separation of Church and State in the United States; they oppose it in Spain. You see, therefore, what unprincipled power-politicians they are; they act solely on immoral grounds of expediency.'"[60]

He likewise expressed concern over the Protestant fear that Spain represented the "ideal" application of the relationship of Church and State and the related Protestant concern which had resulted from an essay by the late Monsignor John A. Ryan in *The State and the Church*, "wherein the author supposedly let slip the episcopal plan of altering the U.S. Constitution and instituting legal persecution of Protestants."[61]

These articles were accompanied by a more comprehensive examination of the notion of the "governmental repression of heresy," in which he began to explain his conviction that an historical approach was essential for the problem's resolution.

Our whole question then has to be viewed in historical perspective. The doctrine of the two powers has had a long history and has seen much development; and there is no reason to suppose that the development is entirely ended. Apart from a view of this development it is impossible for the theologian to succeed in his task, which is to vindicate the internal consistency of Catholic doctrine at any given moment, and to show forth the fact that the development has been truly organic, in *eodem scilicet dogmate, eodem sensu, eademque sententia.* In a matter in which the relativities of the political order have played so large a part it is not the theologian's task to defend as necessarily permanent and of divine origin every right that the Church or the state has asserted or exercised in particular periods of history. His task is the formulation of principles in such terms that they may be asserted as constantly valid, and their organization into a coherent system that will cover all contingencies because it is dependent on none.[62]

Murray rejected the assertion that to do this meant " 'minimizing' Catholic doctrine, diminishing the exegencies of truth, making concessions to the 'liberal spirit.' "[63]

In this connection he went immediately to the heart of the controversy by questioning whether the distinction between "thesis" and "hypothesis" "supplies irrevocably and for all the time the categories in which we must continue to debate the problem of Church and State?" He answered the question in this way:

For my own part, I incline to think that the usefulness of this particular distinction is increasingly outweighed by its tendency to mislead, and that its categories are too facile to admit of fruitful theological and political thought. If, for instance, on this basis one says that the thesis obtains in Spain, whereas only the hypothesis is verified in the United States, one steps off on the wrong foot into a morass of futile controversy, that centers on an irrelevance— whether the particular political form of the Spanish state is in any sense part of some Catholic "ideal." It may or may not be ideal for the Spanish people—that is their problem. But to predicate "Catholic thesis" or "Catholic ideal" of this particular mode of religio-political organization is, I say, at least misleading.[64]

He concluded this first serious attempt at reformulation of the Church-State theory by asserting:

It would remain to confront this theory with the monuments of tradition. Unable to do this here, I can only say I think it would stand the confrontation, if only each monument were itself squarely confronted to see and distinguish the Catholic tradition—*quod semper, quod ubique, quod ab omnibus*—from the contingent modalities of its application, which have long been historically dependent on political conceptions, which evolve, and on social situations, which alter.[65]

At this point the lines of the controversy were already clearly drawn. The first was based on a misunderstanding by his opponents who felt that he was attempting to make the American arrangement the "Catholic ideal." As they saw it this was condemned in *Longinqua oceani*. Secondly, they understood that Murray was "passing over" officially defined doctrine on the relation of Church and State in order to be more accommodating to non-Catholic critics. To his opponents this error was clearly condemned in *Testem benevolentiae*.

A month after his publication of "The Governmental Repression of Heresy," Murray's historical method was attacked by Fenton. Without mentioning Murray by name Fenton criticized the belief that certain "technical terms" used in dogmatic formulae are "completely extraneous to the original deposit of Christian revelation."

The belief that technical historical terms, while not entirely unrelated to the original deposit of revelation, are primarily expressions of concepts assimilated into the body of Christian doctrine to serve as "contingent" instruments in proposing and defending that doctrine has attracted a certain amount of notoriety in our own day. . . . The proponents of this viewpoint hold that these philosophical concepts remain "contingent," even after they have been integrated into the dogmatic formulae of the Church itself. Hence they believe that progress in Sacred theology in our own time must involve the abandonment of those concepts which have ceased to be "vital," and the replacement of these notions by others more in line with modern thought.[66]

For Fenton this assertion involved a misunderstanding or at least a highly confused notion of the Church's own infallibility and a serious misunderstanding of the role of theology which is to give "only a clear, unequivocal, and certain statement of the Church's teaching." To him theological progress connoted, "not the substitution of one set of 'contingent' concepts for another, but a restatement in terms understood by men of the present day of those very truths which were expressed and are still expressed in the technical language of scholastic theology."[67]

This was followed by another article critical of the indifferentist attitude of those suggesting cooperation by "all men of good will." This error, as Fenton saw it, was based on a misunderstanding of the interrelationship of the Church and the world and on the false understanding of the Church as God's kingdom. To Fenton, the Church as a "visible society" was "actually the kingdom which alone does God's will in the religious order. This, and this alone, is the company of Christ."[68]

The following month Fenton provided a lengthy analysis of what he saw as emerging in this controversy. Using Cardinal Emmanuel Suhard's 1947 pastoral letter, Growth or Decline? The Church Today, as a point of departure he analyzed the "two distinct and even divergent viewpoints within the Church today." According to Suhard, "one group of Catholics urges a predominantly 'defensive' attitude with reference to the contemporary world-civilization. The other group is represented as seeking rather to 'permeate' the world so as to bring about a new culture along Catholic lines." As Fenton viewed it, "approximately the same conditions and precisely the same two viewpoints are to be found among our American Catholics today."[69] The two tendencies were developments of attitudes which came into existence during the previous century. While recognizing that neither of these tendencies is objectively reprehensible, he explained the dangers of each in regard to Church orthodoxy.

Using again the terminology of Suhard, Fenton warned against the dangers of Modernism and integralism both of which were to be avoided. Departing somewhat from Suhard he added: "We must not forget the fact that Modernism, as such, is a definite heresy or collection of heretical teachings, while integralism, as such is nothing of the sort." He reasoned, however, that if integralism referred specifically to the antimodernistic teaching of Lamentabile, Pascendi, and the Sacrorum antistitum, "then integralism is nothing more than a statement of Catholic truth, implied in a denial of errors which are incompatible with the divine message of the Catholic Church."[70]

Reminding his readers that Modernism was still rampant, he concluded with passages from Leo XIII's Testem benevolentiae which condemned those who soften or minimize Catholic dogma to make Church teaching more acceptable to the modern mentality.

Murray made no effort to respond to Fenton's criticisms directly. Rather he continued his comprehensive examination of various facets of the religious liberty issue. First came his "St. Robert Bellarmine on the Indirect Power," in December, 1948. This was followed by a further treatment of the historical method in "Contemporary Orientations of Catholic Thought on Church

and State in the Light of History," in June, 1949. In this last article Murray
sought to answer directly Fenton's accusation that he was attempting to make
the American arrangement the ideal application of the Church-State relationship.

> I am not of course suggesting that the American state exhibits the
> pure embodiment of all the principles stated in the treatise *de
> ethica sociali*; no political realization is ever pure. Nevertheless, I
> do think it offers a political category in which the contemporary
> problem of religious freedom can receive its valid theoretical ar-
> gument.[71]

In another place he insisted that his theory did not mean to suggest "a political canonization of the American state, which, like any political realization,
labors under ambiguities and defects. Still less does it mean that the American state receives a sort of religious canonization by the Church."[72] In explaining that the "vital law of continual adaptation" was "essentially relevant" to the Catholic Church's Church-State doctrine, Murray argued that
history and experience had contributed in a positive way to the Church's understanding of her relationship to the state.

This was followed by another article in which Murray again strongly
rejected the belief that the Spanish constitutional concept of "religion of the
state" was a permanent and unalterable part of the Catholic thesis, and
obligatory from the nature of both Church and State in any "Catholic society."[73] And as if to add more fuel to the fire Murray attacked F. Cavalli's article, referred to earlier,[74] by saying: "It is probable that nothing has been
written in decades better calculated to produce in the U.S. a blind reaction of
total hostility to all things Catholic than the author's ruthlessly simplifying
paragraphs on the Church's unblushing intolerance."[75]

Without mentioning Murray by name, Fenton argued in return that
the infallibility of encyclicals "demand acceptance and true internal consent."
Calling *Testem benevolentiae* "a real definition," Fenton urged an end to the
Church-State discussion. As he saw it the discussion was to be considered
closed and the traditional theory accepted by all until the Pope indicated
otherwise.[76] It was clear that Fenton was referring to Murray when he gave
the example of a theologian dissecting the encyclicals of Leo XIII and Gelasius as the kind of error he was rejecting.

> There is, however, an attitude towards the encyclicals which can
> be productive of doctrinal evil, and which can lead to a practical
> abandonment of their teaching. According to this attitude, it is the
> business of the theologian to distinguish two elements in the con-

tent of various encyclicals. One element would be the deposit of genuine Catholic teaching, which, of course, all Catholics are bound to accept at all times. The other element would be a collection of notions current at the time the encyclicals were written. These notions, which would enter into the practical application of the Catholic teaching, are represented as ideas which Catholics can afford to overlook.

Fenton called this attitude "radically destructive of a true Catholic mentality."[77]

As if Fenton's assertion that encyclicals were infallible and demanded internal consent was not enough, he reiterated his case and argued that any denial of doctrinal propositions, particularly regarding questions of Church and State, may be "qualified or censured as at least temerarious." And he added: "Objectively the man who teaches or who accepts such a temerarious proposition is morally at fault."[78]

On August 12, 1950, as has been mentioned, Pius XII issued the encyclical *Humani generis*. Fenton expressed happiness with its content while Murray promised loyalty to its teaching.[79] Fenton characterized the encyclical as reinforcing his understanding of the authority of encyclicals.

> Consequently, despite the fact that the Church has issued no solemn definition on this point, Catholic writers and teachers can definitely not consider themselves free to state explicitly or even to suggest that a civil society composed of members of the true Church can act as God wills that it should by withholding an explicit and specific profession of the Catholic faith and by refusing an explicit and specific recognition of the Catholic Church. The truth that the state, like every other human society, is objectively obligated to worship God according to the one religion He has established and commanded is so obviously a part of Catholic doctrine that no theologian has any excuse to call it into question.[80]

Fenton understood *Humani generis* to be condemning first those "seeking imprudent and unenlightened desire for religious concord and unity." Secondly, the encyclical reproved those who held that diversity of religious belief was desirable in a democracy. Thirdly, it reproved those who hoped that the theology and theological method taught in the past "should not only be perfected, but completely reshaped." Fourthly, the encyclical also dealt with errors concerning the terminology and the concepts used in Catholic dogma. The encyclical characterized as dogmatic relativism the opinion that dogma could be clothed in a different language for different ages. Finally there was the error of those who would undermine the authority of papal encyclicals. "The *Humani generis* presents as a general norm to cover teaching on this point the statement that, when the Holy Father gives his decision on any subject which has hitherto been subject to controversy, his judgment is no longer open to question among theologians."[81]

In conclusion, Fenton warned American theologians not to brush aside the lesson of this papal encyclical "with the statement that it refers to controversies that have aroused no interest and exercised no influence in this part of the world. Such an assertion about the *Humani generis*, made in our own country, would be manifestly false."[82] As far as he was concerned, certain of these errors existed here in this country and Murray was one of those responsible for these false opinions. In a further article on the subject of this encyclical, Fenton compared the errors to those condemned in *Quanta cura* and *Pascendi*. To him all represented a rejection of "new opinions."[83]

In no place did Murray admit that he saw *Humani generis* as condemnatory of some of his theological opinions. Nor did he cease writing and lecturing on the issue of Church and State. Rather, he began his analysis of Leo XIII. His year of lecturing at Yale provided a forum in which he could test his ideas.

In May, 1951, Murray's first article on the notion of "Religion of the State" appeared in *The American Ecclesiastical Review*.[84] It was meant to be a strong refutation of George W. Shea's "Catholic Doctrine and 'The Religion of the State.' " Shea had asserted that until now Murray had not "successfully vanquished the 'old thesis.' "[85] He understood Leo XIII to have vindicated the notion of "religion of the state" as a permanently valid concept and a theological necessity. For Shea the question: "What is the veritable 'Catholic thesis'?" remained unanswered by Murray.[86]

Murray's reply provided a detailed outline of his historical argument. Notable in this article is his daringness in attacking the Spanish approach to the problem,[87] and his assertion that Pope Leo's social theory never really attempted to answer the great question: "Who are the people?" Murray added:

> Actually, the first great historic answer to the question was given in the United States; but the din raised by the conflict with Continental Liberalism was too great to permit the voice of America (ironically, a deist and Protestant voice giving a Catholic answer) to be heard in European canon-law classrooms. In fact, to this day European authors of textbooks *de jure publico* seem unaware that there is any difference between Jacobin democracy and Anglo-Saxon democracy, or between "the sovereignty of the people" in the sense of the men of '89 and "government of the people, for the

people, and by the people" in the sense of Lincoln. *Hinc illae lacrimae*, spilled by an American on reading books *de jure publico*.[88]

The following month Fenton characterized the Church-State debate as "one of the most important doctrinal controversies of our time." He criticized Murray for his disdain of public ecclesiastical law and theological treatises. He called Murray's method ambiguous and his terminology vague. He concluded by insisting that one has no right to put aside true teaching in order to please anti-Catholics.[89]

In July, 1951, Connell joined the debate with a reply to Murray's refutation of Shea.[90] Murray's response showed that he was genuinely offended by Connell's comments:

> Fr. Connell credits me with the intention of trying to "smooth the way toward a better understanding of the Catholic Church on the part of non-Catholics in America," by a process of compromising Catholic principles, or concealing them, or understating them. The suggestion is mistaken and injurious. I reject it.[91]

To Murray, Connell's comments "betrayed a blindness to the present-day problem," and a refusal to look at the problem in its "new form."

> . . . The Church has never consciously and adequately faced the problem, theoretical as well as practical, put to it by a state organized on the constitutional and political lines proper to the tradition of Anglo-American democracy. The practice of Church-State relationships, and therefore to some extent their theory, has been conceived in function of the European Continental political tradition. In fact, one could say without great exaggeration that for centuries the problem of Church and State has been the problem of the Church and France. And "France" here means two things— royal absolutism and the Revolution, both of which, after the French example became international phenomena.[92]

Murray characterized the attitude expressed by Connell as a "nostalgia for the dear dead days of the 'Catholic state' on the monarchic or dictatorial model," and said of his opponent:

> Connell's single concern is for the powers of the powers, not for the freedoms of the people. And he considers the theory and practice of Church-State relations to be "all finished." There is no more

problem; it has been solved. Leo XIII said the last word. The theologian's task is that of repetition of what has been said. He has not to search, explore, explain, develop; he has simply to impose the finished formula.[93]

It was Connell's rejoinder which suggested that Murray's theory was contrary to the teaching of *Longinqua oceani*. According to Connell, Leo XIII's assertion in *Longinqua oceani* "which clearly proposes special favor to the true Church as possible and desirable even under a government such as that of the United States," could in no way be considered in agreement with Murray's assertion that Leo XIII was inclined to base his doctrines on the state conditions prevailing in France during his pontificate.

Connell was prepared to accept that in *Longinqua oceani* the Pope admitted that because of the particular situation in the United States and therefore for practical reasons it was expedient and perfectly reasonable to allow this arrangement. "But this does not prove that in other circumstances it would not be the required condition for the government to recognize the true religion, whatever form of government it may be."[94]

Connell's reply was followed by a Fenton article the next month. It was extremely critical of the historical method and the new theology. In it Fenton did not hesitate to identify himself with the integralist movement.[95]

It was in a June, 1952, article that Fenton himself questioned Murray's interpretation of *Longinqua oceani*. "By clear implication," said Fenton, "the *Longinqua oceani* reminds us that this condition is both licit and expedient as it stands in the United States." According to him those defending this encyclical "have always maintained that, since this is the authoritative teaching of a Roman Pontiff, it is something which all Catholics should accept with a true and sincere internal consent."[96] Certain clear conclusions resulted from this assertion.

> Hence it follows that religion and the Church are not in the best or the most desirable position in a land where, even for perfectly valid and acceptable reasons, the civil society itself does not worship God according to the rites of the Church. This holds true even where the Church shows a freedom and vitality greater than those it manifests in some of the countries where the civil society has offered the true and Catholic worship of God.[97]

For Fenton this was precisely the point the Pope was making so forcefully in his letter to the American bishops. As a result, Fenton concluded, if theologians are to be faithful to the teaching of the true Church it would be false to believe "that this situation is absolutely the best and ultimately satisfactory for our fellow-Americans, for our country itself, or for the Church. As the Pope taught in this encyclical: "it would be very erroneous to draw the conclusion . . . that it would be universally lawful or expedient for State and Church to be, as in America, dissevered and divorced." Fenton inferred from this passage that the Pope considered the situation here to be "allowable" and "expedient" "as the only means by which the civil society can operate properly in the situation in which Americans profess many different religions or none at all." But, there was also "the clear inference that in some cases the non-profession of the Catholic religion by the civil society was a definite moral wrong."[98]

Murray's reply a few months later served to indicate that Fenton understood him to be saying more than he was. His response was clear and straightforward.

> The Encyclical Letter, *Longinqua oceani* (1895), is not an attempt to evaluate the political genius of the American system. The Pope gladly recognizes the fact that the Church in America enjoys "tutam . . . vivendi agendique sine offensione facultatem." . . . But he does not pause to reflect on the uniqueness of the political structure that makes possible this security and freedom.

Murray explained that in immediately noting the "error tollendus," Pope Leo's warning was both timely and meant to be for the European reader. The Pope was working within a political framework where the Vatican's policy in Europe was still linked to the Concordat, and, therefore, where the necessary condition for the Church's life depended on a theory of government which provided favor and patronage.

Murray went on to describe how the encyclical was meant to reject an error that had arisen in France. The Church's search for the kind of favoritism described above finally came in the presidency of Félix Faure (Fifth President of the Third Republic, 1894-1899).

> It was the beginning of the last flowering of "clerical republicanism." In two years the Dreyfus affair, and the unfortunate Catholic attitude towards it, would shatter the *Ralliement* and usher in the second great anti-clerical campaign, which was to culminate in the abrogation of the Concordat and in the legislation of the 1905 Law of Separation. At the moment, however, the *Ralliement* seemed almost to have gone too far, in the direction of a rally to republican principles. And Catholics were citing the American example, doubtless without understanding it. The Pope warns them against the error.

After having described the French situation which led to publication of *Longinqua oceani*, Murray clearly isolated the error rejected by the Pope as that of exporting the American approach to Europe.

> The error, of course, is not a proposition formulated by Americans. And any American would disavow it, for the same reason that he would accept the papal denial that *"universe licere vel expedire, rei civilis reique sacrae distractas esse dissociatasque, more Americano, rationes."* The reason is that the American political system, as Gambetta said of French anticlericalism, was not conceived by its founders as an article of export. No more, therefore, is the American type of separation of church and state which is based on this political system. Moreover, the American Catholic does not pretend that the status of the Church in this country is "the best" for all possible situations. He is content to say that it is a good status, that it is grounded on good political principles, that its basis is not mere expediency, that it is not a makeshift to be endured pending the arrival of Catholics to the point of political power necessary to change it. The American Catholic might indeed say that the status of the Church is better than her status in a number of other places, e.g., better than it was in the Third Republic. But the adjective "best" when applied absolutely to a concrete political system is meaningless—especially in the light of the sound Anglo-Saxon, and basically Catholic, principle of the relativism of political forms.

Murray concluded this brief analysis of *Longinqua oceani* with the following evaluation of Pope Leo's intention:

> Leo XIII concludes with the statement that the Church in America "would make far greater gains if, in addition to freedom, she were to enjoy the favor of the laws and the patronage of the public power." This statement is ambiguous. On the face of it, it would seem to be a statement of fact, not of doctrine, a manner of prophecy, an essay at history in the conditional mood. Yet it is hard to believe that the Pope was trying to play the role of the seer of history.[99]

The only immediate response Murray received was another article by Fenton insisting on the infallibility of papal encyclicals and particularly those concerned with the official teaching on Church and State.[100] This coincided with the publication of another Murray article on Leo XIII. It is noteworthy for its attempt to answer directly the accusation that his method contradicted the teaching of *Testem benevolentiae*.

Murray explained that Leo XIII's polemic was not intended to "canonize any positive and determinate institutionalization of the Church-State relation." While in a polemical way he attacked a real existing error, his doctrine simply stated essential principles. "In a word, his polemic moves onto the historical plane, his doctrine stops short of it." This was the principle outlined by Leo XIII in the Encyclical *Au Milieu*, when he said:

> When one comes down from abstractions onto the solid earth of facts, one must indeed be careful not to deny the principles just established; they remain firm. However, in becoming incarnate in factual situations the principles are invested with a stamp of contingency determined by the environment in which they find application.[101]

While Murray explained that the above statement was made to refer to principles governing the political order, "it is susceptible of generalization to include the principles that govern the Church-State relation." He added: "For these principles likewise require to become incarnate in factual situations which are created in considerable part by historical forces. And this descent into the historical inevitably invests them with the stamp of contingency."

He quoted the following section from Leo XIII's *Testem benevolentiae* to back up his assertion that the Church in her institutional nature is bound to the contingent and the historical. Because the Church is inserted in history she is involved in commitments to history's dissolving situations.

> The history of all past ages bears witness that this Apostolic See, to which there have been committed both the teaching office and the supreme rule of the whole Church, has constantly gone forward in *eodem dogmate, eodem sensu, eademque sententia*. At the same time, it has been wont so to temper its discipline of life that, under safeguard of divine law, it may never disregard the habits and customs of the very different peoples which it embraces. If the salvation of souls demands it, the Holy See will certainly follow the same course today. However, this is not a matter left for settlement to the opinion of private individuals. It must fall to the judgment of the Church. And in this judgment all are to acquiesce. . . .[102]

Murray concluded that according to this principle Leo XIII made it clear that the Church-State relation could not be considered "an end in itself." It was rather "a manner of *vivendi disciplina*, which looks to the temporal and eternal welfare of man, who is both citizen and Christian."

> In a word, his sense of the relativities of history was as fine as his sense of the absoluteness of doctrine. It is therefore entirely in accord with his spirit to say that the Church-State relation, insofar as it necessarily becomes incarnate in "human institutions and laws," is subject to the law of history stated by Rampolla [Cardinal Secretary of State to Leo XIII, 1887-1903]. These institutionalized forms of the relation tend to become "out of date, or useless, or even harmful." The principles themselves remain—timeless, immutable, constantly applicable, always vital.[103]

At this point the controversy was seriously complicated by the introduction of Rome into the debate. This occurred with the publication of Alfredo Cardinal Ottaviani's "Church and State: Some Present Problems in the Light of the Teaching of Pope Pius XII," in which the Cardinal argued that the "confessional state" was the only modern polity which met Leo XIII's strict requirements.[104] Of course, Fenton defended Ottaviani's contention.[105]

Nonetheless, Murray persisted in his efforts to clarify his position. The second of his series of articles on Leo XIII sought to explain carefully that at the foundation of his theory was the belief that the American Church has had a distinctive history which has meant "a new kind of spiritual existence, not tasted on the Continent,—the experience of reliance on its own inner resources under a regime of constitutional law that has been equitable . . . but not creative of legal privilege. . . ." For Murray the all important question was:

> Is the Church in America to be allowed to travel her own historical path and fashion her own particular solution to the Church-State problem, remaining faithful to essential Catholic principle, but likewise striving for effective application of principle to the specific character of the political tradition within which her institutional life is lived? Or, on the other hand, is the Church in America to repudiate the history of America in what is most unique about it—its installation of a political tradition sharply in contrast with that of modern Continental Europe? Is she to be bound to those special applications of principle which were necessary and legitimate within political contexts alien to her own?[106]

For Murray it was clearly essential that the Church here should be permitted to approve in principle her own distinctive solution to the Church-State problem. The rejection of this belief, he thought, was based on a lack of appreciation of the uniqueness of the American system and a failure to clearly distinguish it from the "systems familiar to Continental Europe." In this regard he criticized Cardinal Ottaviani's identification of Count Cavour's formula: "A free Church in a free state," with America's First Amendment, as misleading. "Cavour's formula cannot be used to describe the situation of the Church in the United States."[107]

In August Fenton followed up Murray's June article with a lengthy comparison of the errors reproved in *Testem benevolentiae* and *Humani generis*. He explained that both encyclicals repudiated the same error; that the Church should disregard doctrine in which the deposit of faith is contained in order to become more adaptable to contemporary civilization; and that in order to make Catholic teaching more acceptable to non-Catholics, it was appropriate to "pass over certain statements contained in it."[108] This was followed the next month with Fenton's "Theology and Nationality."

> Within the past few months there has been an increasingly obvious tendency in some quarters to insinuate or even assert that the American theologians, as a group, contradict the teachings of their Spanish and Italian confreres on certain sections of Christian doctrine, particularly on that portion that deals with the interrelations of Church and state.

Calling the tendency unfortunate, Fenton added: "The very concept of sacred theology itself is completely misrepresented when nationality, American or any other, is depicted as an effective factor in determining theological opinions."[109] He branded as untrue the insinuation that American Catholic theologians would hold opinions contrary to those held by theologians in Europe.

It was the publication of Pope Pius XII's papal allocution, *Ci riesce* that brought the theological controversy to a head. As we have already seen in the historical section of this study, interpretations of *Ci riesce* were many and quite diversified. Fenton was the first to comment on its content. For him *Ci riesce* repeated Leo XIII's conditions of Church and State relationship as set down in *Immortale Dei*. He asserted that it would be an error to believe that the Church could improve "in principle" or as a thesis the complete separation of Church and State. After *Ci riesce* there should be no more disagreement with the terms "Catholic State" and "Error has no rights" and the thesis-hypothesis explanation must receive acknowledgment by all.[110]

As we have already seen, Murray's response to *Ci riesce* in his Catholic University of America lecture of that same month was a direct refutation of this interpretation.[111] Beyond that it was understood by Ottaviani and his supporters as a personal attack on the Cardinal.[112] Fenton came to the Cardinal's defense by calling incorrect the impression that *Ci riesce* was meant to be a denial of the Ottaviani position. Fenton reiterated his belief that one could not support the assertion that there was development in the principles enunciated by Pius IX, Leo XIII, and the present Pontiff. For him the position outlined by Ottaviani was the only acceptable one.

Besides Murray's address at the Catholic University, the month of March saw the publication of his fourth article on Leo XIII. It is noteworthy for its daring statement that "Only the superficial or the man of ill will—only those who are by definition not scholars—can maintain that Leo XIII was against democracy, as this term is understood in the Anglo-American tradition." The contrary is true, insisted Murray. Pope Leo "combatted a conspiracy against the moral principles upon which Anglo-American democracy rests!"[113]

Murray's final unpublished article on Leo XIII considered the relation of government to the order of religion, especially as institutionally embodied in the Church. Scheduled for the summer of 1954, its publication would have answered some of the questions raised by Fenton. But its boldness would have greatly embittered the controversy. In it Murray provided a lengthy explanation of his interpretation of *Longinqua oceani*. Quoting the paragraph in which Leo XIII praises the American arrangement while warning against seeing it as the ideal situation, Murray isolated the controversial statement: ". . . nevertheless they would produce more plentiful results if, in addition to freedom, they enjoyed the favor of the laws and the patronage of the public power." Murray then explained:

In the last sentence the Pope is not undertaking to predict, as it were, by hindsight what the history of the Church in America would have been, had it been other than it has been. Nor is he suggesting that the future would be more blessed, if America were to alter the constitutional situation to which the blessings of the past have been largely due. Nor is he in any sense implying that there is in the American constitutional situation, as it exists in America, an *error tollendus*, an error to be done away with. On the contrary, in the immediately preceding context he has said that the Church in America "owes a debt of gratitude to the justice of the laws under which America lives and to the whole character of a good constitutional commonwealth." Certainly there is no error in laws that are just and in a constitution that is good.

Then Murray goes on to explain what error *Longinqua oceani* was indeed rejecting:

What Leo XIII has in mind is a theoretical error bearing on a point of principle. The error was on the part of those who wished to take the American constitutional situation, in which the Church does not enjoy the favor of the laws and the patronage of the public power, as the premise for a generalization to a universal principle. It should be said here that these men were not American Catholics; they were Europeans, who were either doctrinaire theorists, or simply desperate men, striving to break out of the impasse created by the confusion of religion and politics that had for so long been characteristic of the Latin countries. In either case it is highly unlikely that they understood the United States any better than Montesquieu understood England. These men, I say wished to take the legal experience of the Church in America as the premise upon which to erect a definition of an ideal of legal experience that would be everywhere valid, everywhere permissible, everywhere advantageous.[114]

In brief Murray was saying that systems of law could not be divorced from their *Sitz in Leben*, packed up and labelled, and made articles of export. For those men to say that the American constitutional system would be good for all peoples because it was good for the American people was to Murray "political and legal nonsense."

That Murray's opponents were accusing him of making this generalization seemed clear enough. And in this article he tried to answer that accusation directly.

I do not think I have myself ever made this generalization consciously and advertently; if I have ever given the impression of making it, I wish here to correct the impression. Certainly I do not erect the American fact of a religiously pluralist society into a principle, as if somehow society ought to be religiously pluralist. Nor do I erect the American constitutional law which deals with this fact into an ideal in some absolute sense. I have indeed maintained, and do maintain, that the First Amendment, within the American religious, political, and social situation, can be defended in principle. . . . But this is not to make a dogma out of American law, to transform a law that is good *in situ* into a principle that would be valid *universim*. Nor do I argue that full religious liberty ought to obtain within particular societies simply because they are democratically organized. Political forms do not alter theological or ethical principles, or invalidate the norms of human law that derive from traditional legal philosophy. Finally, I do not hold that the freedom of the Church ceases to be in principle a privileged freedom, simply because a democratic form of government obtains. Nor do I say that a general guarantee of freedom of religion is the absolutely sufficient and ideal way to guarantee the freedom of the Church. I do not hold that the case for American constitutional law—"no establishment" and "no intolerance"—can be legitimately made simply on the grounds that the U.S. is a democracy in the Anglo-American tradition. Anymore than I hold that the case for Spanish constitutional law—establishment and intolerance —can be made simply on the ground that a manner of religious unity obtains in Spain and makes possible these institutions. No such simplism of argument is valid.[115]

In the concluding section of this unpublished article, Murray introduced the outline of the "unitary theory" he sought to get accepted. According to this theory the American and the Spaniard could both be arguing from a unitary premise which would be mutually shared as the doctrine of the universal Church. As we have seen, Murray would not return to this until 1958 when he sought McCormick's permission to get an article on the subject published with the Pope's approval in Civiltà Cattolica. Rather word came from McCormick suggesting Murray stop writing on the subject for the moment and get everything else he wanted published approved by the Jesuit censors in Rome.[116]

It would seem that Pius XII's May 31, 1954, allocution, Si diligis was partly an attempt to warn those whose method questioned papal authority. It was delivered to the Cardinals, Archbishops, and Bishops who had come to Rome for the canonization of Saint Pius X. It spoke of those who

care little for conformity with the living Teaching Authority of the Church, pay little heed to her commonly received doctrine clearly proposed in various ways; and at the same time they follow their own bent too much, and regard too highly the intellectual temper of more recent writers, and the standards of other branches of learning, which they declare and hold to be the only ones which conform to sound ideas and standards of scholarship.[117]

Fenton characterized the allocution as "among the more important doctrinal pronouncements of Pope Pius XII, and, indeed, among the more important doctrinal declarations of modern times."[118] Fenton also pointed out that this allocution brought out more explicitly than ever before that "the Roman Pontiff and the residential Bishops within the Catholic Church are the only persons who have been entrusted with the power of teaching in an authorita-

tive manner in the name and by the power of Jesus Christ."[119] In the same
issue of *The American Ecclesiastical Review*, Fenton continued his attack on
Murray's thesis as one condemned by *Ci riesce*.[120]

While Murray stayed clear of the subject in accordance with Rome's
advice, Fenton continued to insist on the doctrinal authority of the papal
position on Church and State. He used the publication of the Holy Father's
allocution *Vous avez voulu* to reaffirm the fact that the teaching here on
Church and State "must clearly be normative for all future teaching and
writing on Church-state relations by Catholics."[121]

The Pope's address had referred specifically to the American arrangement as an example "of the way in which the Church succeeds in flourishing
in the most disparate situations."[122] And Fenton was quick to remind his
readers that this arrangement according to Pius XII could not be considered a
good thing in itself since it is a tendency away from the ideal.[123]

Fenton's interpretation of the authority of papal allocutions served as a
striking example of the extent to which the understanding of papal authority
had grown since the First Vatican Council. In Fenton's view, papal allocutions were to be understood as actual expressions of the Pope's ordinary
magisterium. Referring specifically to the Church-State debate and using the
allocutions *Ci riesce*, *Si diligis*, and *Vous avez voulu* as examples of this kind
of papal teaching, Fenton explained that all were obliged to accept these
"under penalty of serious sin," and added that controverted questions must
be regarded as settled allowing for no more free debate among theologians.

Beyond this, he insisted that, as a direct implication of the above, the
Pope did not have to state explicitly or specifically that he was making a doctrinal decision on a certain point. Nor did private theologians have the right
"to establish what they believe to be the conditions under which teaching
presented in *Acta* of the Pope may be accepted as authoritative." To Fenton
Humani generis had clearly asserted that it was morally wrong to defend a
thesis that contradicted teaching which the Pope had set forth in *Acta* as doctrinal. Beyond that the teaching held true always and everywhere even when
it was not infallible teaching. Nor did the obligation mean simply to refrain
from debating or arguing against it. The Pope's position was to become normative with obligatory internal consent by all.[124]

With Murray's "silencing" virtually in full effect, he did not respond to
Fenton's explanation of papal allocutions nor did he comment on the Holy
Father's assertions in *Vous avez voulu*. Fenton continued warning against
minimism, doctrinal indifferentism, and Americanism and often referred to
the encyclical *Testem benevolentiae*.

In only one other article some four years later did he specifically refer to
Murray as contradicting *Longinqua oceani*. He understood Murray's *We
Hold These Truths* (1960) to be distinguishing between assertions of Chris-

tian doctrine and statements of ecclesiastical policy in his interpretation of teachings set forth on the subject of Church and State by previous Popes. In Fenton's interpretation Murray held that when the magisterium condemned the separation of Church and State it was acting only in the line of policy or tactic. The implication of this is that separation of Church and State could be proposed as the ideal good. To Fenton the thesis of separation of Church and State was rejected as undesirable in itself and contrary to the "unchangeable doctrine of the Catholic doctrine itself." He insisted that Murray's position denied the Catholic doctrine "that in itself and objectively the state or the civil society is obligated to give public and corporate worship to God." Murray's thesis, Fenton said, ignored the teaching of *Longinqua oceani*. In this encyclical, Fenton concluded, Leo XIII

> did not lose sight of the fact, and did not want us to lose sight of the fact, that our American separation of Church and state is predicated upon a condition which definitely is not good in itself, a situation in which a great number of those whom we love as our fellow citizens fail, for one reason or another, to give to God and to Jesus Christ the true and rightful worship really due to God. Furthermore, even considered in itself, the failure of this, the greatest of the nations of history, to thank God according to the rite of the one true religion cannot be considered as objectively anything other than undesirable.[25]

Conclusion

Along with our historical study the preceding analysis provides sufficient evidence to show that Murray was indeed being censored by Rome at the insistence of theologians here in the United States for holding opinions contrary to the teachings of *Testem benevolentiae* and *Longinqua oceani*. Without any doubt Fenton and his associates understood Murray to be teaching some of the false opinions condemned in these encyclicals.

As we have seen, Fenton's final accusation directed against Murray for his misinterpretation of *Longinqua oceani* came as late as October, 1961. For all practical purposes neither side's position had changed through the long debate of the 1950s. Time, however, was on Murray's side. This was already the eve of the Second Vatican Council and the theological climate would change drastically during the early sessions of the Council. The historical method so essential to Murray's thesis would not only become acceptable but the method commonly used by Council theologians. By the beginning of the third session Murray had the solid backing of the American hierarchy, something he lacked during the forties and fifties.

Because of the time spent preparing the dogmatic statement on papal

infallibility, the American bishops at Vatican I were never given the opportunity to explain and defend the American arrangement of Church and
State.[126] For all practical purposes this was the only important contribution of
the Americans at Vatican II. As Murray later insisted, if it had not been for
the American hierarchy *The Declaration on Religious Freedom* would never
have been approved.

> . . . During the long course of its legislative history, the schema
> had the solid and consistent support of the American bishops, and
> their numerous interventions had considerable influence in deter-
> mining its substance and language. There were those who said that
> the American bishops supported the schema simply for pragmatic
> reasons. But this is an inadequate view. Undoubtedly, the support
> derived its basic inspiration from the American experience, from
> which the Church had learned the practical value of the free-exer-
> cise clause of the First Amendment. At the same time, American
> Catholics have understood that the practical value of this constitu-
> tional provision derives from the truth of the principle that it em-
> bodies. It is apparent from their interventions that the American
> bishops made important theoretical contributions toward the illu-
> mination of the principle.[127]

As Murray had insisted in his August, 1962, letter to Archbishop Shehan[128]
there was a need for something beyond a pastoral or pragmatic solution to
the problem. Murray himself brought both a practical and a theoretical solution to the issue.

In retrospect McCormick's insistence in his 1958 letter to Murray[129]
that he wait quietly on the sidelines until "the opportune time" would arrive
and "the present Roman atmosphere" had changed seems almost prophetic.
The opportune time had come and Murray was ready with a more clarified
and refined position to renew the debate in a climate more acceptable to
what he was saying.

One can easily find a number of similarities between the Americanist
debate in the 1890s and its reemergence in the 1940s and 50s. The fear of
indifferentism has already been mentioned. During both periods a disagreement over the proper interpretation of the dogma "no salvation outside the
Church" was at issue. However, by the time Vatican II was in full swing a
number of different ecclesiological models were emerging which more or less
allowed theologians to work through the problem.[130]

A more important similarity, of course, was the fear of exporting
Americanism to other countries. In the 1890s, as we have seen, the Americanist controversy arose over French enthusiasm toward Americanism. In

Murray's own time, his position was being attacked for fear that he was trying to say that the American arrangement was not only better than Spain's
but should become a model for the universal Church. This was no doubt the
basis of Murray's fear concerning the publication of his "The Problem of
Pluralism in America" in the German periodical *Dokumente* in 1956.[131]

Unlike the Americanists of the 1890s, Murray did not expect the American situation to become paradigmatic for the entire Church. Nevertheless, as
his last unpublished article on Leo XIII admitted, he had perhaps given that
impression. In any case, Fenton and Ottaviani understood him to be saying
that. Murray's position, however, was rather that Ottaviani's Spanish "confessional state" arrangement could not become universally paradigmatic.
Since, in the 1950s, the Vatican was trying to renegotiate concordats with
Spain and Germany, a statement of this kind was politically dangerous for
the Vatican. The deeper issue, however, was the emergence of a theological
and ecclesiological pluralism which remained in continuity with authentic
Church tradition. Murray's unitary theory provided this.

Like the Americanists, Murray was very familiar with the distinc-
tiveness of American Church history. This is shown by his articles on Leo
XIII. John Tracy Ellis had provided Murray with the necessary historical
background needed to understand the Americanist tradition. One need only
recall Murray's enthusiasm for Ellis's article "Church and State: An American Catholic Tradition."[132] Murray thus stood on solid ground.

Murray was as enthusiastic about America as were the Americanists
but he was more tempered in his approach. As was shown by *We Hold
These Truths: Catholic Reflection on the American Proposition*, he could be
very critical of the failings of the American system. But he was firmly convinced as were the Americanists of the 1890s that the American system was
providential for American circumstances.

While he could not be accused of being over-optimistic about America's
"manifest destiny" and its implications for the Church here, he was as enthusiastic as the prelates of the 1890s over the values of the democratic system
for the Church's mission.

While developing and elaborating his thinking on the Church-State
theory, Murray also gave much time to developing the theme of the Church's
mission. As early as 1949, in his analysis of Leo XIII's teaching, Murray
described what he understood to be part of the Christian's missionary task.

The Church's faith in herself as the Catholic Unity of mankind is
displayed to you in her missionary enterprise. And that is why I
would have you understand the missions, in order that you may
understand the Church, and understanding her, confidently take
up your share in her total missionary task.

It was in this context that he asked if there was "not a task that lies to hand in the United States that might in a true sense, with no exaggeration, be called a missionary task?" Murray proceeded to answer this question for his audience. There was such a task, he claimed:

I do not mean simply the task that is incumbent on the Church understood as the priesthood, which is the task of building the Body of Christ. I mean more particularly the task that is incumbent on the Church as the Christian people, which is the task of building the earthly City. This is not the task of bishops and priests; as such they stand outside the order of the City, empowered to teach with spiritual authority the Christian conscience but not the City's own structure. Here is a task for the Christian people.

As Murray went on to explain, the task he spoke of centered on all that is meant when men speak of "the problems of democracy."

As Christians you are actively to see it that democracy as a natural demand imposed by reason itself is given a more perfect expression in political and economic and social life than it has hitherto had in American democracy.

He also pointed to the new openness in the United States to the role of religion in society, in education, in the direction to all human affairs while situating the problem of democracy in all these areas as "at bottom a religious and moral problem."

In a critical way Murray pointed to the American Catholic attitude of "exclusiveness"—building the Church in the United States—by erecting churches, its own schools and hospitals, creating societies and pursuing its own interests. While this was a necessary task, Murray saw greater urgency in helping to build the City, and thereby finding solutions for American and world democracy. He challenged his listeners to bring their "Christian sense of justice and of charity into contact with the American democratic culture." Murray saw the basic task as a work of human unity, a unity which is first civic and then religious. As he saw it, the grand old American concept of "We, the People" found solid basis in Christianity and he was convinced that to allow the unity of the above concept to be broken down into "We" and "They" amounted to an "indirect betrayal of the missionary spirit of the Church."[133]

Murray thus shared much of the enthusiasm of Ireland, Gibbons, and O'Connell for American democracy. He reaffirmed, as he clarified their position, that the appearance of American democracy obviated many of the problems which existed when a monarch could declare that he himself was the state. Murray's reformulation provided a reassertion and a refinement of the liberal tradition by answering some of the more difficult questions of the Church-State contention.

Murray especially reemphasized Hecker's familiar contention that the American system emerged not from the Jacobin principles of the French Revolution, but from medieval constitutionalism and English political practice. He was able to reorient the discussion to the larger question confronting all religious leaders of how to secure the "freedom of the human person, Christian and citizen, to live at peace in Christ and in society that he may thus move straight on to God."[134]

Indeed the most important event in our recent American Catholic history has been the reopening of the debate on the relationship of Catholic and American life, a debate which had been suddenly terminated with the condemnation of Americanism. No doubt it was a misunderstanding of our incarnationalism that was condemned under the unfair label of Americanism. Murray brought to the problem the theological expertise needed for its clarification and resolution. Over the years he clarified the task of the Church as a presence in contemporary secular society and contributed considerably to a clearer understanding of how the Church is incarnated in history. As he himself said in appraising the progress made, the statements on the Church in *Gaudium et spes* just as those in *Dignitatis humanae* represented *aggiornamento*. And they are to be "programmatic for the future."

> From now on, the Church defines her mission in the temporal order in terms of the realization of human dignity, the promotion of the rights of man, the growth of the human family towards unity, and the sanctification of the secular activities of the world.[135]

Notes

1. James Cardinal Gibbons, "The Roman Sermon," in *Documents of American Catholic History*, ed. John Tracy Ellis (Milwaukee: The Bruce Publishing Co., 1956), p. 478. See also Ellis. *The Life of James Cardinal Gibbons* (2 vols.; Milwaukee: The Bruce Publishing Co., 1952), especially "An Essay on the Sources," II, pp. 651-59, where all the leading manuscript and printed sources for Gibbons's life are listed with critical comments. The occasion for the Roman address was Gibbons's taking possession of his titular Church of Santa Maria in Trastevere on March 25, 1887.
2. James Cardinal Gibbons, "Civil and Religious Liberty," in *The Faith of*

Our Fathers (47th carefully revised and enlarged edition; Baltimore: John Murphy & Co., 1896), p. 264.

3. *Ibid.*

4. *Ibid.*, pp. 273-74.

5. *Ibid.*, p. 281.

6. *Ibid.*

7. Bishop John Ireland, "The Catholic Church and Civil Society," in *The Church and Modern Society* (2d ed.; New York: D. H. McBride & Co., 1897), pp. 34-35. For a biography of Ireland, see: James H. Moynihan. *The Life of Archbishop John Ireland* (New York: Oxford University Press, 1959).

8. Bishop John Ireland, "American Citizenship," in *The Church and Modern Society*, p. 96.

9. "Catholic Church and Modern Society," pp. 13, 14.

10. *Ibid.*, p. 24.

11. *Ibid.*, p. 25.

12. *Ibid.*, p. 37.

13. *Ibid.*, p. 44.

14. "Liberty is the exemption from all restraint, save that of the laws of justice and order, exemption from submission to other men, except so far as they represent and enforce those laws. The divine gift of liberty is God's recognition of man's greatness and man's dignity. In liberty lie the sweetness of life and the power of growth. . . . Not until the Republic of the West was born, not until the star-spangled banner rose towards the skies, was liberty caught up in humanity's embrace and embodied in a great and abiding nation.

"In America the government takes from the liberty of the citizen only so much as is necessary for the weal of the nation. In America there are no masters who govern in their own right, for their own interest, or at their own will. . . .

"In America, rights begin with, and go upward from the people. In other countries, even in those which are apparently the most free, rights begin with, and come downward from the state; the rights of citizens, the rights of the people, are concessions which have been wrested from the governing powers."

Bishop John Ireland, "Patriotism," in *The Church in Modern Society*, pp. 148-49.

15. Bishop John Ireland, "America in France," in *The Church in Modern Society*, p. 363.

16. *Ibid.*, pp. 366-67.

17. Bishop John Ireland, "The Church and the Age," in *The Church in Modern Society*, p. 99.

18. "Catholic Church in Civil Society," p. 45.

19. "An inestimable advantage to us is the liberty which the Church enjoys under the Constitution of the United States. Here no concordat limits her action, or cramps her energy. Here she is as free as the eagle upon Alpine heights, free to unfold her pinions in unobstructed flight, and to soar to loftiest altitudes. The law of the land protects her in her rights, and asks in return no sacrifice of these rights, for her rights are those of American citizenship."

Bishop John Ireland, "The Mission of Catholics in America," in *The Church in Modern Society*, pp. 64-65.

20. "The Church and the Age," p. 100.

21. Denis O'Connell, "Fribourg Address," in Félix Klein. *Americanism: A Phantom Heresy* (Cranford, N.J.: Aquin Book Shop, 1951), p. 75. For a study on

O'Connell see: Gerald P. Fogarty, *The Vatican and the Americanist Crisis: Denis J. O'Connell, American Agent in Rome, 1885-1903* (Roma: Università Gregoriana Editrice, 1974).

22. O'Connell, "Fribourg Address," p. 75.

23. See Chap. II, pp. 37-38.

24. *The Catholic Encyclopedia*, I (New York: The Encyclopedia Press, Inc., 1907), p. 428.

25. Thomas T. McAvoy. *Great Crisis in American Catholic History* (Chicago: Henry Regnery Co., 1957); Robert D. Cross. *The Emergence of Liberal Catholicism* (Cambridge: Harvard University Press, 1958); Margaret M. Reher, "The Church and the Kingdom of God in America: The Ecclesiology of the Americanists" (Ph.D. dissertation, Fordham University, 1972). Both McAvoy and Cross have done excellent work in treating a very difficult subject. Both show evidence of extensive research and present the findings and conclusions in a scholarly manner. Of the two, however, McAvoy's is the better. Cross often creates false impressions which might go easily unnoticed by someone not well acquainted with the Church's experience in this country. Cross also tends to oversimplify the term "liberalism," which is no doubt difficult to define. But simply to say that the entire American Church was divided into conservative or liberal camps is not actually the case. The controversy was actually carried on by a few leaders on both sides with a number of prominent members of the hierarchy like Williams of Boston, Ryan of Philadelphia, and Feehan of Chicago not belonging to either party. Nonetheless, both books make a significant contribution to American religious history. Margaret Reher's unpublished Fordham University dissertation examines the Americanist controversy from an ecclesiological stance, specifically through the thought of the principal figures involved: Isaac Hecker, John Keane, John Ireland, and Denis O'Connell. She concludes that each in his own way was attempting to implement the universalization of Americanism for "all unquestionably accepted the situation of the American Church as the future model for the Church universal," p. 92.

26. Archbishop Ireland, quoted in Daniel Callahan, *The Mind of the Catholic Layman* (New York: Charles Scribner's Sons, 1963), p. 60.

27. The best translation of the encyclical can be found in John J. Wynne, S.J. (ed.). *The Great Encyclical Letters of Pope Leo XIII* (New York: Benziger Bros., 1903), pp. 320-35. This translation also appears in John Tracy Ellis (ed.). *Documents of American Catholic History* (Milwaukee: Bruce Publishing Co., 1956), pp. 515-27. The passage quoted above is from Wynne, pp. 323-24.

28. E.E.Y. Hales. *The Catholic Church in the Modern World* (New York: Doubleday, 1958), p. 170. Hales's treatment of the "Americanist Heresy" appears in Chap. XIV of this book. This historian presents a brief but clear and good examination of this period in American Church history which is valuable for the average reader.

29. The letter in its original form, without translation and without comment was printed in *The Ecclesiastical Review*, XIII (November, 1895), p. 395. For a translation of the letter and a commentary on its application to the call for intercredal cooperation in the 1940s see: Francis J. Connell, "Pope Leo XIII's Message to America," *AER*, CIX (October, 1943), pp. 249-56.

30. Isaac T. Hecker was a convert, former Redemptorist and founder of the Paulists. He was one of the American Church's intellectual giants and accompanied Archbishop Martin J. Spalding of Baltimore to the First Vatican Council as his personal theologian. As a young man he had been closely associated with Brook Farm

and the Transcendentalist movement, and men like Ralph Waldo Emerson and Henry Thoreau, also members of this New England intellectual community. After converting to Catholicism he later joined the Redemptorists, a predominantly German religious order. Hecker along with a number of other Redemptorists dissociated themselves from the parent group to form the Congregation of St. Paul (Paulist) under Hecker's leadership. In his treatment of "Diocesan and Religious Clergy: The History of a Relationship, 1789-1969" in a recent book, *The Catholic Priest in the United States: Historical Investigations*, ed. John Tracy Ellis, J. P. Marschall said of this group: "The basic cause of separation was a lack of sympathy on the part of the Redemptorist superiors for the establishment of an 'American House' dedicated to the ministry among native Americans. In addition, the fledgling group showed its own bias against the traditional style of religious life by insisting on the 'voluntary principle' for its members rather than on the profession of formal vows of poverty, chastity and obedience. The older form of the religious life did not appear to these men to be an appropriate style of life for Americans" (p. 398). Hecker was himself a prolific writer. He was founder and editor of the periodical *Catholic World*. For a popular but good treatment of Hecker, see Andrew Greeley, "Converts from Brook Farm: Brownson and Hecker," *The Catholic Experience* (New York: Doubleday, 1967), pp. 127-49.

31. See Thomas T. McAvoy, "American Cultural Impacts on Catholicism," in *The Religion of the Republic*. ed. Elwyn A. Smith (Philadelphia: Fortress Press, 1971), pp. 62-65.

32. Wynne, *Great Encyclicals*, p. 442.

33. *Ibid.*, p. 452.

34. McAvoy, *Great Crisis in American Catholic History: 1895-1900* (Chicago: Henry Regnery, 1957), p. 349.

35. *Ibid.*, p. 353. It was Archbishop Ireland who especially saw the encyclical as a condemnation of a "phantom heresy." His adversaries interpreted the papal letter as a silencing of Ireland and a vindication of their point of view that he had gone too far in accommodating Catholic teaching to the American scene. Ireland, however, felt quite differently when he wrote: "In Europe, Americanism was cradled as well as entombed; in America it was unknown until it was condemned." From: Moynihan, *The Life of Archbishop Ireland*, p. 129.

36. McAvoy, *Great Crisis*, p. 349.

37. Gibbons to Leo XIII, Baltimore, March 17, 1899, in Ellis, *The Life of James Cardinal Gibbons*, II, p. 71.

38. Cross says of the conservative reaction: "Corrigan, with the approval of most of the suffragans, wrote in March 1899 to thank the Pope for his timely warning against the 'multiplicity of fallacies and errors . . . under the specious title of Americanism.' The Archbishop made clear that the letter had been badly needed in America"; Cross, *The Emergence of Liberal Catholicism*, p. 201; see also F. J. Zwierlein, *Letters of Archbishop Corrigan to Bishop McQuaid and Allied Documents*, Rochester, New York, The Art print shop, 1946.

39. McAvoy, *Great Crisis*, p. 351.

40. *Ibid.*, p. 353.

41. Reher, "The Church and the Kingdom of God in America," abstract.

42. Fenton, "The Teaching of the *Testem Benevolentiae*," AER, LXXIX (August, 1953), p. 133.

43. Connell, "Pope Leo XIII's Message to America," p. 254. See Chap. I, pp. 15-16.

44. *Ibid.*, p. 255. Connell returned to this subject again in 1956. There is no

evident change in his position. "Co-operation of Catholics in Non-Catholic Religious Activities. Part I," *AER*, CXXXIV (February, 1956), pp. 98-108; the second and third parts of this article appeared in March and April under the same title, Part II, pp. 190-200; Part III, pp. 240-50. By this time Connell had the backing of an influential member of the American hierarchy. Archbishop Stritch banned participation in the World Council of Churches meeting at Evanston, Illinois, in the summer of 1954. His pastoral letter of June 29, 1954, was issued just before the mid-August meeting of the World Council of Churches. As Cardinal Archbishop of the place where these meetings would be held, Stritch reiterated authoritative Catholic teaching on the meaning of religious unity. While encouraging Catholics to do as much as possible on the civic and social levels to prepare the way for further understanding, he forbade both clergy and laity from participating in the assembly. As chairman of the American Bishops' Special Committee on the Pope's Peace Plan he was responsible for encouraging some kind of cooperation. But he would not encourage activities that might imply an indifferentist attitude. He thus stated that he could not see how a Catholic could participate in an assembly based on the false assumption that Roman Catholics, too, were still searching for the truth of Christ. While it appears Stritch had a mind that could quickly grasp all aspects of a problem, he was often slow to arrive at decisions. We have already seen his cautious hesitation on the Church-State issue. See, Chap. II, pp. 39-40; also, Stritch, "Pastoral Letter on Church Unity," *Unitas*, VI (Autumn, 1954), pp. 180-91; "The Gulf," *Christian Century*, LXXI (July 21, 1954), pp. 869-71.

45. Murray, "Current Theology: Cooperation, Some Further Views," *TS*, IV (March, 1943), p. 103.

46. Paul Furfey, "Correspondence: To the Editor," *TS*, IV (September, 1943), pp. 467-72; Fenton, "The Church and the Non-Catholic," *AER*, CXIII (July, 1945), pp. 44-58; "Our Lord's Presence in the Catholic Church," *AER*, CXV (July, 1946), pp. 50-61.

47. Murray, "Current Theology: Intercredal Co-operation: Its Theory and Its Organization," *TS*, IV (June, 1943), p. 275; also, "Correspondence, Editor's Reply to Father Furfey," *TS*, IV (September, 1943), pp. 472-74.

48. Murray, "Current Theology: Intercredal Co-operation: It's Theory and Organization," p. 286.

49. Fenton, "The Church and the State of Siege," *AER*, CXII (January, 1945), p. 63. See Chap. I, p. 24, n. 32.

50. *Time*, XLVII, no. 8 (February 25, 1946), p. 44.

51. Fenton, "*Time* and Pope Leo," *AER*, CXIV (May, 1946), pp. 370-71.

52. *Ibid.*, p. 375.

53. Murray, "Current Theology: Freedom of Religion," *TS*, VI (March, 1945), pp. 87-88.

54. *Ibid.*, p. 90.

55. Fenton, "The Proofs of the Church's Divine Origin," *AER*, CXIII (September, 1945), pp. 203-19; "The True Church and the Notes of the Church," *AER*, CXIV (April, 1946), pp. 282-97.

56. Fenton, "The Catholic and the Church," *AER*, CXIII (November, 1945), p. 383.

57. Murray, "Freedom of Religion, I: The Ethical Problem," *TS*, VI (June, 1945), p. 229.

58. Murray, "On Religious Liberty: An Inquiry," *TS*, VII (March, 1946), pp. 151-63. See Chap. I, p. 23, n. 29.

59. Murray, "How Liberal Is Liberalism?" *America*, LXXV (April 6, 1946),

pp. 6-7; "Separation of Church and State," *America*, LXXVI (December 7, 1946), pp. 261-63; "Separation of Church and State: True and False Concepts," *America*, LXXVI (February 15, 1947), pp. 541-45; "Religious Liberty: The Concern of All," *America*, LXXVIII (February 7, 1948), pp. 513-16.

60. Murray, "Separation of Church and State," p. 263.

61. "Separation of Church and State: True and False Concepts," p. 542; also John A. Ryan and M.F.X. Millar, *The State and the Church* (New York: Macmillan Company, 1946), p. 38.

62. Murray, "Governmental Repression of Heresy," *Proceedings of The Catholic Theological Society of America*, Chicago, 1948, p. 34.

63. *Ibid.*, p. 36.

64. *Ibid.*, p. 37.

65. *Ibid.*, p. 98.

66. Fenton, "New Concepts in Theology," *AER*, CXIX (July, 1948), p. 57.

67. *Ibid.*, pp. 60-61.

68. Fenton, "The Church and the World," *AER*, CXIX (September, 1948), p. 211. See Chap. I, p. 15.

69. Fenton, "Two Currents in Contemporary Catholic Thought," *AER*, CXIX (October, 1948), pp. 293-94.

70. *Ibid.*, p. 298.

71. Murray, "Contemporary Orientations of Catholic Thought on Church and State in the Light of History," *TS*, X (June, 1949), p. 190.

72. *Ibid.*, p. 226.

73. Murray, "Current Theology on Religious Freedom," *TS*, X (September, 1949), p. 430.

74. See Chap. I, p. 18.

75. *Ibid.*, p. 414, n. 26.

76. Fenton, "The Doctrinal Authority of Papal Encyclicals, Part II," *AER*, CXXI (September, 1949), p. 216. There is an important implication in Fenton's position. He also admitted the possibility of development, if it came from the Pope.

77. *Ibid.*, p. 217.

78. Fenton, "The Religious Assent Due to the Teachings of Papal Encyclicals," *AER*, CXXIII (July, 1950), pp. 64-65.

79. I have described this in Chap. II, pp. 34-35.

80. Fenton, "The Relation of the Christian State to the Catholic Church According to the *Pontificale Romanum*," *AER*, CXXIII (September, 1950), p. 218.

81. Fenton, "The Lesson of *Humani generis*," *AER*, CXXIII (November, 1950), pp. 360-69.

82. *Ibid.*, p. 378.

83. Fenton, "The *Humani generis* and its Predecessors," *AER*, CXXIII (December, 1950), pp. 452-58.

84. It was this article that Fenton attacked in his editorial note attached to Murray's article. See Chap. II, p. 35.

85. George W. Shea, "Catholic Doctrine and 'The Religion of the State,'" *AER*, CXXIII (September, 1950), p. 162.

86. *Ibid.*, p. 170.

87. Murray, "The Problem of 'The Religion of the State,'" *AER*, CXXIV (May, 1951), pp. 334-35, n. 9.

88. *Ibid.*, pp. 336-37, n. 10.

89. Fenton, "The Status of a Controversy," *AER*, CXXIV (June, 1951), pp. 451-58.

90. Connell, "The Theory of the 'Lay State,' " *AER*, CXXV (July, 1951), pp. 7-18.

91. Murray, "For the Freedom and Transcendence of the Church," *AER*, CXXVI (January, 1952), p. 43.

92. *Ibid.*, pp. 43-44.

93. *Ibid.*, pp. 47-48.

94. Connell, "Reply to Fr. Murray," *AER*, CXXVI (January, 1952), pp. 56-57.

95. Fenton, "Reform and Integralism," *AER*, CXXVI (February, 1952), pp. 126-39. The article was specifically a criticism of Y. Congar's *Vraie et fausse réforme dans l'église* (Paris: Editions du Cerf, 1950).

96. Fenton, "Principles Underlying Traditional Church-State Doctrine," *AER*, CXXVI (June, 1952), p. 453.

97. *Ibid.*, p. 457.

98. *Ibid.*, pp. 459-61.

99. Murray, "The Church and Totalitarian Democracy," *TS*, XIII (December, 1952), pp. 151-52, n. 58.

100. Fenton, "Infallibility in the Encyclicals," *AER*, LXXVIII (March, 1953), pp. 177-98.

101. Encyclical, *Au Milieu*, ASS, XXIV (1891-92), p. 523, as quoted by Murray in "Leo XIII on Church and State: The General Structure of the Controversy," *TS*, XIV (March, 1953), p. 15.

102. *Ibid.*, pp. 15-16.

103. *Ibid.*, pp. 17-18.

104. Ottaviani, *AER*, CXXVIII (May, 1953), pp. 321-34. See Chap. II, pp. 37.

105. Fenton, "Toleration and the Church-State Controversy," *AER*, CXXX (May, 1954), pp. 330-43; "Catholic Polemic and Doctrinal Accuracy," *AER*, CXXXII (February, 1955), pp. 107-17.

106. Murray, "Leo XIII: Separation of Church and State," *TS*, XIV (June, 1953), pp. 179-80.

107. *Ibid.*, p. 146, n. 2. He said of Ottaviani: "In his work, *Institutiones iuris publici ecclesiastici*, II (3d ed.; Rome: Typis Polyglottis Vaticanis, 1948), p. 82, the present Cardinal Ottaviani states that the 'most common system of separation is that which is enunciated in the well-known formula, "A Free Church in a free state," ' he adds . . . that this system was proclaimed in Italy by Count Cavour in 1861, but has 'obtained in the United States since Sept. 17, 1787,' " p. 146, n. 2.

108. Fenton, "The Teaching of the *Testem Benevolentiae*," p. 131.

109. Fenton, "Theology and Nationality," *AER*, CXXIX (September, 1953), p. 192.

110. Fenton, "The Teachings of the *Ci riesce*," *AER*, CXXX (February, 1954), pp. 114-23.

111. See Chap. II, pp. 46ff.

112. Giuseppe Di Meglio, "*Ci riesce* and Cardinal Ottaviani's Discourse," *AER*, CXXX (June, 1954), pp. 384-87; Fenton, "Toleration and the Church-State Controversy," pp. 340-43.

113. Murray, "Leo XIII: Two Concepts of Government; II: Government and the Order of Culture," *TS*, XV (March, 1954), p. 21.

114. Murray, "Leo XIII and Pius XII: Government and the Order of Religion," Unpublished manuscript, galley page R—79, WCA.

115. *Ibid.*, galley page B—70, n. 9.

116. See Chap. II, p. 58.

117. The Latin and English text of *Si diligis* appeared in *AER*, CXXXI (August, 1954), pp. 127-37. The quotation comes from pp. 134-35.

118. Fenton, "The Papal Allocution *Si diligis,*" *AER*, CXXXI (September, 1954), p. 186.

119. *Ibid.*, p. 190.

120. Fenton, Review of *The Catholic Church in World Affairs*, ed. Waldemar Guaian and M. A. Fitzsimons (Notre Dame: University of Notre Dame Press, 1954). The review is in *AER*, CXXXI (September, 1954), p. 215.

121. Fenton, "The Holy Father's Statement on Relations Between the Church and the State," *AER*, CXXXIII (November, 1955), p. 323. The English translation of the address appeared in this same issue of *AER*, pp. 340-51. The discourse was given by Pius XII on September 7, 1955, to the Tenth International Congress of Historical Sciences. See Chap. II, p. 70, n. 104.

122. Fenton, "The Holy Father's Statement," p. 347.

123. *Ibid.*, p. 330. A copy of the address *Vous avez voulu* can be found among Murray's personal notes, WCA. The points that Murray considered the most significant are underlined without marginal comment. The passages that are underlined are especially noteworthy. They all refer to elements important to Murray's method. For instance, "The Catholic Church is herself an historical fact." "The Church believes that she can in any case expect him (the historian) to inform himself of the historical consciousness the Church has of herself." Or, "The mission and development of the Church are historical facts." For obvious reasons Murray never wrote anything on this address. But it would seem that his interpretation would have been considerably different from Fenton's. It stands solidly behind Murray's method.

124. Fenton, "The Doctrinal Authority of Papal Allocutions," *AER*, CXXXIV (February, 1956), pp. 109-17.

125. Fenton, "Doctrine and Tactic in Catholic Pronouncements on Church and State," *AER*, CXLV (October, 1961), p. 274.

126. Hennesey, *The First Council of the Vatican*, pp. 139-40.

127. Murray, "Declaration on Religious Freedom," in Vincent A. Yzermans, ed. *American Participation in the Second Vatican Council* (New York: Sheed and Ward, 1967), p. 668.

128. See Chap. III, pp. 79-80.

129. See Chap. II, p. 59.

130. Avery Dulles. *Models of the Church* (New York: Doubleday & Company, 1974). This study provides an excellent survey of five major approaches or "models" of the Church that emerged at Vatican II. His analysis of the traditional "institutional model" of the Church explains how the dogma no salvation outside the Church was an essential element in this model (p. 41). In the "communion model" this maxim becomes "almost a tautology" (p. 53). "The institutional model seems to deny salvation to anyone who is not a member of the organization, whereas the communion model leaves it problematical why anyone should be required to join the institution at all" (p. 58). For a detailed examination of this problem as it relates to the other models: the sacramental model, the kingdom model, and the servant model, see Chap. VIII: "The True Church," and Chap. IX: "The Church and the Churches," pp. 116-50.

131. See Chap. II, pp. 53-54.

132. See Chap. II, p. 37-38.

133. Murray, "The One Work of the One Church," *The Catholic Mind*, XLVIII (June, 1950), pp. 361-63.

134. Murray, "Freedom of Religion," *TS*, VI (June, 1945), p. 238.

135. Murray, "The Issue of Church and State at Vatican Council II," *TS*, XXVII (December, 1966), p. 601.

Epilogue

Historical conditions focused John Courtney Murray's lifelong effort on the "distracting debate on religious freedom," a debate which he not only initiated and persuasively argued but which he led to a concluding consensus in the official statements of Vatican II. Few theologians have seen their efforts so crowned. In Murray's eyes, the debate had little importance as a point of arrival. Its significance lay rather in its resolution of long-delayed and unfinished business, crucial for the confrontation of deeper issues affecting the Church's effective presence in the modern world. The satisfactory resolution of the debate on freedom thus constituted one of the conditions for carrying out the much vaster program outlined in the Council's total achievement. So situated, Murray's contribution must be recognized not only as vital to the life of the Church in America, but as universally significant.

The importance of Murray's role in developing a Roman Catholic theology of freedom called for both historical and theological analysis. Such was the task of this study. The import of Murray's work for future theological and especially ecclesiological discussion, however, remains unexplored. If Murray's achievement is to be taken seriously, theological reflection must now turn to at least three areas of inquiry, that of development of doctrine, that of the democratization of the Church, and that of Catholic presence in American secular society. The following is an effort to outline the implications of Murray's thought with regard to each of these three areas.

Development of Doctrine

Murray's achievement directs our attention to several questions and approaches relative to doctrinal development. First, theological reflection must derive from human experience. Theology raises critical questions concerning that experience. What does it say about God and humanity? How does it relate to the broader range of Catholic experience? What is its validity and what criteria are needed for its evaluation? Murray's own theology was an example of such reflection in that it arose from the needs of the Church in

America and attempted to respond to those experiential needs. Second, theology must be interdisciplinary. Murray succeeded in developing the Church's teaching on religious freedom because he raised this limited issue to the light of his own historical, political, philosophical, and anthropological expertise. Theology has little validity apart from intimate contact with other sciences and disciplines. Third, theological reflection must be collaborative. Murray was well aware that he could hardly succeed in achieving a development in the Church's teaching if it was not done in collaboration with the Church's authoritative teachers. In his early years Murray received but cautious and frequently unspoken, or at least unpublicized, support from all too few members of the American hierarchy. His vindication came with the solid and enthusiastic support of the majority of the American bishops present at the Council. Murray was well aware that he could achieve extremely little on his own. His experience points to the need for hierarchical sensitivity to the importance of intellectual freedom in scholarly research. Excellence is needed for the emergence of new ideas, new techniques, and new answers in response to both old and new questions. The Church is thus in need of scholarly masters with intellects stimulated by an atmosphere of faith and trust and free to range widely in their theological task.

Democratization of the Church

There is need for further development and clarification of Murray's theology of the democratic process. Since his thought is incorporated in the *Declaration on Religious Freedom*, this second task appears especially important. From the point of view of strategy in the resolution of socio-ethical dilemmas this document contains far-reaching implications for the application of the democratic process in secular society as well as in the Church. It appears that the philosophical and theological principles which permitted a reformulation of Catholic teaching on religious freedom and Church-State theory might also justify a continuing democratization of the Church's internal structures. It is in this connection that Murray's thought might well have its greatest impact on the institutional life of the Church. Indeed, the influence of his thought already can be seen in the collegial response of some bishops to *Humanae vitae*, in movements for the democratic election of bishops, and in the formation of groups such as the National Federation of Priests' Councils. It remains to be seen how these events and various movements which inspired them can be theologically reconciled with the role traditionally attributed to the papacy. In thinking through the democratization of Church structures the Catholic community will have the benefit of centuries of Protestant experience.

Catholic Presence in American
Secular Society

It also appears necessary to reevaluate the Catholic community's actual role in American society and to project its future direction with regard to the critical issues facing all Americans. Since Murray's death in 1967, the Church in America has evolved from the liberal Catholicism espoused by Murray to the radical left represented, for example, by the Berrigans. Murray's Catholicism was based on the need to bring religion into harmony with the American consensus. Catholic radicalism represents a reassertion of the central importance of religious values in political life. The latter has rejected liberal Catholicism with its emphasis on civility, dialogue, and consensus, as an accommodation to a fundamentally dishonest and exploitative system. Out of eagerness for its own acceptance, American Catholicism would thus have uncritically accepted the basic ideologies of the American way of life.

Murray's position, however, was a good deal more sophisticated than such a caricature would allow. Never would Murray have accepted that religious values be compromised for the sake of political civility. His position may have been somewhat confined in its vision and limited in its critical edge. Its expression was perhaps too often shaped by the position of conservative Catholics and anti-Catholic Americans. As a result, it often may have lacked a critical sense of the character of the religious situation in America and the dynamics of American society itself. Murray may have been more optimistic than realistic about the American ideal and its possibilities. What Murray meant by the American ideal was the American consensus which is expressed by a free people under a limited government. Although, as he saw, such an ideal was never fully realizable, it was constantly to be striven for. Murray, however, was clearly critical of gross inadequacies in the realization of that consensus.

It was Murray's deep concern to respond to the social and moral issues of his day through theological reflection. He was primarily a thinker and not an activist. His method and style were not that of the radical Catholic Left. From their standpoint, he would be presented as a conservative. Those who prefer to storm the battlements will obviously become disenchanted with his meticulous approach. Murray's scholarly work, however, helped to liberalize the Church. He succeeded because he was essentially a conservative man who always moved within tradition, presenting his liberal conclusions as normal developments of the past.

In retrospect, the Catholic Left has not been any more successful at permanently shaping American secular values. While for a short period of time it has had a considerable effect on the general climate of opinion in America, the movement has not represented and is never likely to represent more than a small minority of the Church.

For Murray, dialogue between serious men about serious things was the *sine qua non* of civilized society. The end in view was not necessarily agreement but frequently that kind of understanding which is presupposed by honest disagreement. Such Christian realism might well prove an excellent norm for those who have accepted his challenge to commit themselves as Catholics to America's role in history.

Bibliography

Primary Sources

Archives of the Woodstock College Library, Georgetown University, 37th and O Sts., Washington, D.C. 20057. This collection contains the John Courtney Murray Papers. The material includes his personal class notes, early sermons, unpublished manuscripts, particularly from his later years. There are also numerous letters from Murray to various individuals involved in both the Church and government, along with personal recollections from some of his friends and associates. The collection also includes numerous tapes of lectures or commencement addresses delivered by Murray which have never been published.

Archives of the New York Province of the Society of Jesus, 501 East Fordham Road, Bronx, New York 10458. This collection contains a personal file on Murray which includes much of the important correspondence from Murray's major superiors in the United States and in Rome.

Archives of the Archdiocese of New York, St. Joseph's Seminary, Dunwoodie, Yonkers, New York 10704. This collection contains the Francis Cardinal Spellman papers wherein a few important letters pertaining to Murray can be found.

John Courtney Murray
Complete bibliography
(arranged chronologically)

Murray, John Courtney. "A Crisis in the History of Trent," *Thought*, VII (December, 1932), pp. 463-73.

————. "Taken From Among Men," *Jesuit Seminary News*, XIII (June, 1938), pp. 3-5.

————. "Book Reviews: New Periodicals," *Theological Studies*, III (May, 1942), pp. 290-93. (Hereafter referred to as *TS*.)

————. "Current Theology: Christian Co-operation," *TS*, III (September, 1942), pp. 413-31.

————. "Review of: William R. O'Connor, The Layman's Call, New York: P. J. Kenedy and Sons, 1942," *TS*, III (December, 1942), pp. 608-10.

————. "Current Theology: Co-operation, Some Further Views," *TS*, IV (March, 1943), pp. 100-111.

————. "Current Theology: Intercredal Co-operation: Its Theory and Its Organization," *TS*, IV (June, 1943), pp. 257-68. Also published under "Intercredal Co-operation; Principles." Catholic Association for International Peace, Washington, D.C.: Paulist, 1943.

———. "To the Editor," *TS*, IV (September, 1943), pp. 472-74.

———. "Descriptive Notes," *TS*, IV (September, 1943), p. 466.

———. "Principles for Peace," *TS*, IV (December, 1943), pp. 634-38.

———. "The Catholic, Jewish, Protestant Declaration on World Peace." Published in excerpts of *Verbum* (Guatemala) Tuesday, January 9, 1945 as "La Cooperación Interconfessional Para la Paz." U.S. publication (if any) unlocated. Also published in Vida: Revista de Orientación, VII (1944), pp. 757-71.

———. "The Pattern for Peace and the Papal Peace Program." Catholic Association for International Peace, Washington, D.C.: Paulist, 1944.

———. "Woodstock Wisdom," Three Convocation Addresses. Woodstock, 1944, pp. 1-9.

———. "Towards a Theology for the Layman: The Problem of Its Finality," *TS*, V (March, 1944), pp. 43-75.

———. "Towards a Theology for the Layman: The Pedagogical Problem," *TS*, V (September, 1944), pp. 340-76.

———. "The Juridical Organization of the International Community," *The Wall Street Journal*, October 9, 1944.

———. "World Order and Moral Law," *Thought*, XIX (December, 1944), pp. 581-86.

———. "On the Problem of Co-operation: Some Clarifications; Reply to Father P. F. Furfey," *The American Ecclesiastical Review*, CXII (March, 1945), pp. 194-214.

———. "Current Theology: Freedom of Religion," *TS*, VI (March, 1945), pp. 85-113.

———. "Freedom of Religion, I: The Ethical Problem," *TS*, VI (June, 1945), pp. 229-86.

———. "The Real Woman Today," *America*, LXXIV (November 3, 1945), pp. 122-24.

———. "God's Word and Its Realization," *America*, LXXIV (December 8, 1945), supplement, pp. xix-xxi.

———. "The Papal Allocution: Christmas," *America*, LXXIV (January 5, 1946), pp. 370-71.

———. "Religious Liberty: An Inquiry," *TS*, VII (March, 1946), pp. 151-63.

———. "How Liberal Is Liberalism," *America*, LXXV (April 6, 1946), pp. 6-7.

———. "Operation University," *America*, LXXV (April 13, 1946), pp. 28-29.

———. "Separation of Church and State," *America*, LXXVI (December 7, 1946), pp. 261-63.

———. "Admonition and Grace." Introduction and translation in *The Fathers of the Church: Writings of St. Augustine*. New York: Cima, 1947. IV, pp. 239-305.

———. "Separation of Church and State: True and False Concepts," *America*, LXXVI (February 15, 1947), pp. 541-45.

———. "The Court Upholds Religious Freedom," *America*, LXXVI (March 8, 1947), pp. 628-30.

———. "The Roman Catholic Church." The *Annals of the American Academy of Political and Social Science*, CCLVI (March, 1948), pp. 36-42. Also published as: "What Does the Catholic Church Want?" *Catholic Digest*, XIII (December,

1948), pp. 51-53; and "The Roman Catholic Church," *Catholic Mind*, XLVI (September, 1948), pp. 580-88.

———. "Governmental Repression of Heresy," *Proceedings* of the Third Annual Convention of the Catholic Theological Society of America. Chicago, 1948, pp. 26-98.

———. "Religious Liberty: The Concern of All," *America*, LXXVIII (February 7, 1948), pp. 513-16.

———. "Dr. Morrison and the First Amendment," *America*, LXXVIII (March 6, 1948), pp. 627-29; (March 20, 1948), pp. 683-86.

———. "The Root of Faith: The Doctrine of M. J. Sheeben," *TS*, IX (March, 1948), pp. 20-46.

———. "The Role of Faith in the Renovation of the World," *The Messenger of the Sacred Heart*, LXXXIII (March, 1948), pp. 15-17.

———. "St. Robert Bellarmine on the Indirect Power," *TS*, IX (December, 1948), pp. 491-535.

———. "The Political Thought of Joseph de Maistre," *Review of Politics*, XI (January, 1949), pp. 63-86.

———. "On the Necessity For Not Believing: A Roman Catholic Interpretation," *The Yale Scientific Magazine*, XXIII (February, 1949), pp. 11-12.

———. "Reversing the Secularist Drift," *Thought*, XXIV (March, 1949), pp. 36-46.

———. "Towards a Theology for the Layman," *Jesuit Educational Quarterly*, XI (March, 1949), pp. 221-28.

———. "Free Speech in Its Relation to Self-Government," *Georgetown Law Journal*, XXXVII (May, 1949), pp. 654-62.

———. "Review of: Paul Blanshard, American Freedom and Catholic Power. Boston: Beacon Press, 1949," *The Catholic World*, CLXIX (June, 1949), pp. 233-34.

———. "Contemporary Orientations of Catholic Thought on Church and State in the Light of History," *TS*, X (June, 1949), pp. 177-234.

———. "Current Theology: On Religious Freedom," *TS*, X (September, 1949), pp. 409-32.

———. "The Catholic Position: A Reply," *The American Mercury*, LXIX (September, 1949), pp. 274-83, 637-39.

———. "Law or Prepossessions," *Law and Contemporary Problems*, XIV (Winter, 1949), pp. 23-43. Also published in: *Essays in Constitutional Law*. Ed. by R. G. McCloskey. New York: Alfred Knopf, 1957, pp. 316-42.

———. "The Natural Law." In *Great Expressions of Human Rights*. Ed. by R. M. MacIver. New York: Harper, 1950, pp. 69-104. Also published as: "Natural Law and the Public Consensus." In *Natural Law and Modern Society*. Cleveland and New York, 1962, pp. 48-81.

———. "The One Work of the One Church," *The Missionary Union of the Clergy Bulletin*, XIV (March, 1950), pp. 5-11. Also in: *Catholic Mind*, XLVIII (June, 1950), pp. 358-64.

———. "Paul Blanshard and the New Nativism," *The Month*, New Series, V (April, 1951), pp. 214-25. Also excerpt in *Commonweal*, LIV (May 4, 1951), pp. 94-95.

———. "The Problem of 'The Religion of the State,'" *The American Ecclesiastical Review*, CXXIV (May, 1951), pp. 327-52. Also published as: "The Problem of State Religion," *TS*, XII (June, 1951), pp. 155-78.

———. "School and Christian Freedom," National Catholic Educational Association *Proceedings*, XLVIII (August, 1951), pp. 63-68.

———. "For the Freedom and Transcendence of the Church," *The American Ecclesiastical Review*, CXXVI (January, 1952), pp. 28-48.

———. "The Church and Totalitarian Democracy," *TS*, XIII (December, 1952), pp. 525-63.

———. "Leo XIII on Church and State: The General Structure of the Controversy," *TS*, XIV (March, 1953), pp. 1-30.

———. "Christian Humanism in America," *Social Order*, III (May-June, 1953), pp. 233-44.

———. "Leo XIII: Separation of Church and State," *TS*, XIV (June, 1953), pp. 145-214.

———. "The Problem of Free Speech," *Philippine Studies*, I (September, 1953), pp. 107-24.

———. "Leo XIII: Two Concepts of Government," *TS*, XIV (December, 1953), pp. 551-67.

———. "Leo XIII: Two Concepts of Government: Government and the Order of Culture," *TS*, XV (March, 1954), pp. 1-33.

———. "The Problem of Pluralism in America." In *Catholicism in American Culture*. College of New Rochelle, 1955. Reprinted as "Church, State and Religious Liberty," *The Catholic Mind*, LVII (May-June, 1959), pp. 201-15; and in *Thought*, XXIX (Summer, 1954), pp. 165-208.

———. "On the Structure of the Church-State Problem." In *The Catholic Church in World Affairs*. Ed. by Waldemar Gurian and M. A. Fitzsimons. Notre Dame, Ind.: University of Notre Dame Press, 1954, pp. 11-32.

———. "Catholics in America—a Creative Minority—Yes or No?" *Epistle* (New York), XXI (1955), pp. 36-41. Reprinted as: "Catholics in America—a Creative Minority?" *The Catholic Mind*, LIII (October, 1955), pp. 590-97.

———. "The Catholic University in a Pluralist Society" [St. Louis University Address delivered in November, 1955, at the Founder's Day Commemoration], *The Catholic Mind*, LVII (May-June, 1959), pp. 253-60. Also published as "Unity of Truth," *Commonweal*, LXIII (January 13, 1956), pp. 381-82.

———. "Special Catholic Challenges," *Life*, XXXIX-XL (December 26, 1955), pp. 144-46. Reprinted as: "Challenges Confronting the American Catholic," *The Catholic Mind*, LVII (May-June, 1959), pp. 196-200.

———. "St. Ignatius and the End of Modernity." In *The Ignatian Year at Georgetown*. Georgetown University Press, 1956.

———. "The Thesis Form as an Instrument of Theological Reflection." *Proceedings of the Eleventh Annual Convention of the Catholic Theological Society of America*, Cleveland, 1956, pp. 218-24.

———. "The School Problem in Mid-Twentieth Century." In *The Role of the Independent School in American Democracy*. Ed. by William H. Conley. Milwaukee: Marquette University Press, 1956, pp. 1-16. Reprinted as "The Religious School in a Pluralist Society," *The Catholic Mind*, LIV (September, 1956), pp. 502-11.

———. "Kirche und Demokratie," *Dokumente*, XII (February, 1956), pp. 9-16.

———. "The Quality of Reverence," *Journal of the Newman Club of the University of Minnesota*, June, 1956.

———. "Freedom, Responsibility and the Law," *The Catholic Lawyer*, II (July, 1956), pp. 214-20, 276. Reprinted in: *The Catholic Mind*, LVI (September-October, 1958), pp. 436-47.

——. "Die Katholiken in der americanischen Gesellschaft," *Dokumente*, XII (August, 1956), pp. 10-14.

——. "The Bad Arguments Intelligent People Make," *America*, CXVI (November 3, 1956), pp. 120-23.

——. "Questions of Striking a Right Balance: Literature and Censorship," *Books on Trial*, XIV (June-July, 1956), pp. 393-95. Reprinted as: "Literature and Censorship," *The Catholic Mind*, LIV (December, 1956), pp. 665-77.

——. "The Christian Idea of Education." In *The Christian Idea of Education*. Ed. by Edmund Fuller. New Haven: Yale University Press, 1957, pp. 152-63.

——. "Church, State and Political Freedom," *Modern Age: A Conservative Review*, I (Fall, 1957), pp. 134-45. Also: *The Catholic Mind*, LVII (May-June, 1959), pp. 216-29. Reprinted as: "The Freedom of Man in the Freedom of the Church." In *Modern Catholic Thinkers*. Ed. by A. Robert Caponigri. New York: Harper, 1960, pp. 372-84.

——. "How to Think (theologically) about War and Peace," *Catholic Messenger*, LXXVI (December, 1958), pp. 7-8.

——. "U.S. Policy vis-à-vis the Soviet Union," Catholic Association for International Peace *News*, XIX (1958), pp. 8-10.

——. "America's Four Conspiracies." In *Religion in America*. Ed. by John Cogley. Meridian Books, 1958, pp. 12-41. Reprinted in *The Catholic Mind*, LVII (May-June, 1959), pp. 230-41.

——. *Foreign Policy and the Free Society*. By J. C. Murray and Walter Millis. New York: Oceana Publications, 1958. (Fund for the Republic) Excerpt published as: "Confusion of U.S. Foreign Policy," *The Catholic Mind*, LVII (May-June, 1959), pp. 261-73.

——. "The Making of a Pluralist Society," *Religious Education*, LIII (November-December, 1958), pp. 521-28. Reprinted as "University in a Pluralist Society." In *Religion and the State University*. Ed. by Erich A. Walter. Ann Arbor: University of Michigan Press, 1958. Reprinted as "State University in a Pluralist Society," *The Catholic Mind*, LVII (May-June, 1959), pp. 242-52.

——. "Morality and Modern War." A paper delivered before the Catholic Association for International Peace, October 24, 1958. The Church Peace Union, 1959. Reprinted as: "The Morality of War," *Theology Digest*, VII (Autumn, 1959), pp. 131-37. Reprinted as: "God, Man and Nuclear War," *Catholic Mind*, LVII (May, June, 1959), pp. 274-88. Reprinted as: "Remarks on the Moral Problem of War," *TS*, XX (March, 1959), pp. 40-61. Reprinted as: "Theology and Modern War." In, *In Morality and Modern Warfare*. Ed. by William Nagle. Baltimore: Helicon Press, 1960, pp. 69-91.

——. *We Hold These Truths: Catholic Reflections on the American Proposition*. New York: Sheed and Ward, 1960.

——. "Morality and Foreign Policy, Part I," *America*, CII (March 19, 1960), pp. 729-32.

——. "Morality and Foreign Policy, Part II," *America*, CII (March 26, 1960), pp. 764-67.

——. "On Raising the Religious Issue," *America*, CIII (September 24, 1960), p. 702.

——. "One Fold, One Shepherd," *America*, CIV (January 14, 1961), pp. 459-60.

——. "Hopes and Misgivings for Dialogue," *America*, CIV (January 14, 1961), pp. 459-60.

——. "The American Proposition," *Commonweal*, LXXIII (January 20, 1961),

pp. 433-35.
————. "What can Unite a Religiously Divided Nation," *Catholic Messenger*, LXXIX (April 27, 1961), pp. 1, 4; (May 4, 1961), p. 4.
————. "The Return to Tribalism," *The Catholic Mind*, LX (January, 1962), pp. 5-12.
————. "On the Structure of the Problem of God," *TS*, XXIII (March, 1962), pp. 1-26. Also published as: *The Problem of God, Yesterday and Today*. New Haven: Yale University Press, 1964.
————. "Le droit à l'incroyance," *Relations*, XXII (Avril, 1962), pp. 91-92.
————. "Literatur und Zensur," *Frankfurter Hefte*. Zeitschrift für Kultur und Politik. XVII Jahrgang Heft 12 (December, 1962), pp. 824-33.
————. Foreword to: Richard J. Regan, S.J. *American Pluralism and the Catholic Conscience*. New York: Macmillan, 1963, pp. xiii-xv.
————. "Make the News Good News!" *Interracial Review*, XXXVI (July, 1963), pp. 34-35, 130-31.
————. "Natural Law and Public Consensus." In *Natural Law and Modern Society*. Ed. by John Cogley. Cleveland: World Publishing Co., 1963. Fund for the Republic.
————. "Things Old and New in 'Pacem in Terris,'" *America*, CVIII (April 27, 1963), pp. 612-14. Also in: *American Catholic Horizons*. Ed. by Eugene K. Culhane. New York: Doubleday, 1966, pp. 188-94.
————. "Good Pope John: A Theologian's Tribute," *America, CVIII* (June 15, 1963), pp. 854-55.
————. "The Church and the Council," *America*, CIV (October 19, 1963), pp. 451-53.
————. "On Religious Liberty," *America*, CIX (November 30, 1963), pp. 704-706. Also published in: *American Catholic Horizons*. Ed. by Eugene K. Culhane. New York: Doubleday, 1966, pp. 219-26. Excerpted in: "Fr. Murray Cites Questions Posed by Liberty Questions," *Catholic Messenger*, LXXXII (December, 1963), p. 12. "Religionsfreiheit als Konzilsthema." In *Das Konzil: Zweiter Bildund Textbericht*, Mario v. Galli Olten (Switz.), 1964, pp. 138-40. "Liberté religieuse: la position de l'épiscopat americain," *Choisir* (1964), pp. 14-16.
————. "Kirche und Staat in Nordamerika," *Dokumente*, XIX (December, 1963), pp. 423-33.
————. "Key Themes in the Encyclical 'Pacem in Terris.'" New York: The America Press, 1963, pp. 57-64.
————. Foreword to: Patricia Barrett, *Religious Liberty and the American Presidency; A Study in Church-State Relations*, New York: Herder, 1963, pp. v-vii.
————. "On the Future of Humanistic Education." In *Humanistic Education and Western Civilization*. Ed. by Arthur A. Cohen in honor of the 65th birthday of Robert M. Hutchins. New York: Holt, Rinehart, and Winston, 1964, pp. 231-47. Excerpted in: *The Critic*, XXII (February, March, 1964), pp. 37-43.
————. "The Social Function of the Press," *Journalistes Catholiques*, XII (Janvier-Avril, 1964), pp. 8-12.
————. "Today and Tomorrow; Conversation at the Council; John Courtney Murray, Hans Küng, Gustave Weigel, Godfrey Diekmann, and Vincent Yzermans," *American Benedictine Review*, XV (September, 1964), pp. 341-51.
————. Foreword to: *Freedom and Man*. Ed. by John Courtney Murray. New York: P. J. Kenedy, 1965, pp. 11-16.
————. "Religious Freedom." In *Freedom and Man*. Ed. by John Courtney Mur-

ray. New York: P. J. Kenedy, 1965, pp. 131-40.
———. "The Problem of Religious Freedom," *TS*, XXV (December, 1964), pp. 503-75. Published as: *The Problem of Religious Freedom*. Woodstock Papers, No. 7; Westminster, Md.: The Newman Press, 1965. "De kwestie van de godsdienstvrijheld op het concilie." *Documentation Hollandaise du Concile* dossiers 9. Hilversum/Antwerp, 1965, pp. 7-83. "Le problème de la liberté religieuse." In *La Liberté Religieuse: exigence spirituelle et problème politique*. Paris: Edition du Centurion, 1965, pp. 9-112. "Die Religiöse Freiheit und Konzil II," *Wort und Warheit*, XX (1965), pp. 409-30, 505-36.
———. "Das Verhältnis Von Kirche und Staat in Den USA." In *Das Verhältnis Von Kirche und Staat: Erwägungen Zur Vielfalt Der Geschichtlichen Entwicklung und Gegenwärtigen Situation*. Echter-Verlag-Würzburg, 1965, pp. 51-71.
———. "This Matter of Religious Freedom," *America*, CXII (January 9, 1965), pp. 40-43.
———. "The Status of the Nicene Creed as Dogma," *Chicago Studies: An Archdiocesan Review*, V (Spring, 1966), pp. 65-80. (Delivered 1965.)
———. "Osservazione sulla dichiarazione della libertà religiosa," *La Civiltà Cattolica*, CXVI (18 Dicembre, 1965), pp. 536-54. Also published as: "The Issue of Development of Doctrine," *Documentation Hollandaise du Concile*, CCVI, Rome, n.d., pp. 1-7. "La Déclaration sur la liberté religieuse," *Nouvelle Revue Théologique*, LXXXVIII (January, 1966), pp. 41-67.
———. "The Declaration on Religious Freedom: A Moment in Its Legislative History." In *Religious Liberty: An End and a Beginning. The Declaration on Religious Freedom: An Ecumenical Discussion*. Ed. by John Courtney Murray. New York: Macmillan, 1966, pp. 15-42.
———. "Religious Freedom," pp. 673-74, introduction, and pp. 674-98, text and commentary. In *The Documents of Vatican II*. Ed. by Walter M. Abbott and Joseph Gallagher. New York: An Angelus Book, America Press, 1966.
———. "The Declaration on Religious Freedom," pp. 565-76, and discussion, pp. 577-85. In *Vatican II: An Interfaith Appraisal*. Ed. by John H. Miller. Notre Dame: Association Press, 1966.
———. "The Declaration on Religious Freedom: Its Deeper Significance," *America*, XIV (April 23, 1966), pp. 592-93.
———. "The Vatican Declaration on Religious Freedom." In *The University in the American Experience*. New York: Fordham University, 1966, pp. 1-10.
———. "The Declaration on Religious Freedom." *War, Poverty, Freedom: The Christian Response*. Concilium, XV, New York: Paulist Press, 1966, pp. 3-16.
———. "The Issue of Church and State at Vatican II," *TS*, XXVII (December, 1966), pp. 580-606.
———. "Freedom, Authority, Community," *America*, CXV (December 3, 1966), pp. 734-41.
———. Review of: *The Garden and the Wilderness: Religion and Government in American Constitutional History*. By M. D. Howe. Chicago: University of Chicago Press, 1965. In *Yale Law Review* (March, 1967), pp. 25-27.
———. "Declaration on Religious Freedom." In *American Participation at the Second Vatican Council*. Ed. by Vincent A. Yzermans. New York: Sheed and Ward, 1967, pp. 668-76.
———. "Vers une intelligence du dévelopment de la doctrine de l'Église sur la liberté religieuse." In *Vatican II: La Liberté Religieuse*. Paris: Les Éditions du Cerf, 1967, pp. 111-47. (*Unam Sanctam* 60.)

————— "Zum Verständis Der Entwicklung Der Lehre Der Kirche über Die Religionsfreiheit." In *Über die Religionsfreiheit: Latainischer und Deutscher Text.* Paderborn, Bonifacius Druckerei, 1967, pp. 125-65.

————— "Religious Liberty and Development of Doctrine," *The Catholic World,* CCIV (February, 1967), pp. 277-83.

————— "Our Response to the Ecumenical Revolution," *Religious Education,* XLII (March-April, 1967), pp. 91-92. (Delivered in 1966.)

————— "Murray says Church was Too Sure," *The National Catholic Reporter,* III (May 17, 1967), p. 3.

————— "He Held This Truth." Last published statement of John Courtney Murray, Given to special committee of the Episcopal Church studying the problem of the nature of heresy. *The National Catholic Reporter,* III (August 23, 1967), p. 3. Published as: "A Will to Community." In *Theological Freedom and Social Responsibility.* Ed. by Stephen F. Bayne, Jr. New York: Seabury Press, 1967, pp. 111-16.

————— "Selective Conscientious Objection." Published in pamphlet form by Our Sunday Visitor. (Text of address at Western Maryland College, June 4, 1967.)

————— "The Danger of the Vows: An Encounter With Earth, Woman and the Spirit," *Woodstock Letters,* CXVI (Fall, 1967), pp. 421-27.

————— "Freedom in the Age of Renewal," *American Benedictine Review,* XVIII (September, 1967), pp. 319-24. (Delivered at commencement exercises of St. John's University, Collegeville, Minn., June 3, 1965.)

Joseph Clifford Fenton
(arranged chronologically)

Fenton, Joseph C. "An Accusation Against School Theology,"*AER,* CX (March, 1944), pp. 213-22.

————— "Extra Ecclesiam Nulla Salus," *AER,* CX (April, 1944), pp. 300-306.

————— "The Church and the State of Siege," *AER,* CXII (January, 1945), pp. 54-63.

————— "Theology and Religion," *AER,* CXII (June, 1945), pp. 447-63.

————— "The Proof of the Church's Divine Origin," *AER,* CXIII (September, 1945), pp. 203-19.

————— "The Catholic and the Church," *AER,* CXIII (November, 1945), pp. 377-84.

————— "The True Church and the Notes of the Church," *AER,* CXIV (April, 1946), pp. 282-97.

————— "*Time* and Pope Leo," *AER,* CXIV (May, 1946), pp. 369-75.

————— "The Sources of Modern Attacks Against the Church," *AER,* CXV (September, 1946), pp. 204-18.

————— "The Catholic Church and Freedom of Religion," *AER,* CXV (October, 1946), pp. 286-301.

————— "The Theology of the Church and the State," *Proceedings* of the Second Annual Meeting of the Catholic Theological Society of America. Boston, 1947, pp. 15-46.

————— "New Concepts in Theology," *AER,* CXIX (July, 1948), pp. 56-62.

————— "The Church and the World," *AER,* CXIX (September, 1948), pp. 202-14.

————. "Two Currents in Contemporary Catholic Thought," *AER*, CXIX (October, 1948), pp. 293-301.
————. "Factors in Church Unity," *AER*, CXIX (November, 1948), pp. 375-83.
————. "Review of Cardinal Ottaviani, *Institutiones iuris publici ecclesiastici*, Vols. I and II, Rome," *AER*, CXIX (December, 1948), pp. 471-72.
————. "The Doctrinal Authority of Papal Encyclicals, Part I," *AER*, CXXI (August, 1949), pp. 136-50.
————. "The Doctrinal Authority of Papal Encyclicals, Part II," *AER*, CXXI (September, 1949), pp. 210-20.
————. "The Religious Assent Due to the Teachings of Papal Encyclicals," *AER*, CXXIII (July, 1950), pp. 59-67.
————. "The Relation of the Christian State to the Catholic Church According to the *Pontificale Romanum*," *AER*, CXXIII (September, 1950), pp. 214-18.
————. "The Lesson of *Humani Generis*," *AER*, CXXIII (November, 1950), pp. 359-78.
————. "The *Humani Generis* and Its Predecessors," *AER*, CXXIII (December, 1950), pp. 452-48.
————. "The Status of a Controversy," *AER*, CXXIV (June, 1951), pp. 451-58.
————. "Reform and Integralism," *AER*, CXXVI (February, 1952), pp. 126-39.
————. "Principles Underlying Traditional Church-State Doctrine," *AER*, CXXVI (June, 1952), pp. 452-62.
————. "A Reply to Father Hartnett," *AER*, CXXVII (October, 1952), pp. 286-99.
————. "Infallibility in the Encyclicals," *AER*, CXXVIII (March, 1953), pp. 177-98.
————. "The Teaching of *Testem Benevolentiae*," *AER*, CXXIX (August, 1953), pp. 124-33.
————. "Theology and Nationality," *AER*, CXXIX (September, 1953), pp. 192-95.
————. "The Teachings of *Ci riesce*," *AER*, CXXX (February, 1954), pp. 114-23.
————. "*Magisterium* and Jurisdiction in the Catholic Church," *AER*, CXXX (March, 1954), pp. 194-201.
————. "Toleration and the Church-State Controversy," *AER*, CXXX (May, 1954), pp. 330-43.
————. "The Papal Allocution *Si diligis*," *AER*, CXXXI (September, 1954), pp. 186-98.
————. "The Catholic Church in World Affairs," *AER*, CXXXI (September, 1954), pp. 215-16.
————. "Separation or Too Close a Union?" *AER*, CXXXI (November, 1954), pp. 343-44.
————. "Catholic Polemic and Doctrinal Accuracy," *AER*, CXXXII (February, 1955), pp. 107-17.
————. "The Holy Father's Statement on Relations between Church and State," *AER*, CXXXIII (November, 1955), pp. 323-31.
————. "Appraisal in Sacred Theology," *AER*, CXXXIV (January, 1956), pp. 24-36.
————. "The Doctrinal Authority of Papal Allocutions," *AER*, CXXXIV (February, 1956), pp. 109-17.
————. "The Components of Liberal Catholicism," *AER*, CXXXIX (July, 1958), pp. 36-53.
————. "Technical Excellence in the Teaching of Catholic Doctrine," *AER*, CXL

(May, 1959), pp. 333-42.

————. "The Ecumenical Council and Christian Reunion," *AER*, CXLI (July, 1959), pp. 45-57.

————. "Doctrinal Function of the Ecumenical Council," *AER*, CXLI (August, 1959), pp. 117-28.

————. "The Case for Traditional Apologetics," *AER*, CXLI (December, 1959), pp. 406-16.

————. "The Basis for Conciliar Action in the Catholic Church," *AER*, CXLII (February, 1960), pp. 116-25.

————. "The Vatican Council's Unfinished Business," *AER*, CXLII (April, 1960), pp. 217-24.

————. "The *Sacrorum Antistitum* and the Background of the Oath against Modernism," *AER*, CXLIII (October, 1960), pp. 239-60.

————. "Rome and the Status of Catholic Theology," *AER*, CXLIII (December, 1960), pp. 395-417.

————. "Revolutions in Catholic Attitudes," *AER*, CXLV (August, 1961), pp. 120-29.

————. "Doctrine and Tactic in Catholic Pronouncements on Church and State," *AER*, CXLV (October, 1961), pp. 266-76.

————. "The Council and Father Küng," *AER*, CXLVII (September, 1962), pp. 178-200.

————. "Cardinal Ottaviani and the Council," *AER*, CXLVIII (January, 1963), pp. 44-53.

————. "The Roman Curia and the Ecumenical Council," *AER*, CXLVIII (March, 1963), pp. 185-98.

————. "The Teaching of the Theological Manuals," *AER*, CXLVIII (April, 1963), pp. 254-70.

————. "A Letter From Rome," *AER*, CXLIX (December, 1963), pp. 392-430.

Books

Abbott, Walter M., S.J., ed. *The Documents of Vatican II.* An Angelus Book. New York: The America Press, 1966.

Blanshard, Paul. *American Freedom and Catholic Power.* Boston: Beacon Press, 1949.

Ellis, John T., ed. *Documents of American Catholic History.* Logos. 2 vols. Chicago: Henry Regnery Company, 1967.

Hecker, Isaac. *The Church and the Age.* New York: Office of the Catholic World, 1887.

Ireland, John. *The Church and Modern Society.* New York: D. H. McBride & Co., 1897.

John XXIII. *Pacem in Terris.* English edition by The America Press. New York, 1963.

Ottaviani, Alfredo Cardinal. *Institutiones iuris publici ecclesiastici*, Vol. I, Ius publicum internum, Editio tertia. Rome: Typis Polyglottis Vaticanis, 1947.

————. *Institutiones iuris publici ecclesiastici*, Vol. II, Ius publicum externum, Editio tertia. Rome: Typis Polyglottis Vaticanis, 1948.

Pius XII. *The Major Addresses of Pope Pius XII.* Ed. by V. A. Yzermans. 2 vols. I:

Encyclicals; II: Radio Messages. St. Paul, Minn.: North Central, 1961.
Weigel, Gustave. *Church State Relations: A Theological Consideration.* Baltimore:
   Helicon Press, 1960.
Wynne, John J., ed. *The Great Encyclical Letters of Pope Leo XIII.* New York:
   Benziger Bros., 1903.

Articles

Bowie, W. Russell. "Protestant Concern Over Catholicism," *American Mercury,*
   LXIX (September, 1949), pp. 261-73.
Cavalli, Fiorelli. "La Condizione dei Protestanti in Spagna," *La Civiltà Cattolica,*
   Anno 99, II (April, 1946), pp. 29-47.
Connell, Francis J. "Catholics and 'Interfaith' Groups," *AER,* CV (November,
   1941), pp. 336-53.
———. "Does Catholic Doctrine Change?" *AER,* CXVII (November, 1947), pp.
   321-31.
———. "Pope Leo XIII's Message to America," *AER,* CIX (October, 1943), pp.
   249-56.
———. "Reply to Fr. Murray," *AER,* CXXVI (January, 1952), pp. 49-59.
———. "The Theory of the 'Lay State,'" *AER,* CXXV (July, 1951), pp. 7-18.
Di Meglio, Giuseppe. "*Ci riesce* and Cardinal Ottaviani's Discourse," *AER,* CXXX
   (June, 1954), pp. 384-87.
Ellis, John T. "Church and State: An American Catholic Tradition," *Harper's Mag-
   azine,* CCVII (July-December, 1953), pp. 63-67.
Furfey, Paul H. "Intercredal Cooperation: Its Limitations," *AER,* CXI (September,
   1944), pp. 161-75.
———. "Why Does Rome Discourage Socio-Religious Intercredalism?" *AER,* CXII
   (May, 1945), pp. 364-74.
Ottaviani, Alfredo Cardinal. "Church and State: Some Present Problems in the
   Light of the Teachings of Pope Pius XII," *AER,* CXXVIII (May, 1953), pp.
   321-34.
Pius XII. "*Ci riesce*: A Discourse to the National Convention of Italian Catholic
   Jurists. Official Vatican Press Office English Translation," *AER,* CXXX (Febru-
   ary, 1954), pp. 129-38.
———. "The Holy Father's Address to the 10th International Congress of the His-
   torical Sciences," *AER,* CXXXIII (November, 1955), pp. 340-51.
Shea, George W. "Catholic Doctrine and 'The Religion of the State,'" *AER,* CXX-
   III (September, 1950), pp. 161-74.
———. "Spain and Religious Freedom," *AER,* CXXVII (September, 1952), pp.
   161-72.
Weigel, Gustave. "The Church and the Democratic State," *Thought,* XXVII (Sum-
   mer, 1952), pp. 165-84.
———. "The Historical Background of the Encyclical 'Humani generis,'" *TS,* XII
   (June, 1951), pp. 208-30.
———. "Religious Toleration in a World Society," *America,* XC (January 9, 1954),
   pp. 375-76.

202 BIBLIOGRAPHY

Secondary Sources

Books

Ahlstrom, Sydney E. *A Religious History of the American People*. New Haven: Yale University Press, 1972.
Blanshard, Paul. *Communism, Democracy, and Catholic Power*. Boston: Beacon Press, 1951.
_____. *The Irish and Catholic Power*. Boston: Beacon Press, 1953.
_____. *Paul Blanshard on Vatican II*. Boston: Beacon Press, 1966.
Biechler, James A., ed. *Law for Liberty: The Role of Law in the Church Today*. Baltimore: Helicon Press, 1967.
Buehrle, Maria C. *The Cardinal Stritch Story*. Milwaukee: Bruce Publishing Company, 1959.
Caporale, Rock. *Vatican II: Last of the Councils*. Baltimore: Helicon Press, 1964.
Carrillo de Albornoz, A.F. *Roman Catholicism and Religious Liberty*. Geneva: World Council of Churches, 1959.
Cogley, John. *Catholic America*. New York: The Dial Press, 1973.
Cross, Robert D. *The Emergence of Liberal Catholicism in America*. Cambridge: Harvard University Press, 1958.
Drinan, Robert F. *Religion, the Courts, and Public Policy*. New York: McGraw-Hill Book Co., 1963.
Dulles, Avery. *Models of the Church*. New York: Doubleday and Company, Inc., 1974.
Elliott, Walter. *The Life of Father Hecker*. New York: The Columbus Press, 1891.
Ellis, John T. *American Catholicism*. 2d ed. rev. Chicago: The University of Chicago Press, 1969.
_____. *Catholics in Colonial America*. Baltimore: Helicon Press, 1965.
_____. *The Life of James Cardinal Gibbons*. 2 vols. Milwaukee: The Bruce Publishing Co., 1952.
_____. *Perspectives in American Catholicism*. Baltimore: Helicon Press, 1963.
Ellis, John T., ed. *The Catholic Priest in the United States: Historical Investigations*. Collegeville: St. John's University Press, 1971.
Fogarty, Gerald P. *The Vatican and the Americanist Crisis: Denis J. O'Connell, American Agent in Rome, 1885-1903*. Roma: Università Gregoriana Editrice, 1974.
Gleason, Philip. *Contemporary Catholicism in the United States*. Notre Dame, Ind.: University of Notre Dame Press, 1969.
Gleason, Philip, ed. *Catholicism in America*. New York: Harper & Row, 1970.
Greeley, Andrew M. *The Catholic Experience: An Interpretation of American Catholicism*. Garden City, N.Y.: Doubleday & Co., 1967.
_____. *The Hesitant Pilgrim: American Catholicism after the Council*. New York: Sheed and Ward, 1966.
Goerner, Edward A. *Peter and Caesar: Political Authority and the Catholic Church*. New York: Herder and Herder, 1965.
Hales, Edward E.Y. *The Catholic Church in the Modern World: A Survey from the French Revolution to the Present*. New York: Doubleday & Company, 1958.
Hennesey, James J. *The First Council of the Vatican: The American Experience*. New York: Herder and Herder, 1963.
Houtin, Albert. *L'américanisme*. Paris: Librairie Emile Nourry, 1904.

Kaiser, Robert B. *Pope, Council and World: The Story of Vatican II.* New York: Macmillan Company, 1963.

Klein, Félix. *Americanism: A Phantom Heresy.* Atchison: Aquin Book Shop, 1951.

Leclerq, Jean. *Jean de Paris et l'ecclésiologie du XIIIe siècle.* Paris: J. Vrin, 1942.

Littell, Franklin H. *From State Church to Pluralism.* Garden City, N.Y.: Doubleday and Company, Inc., 1962.

Lonergan, Bernard. *Insight: A Study of Human Understanding.* New York: Philosophical Library, 1957.

──────. *Method in Theology.* New York: Herder and Herder, 1972.

Love, Thomas T. *John Courtney Murray: Contemporary Church-State Theory.* Garden City, N.Y.: Doubleday and Company, Inc., 1965.

Maignen, Charles. *Études sur l'américanisme, le père Hecker, est-il un saint?* Rome: Desclée, Lefèbvre et cie., 1898.

Maynard, Theodore. *The Catholic Church and the American Idea.* New York: Appleton-Century-Crofts, 1953.

McAvoy, Thomas T. *The Great Crisis in American Catholic History: 1895-1900.* Chicago: Henry Regnery Co., 1957.

McSorley, Joseph. *Father Hecker and His Friends.* St. Louis: B. Herder Book Co., 1952.

Mead, Sydney E. *The Lively Experiment: The Shaping of Christianity in America.* New York: Harper and Row, 1963.

Messmer, Sebastian, ed. *The Words of the Right Reverend John England, First Bishop of Charleston.* 7 vols. Cleveland: Arthur H. Clark, 1908.

Miller, John H. *Vatican II: An Interfaith Appraisal.* Notre Dame: The University of Notre Dame Press, 1966.

Moynihan, James H. *The Life of Archbishop John Ireland.* New York: Harper Brothers, 1953.

Muller, Herbert J. *Religion and Freedom in the Modern World.* Chicago: University of Chicago Press, 1963.

Novak, Michael. *The Open Church: Vatican II, Act II.* New York: Macmillan Company, 1964.

O'Brien, David J. *American Catholics and Social Reform: The New Deal Years.* New York: Oxford University Press, 1968.

──────. *The Renewal of American Catholicism.* New York: Oxford University Press, 1972.

O'Connor, John. *The People Versus Rome: Radical Split in the American Church.* New York: Random House, 1969.

O'Neill, James N. *Catholicism and American Freedom.* New York: Harper and Brothers, 1952.

Pavan, Pietro. *Libertà Religiosa e Publici Poteri.* Milan: Editrice Ancora, 1965.

Regan, Richard J. *American Pluralism and the Catholic Conscience.* With a Foreword by John Courtney Murray. New York: Macmillan Company, 1963.

──────. *Conflict and Consensus: Religious Freedom and the Second Vatican Council.* New York: Macmillan Company, 1967.

Rommen, Heinrich. *The State in Catholic Thought.* New York: Herder and Herder Co., 1945.

Ryan, John A. and Millar, Moorhouse F., eds. *The State and the Church.* New York: Macmillan Company, 1922.

Rynne, Xavier. *Vatican Council II.* New York: Farrar, Straus, Giroux, 1968.

Schlesinger, Arthur M., Jr. *A Thousand Days: John F. Kennedy in the White*

House. Boston: Houghton Mifflin Co., 1965.
Serafin, Michael. *The Pilgrim.* New York: Farrar, Straus and Company, 1964.
Shields, Currin V. *Democracy and Catholicism in America.* New York: McGraw-Hill Company, 1958.
Shuster, George N. *The Catholic Spirit in America.* New York: Dial Press, 1927.
Smith, Elwyn A. *Religious Liberty in the United States: The Development of Church-State Thought Since the Revolutionary Era.* Philadelphia: Fortress Press, 1972.
Smith, Elwyn A., ed. *Church-State Relations in Ecumenical Perspectives.* Pittsburgh: Duquesne University Press, 1966.
――――. *The Religion of the Republic.* Philadelphia: Fortress Press, 1971.
Sorensen, Theodore C. *Kennedy.* New York: Harper and Row Publishers, 1965.
Stokes, Anson Phelps. *Church and State in the United States.* New York: Harper & Brothers, 1950.
Swidler, Leonard. *Freedom in the Church.* Dayton, Ohio: Pflaum Press, 1969.
Thiel, Andreas, ed. *Epistolae Romanorum pontificum a S. Hilario usque ad S. Hormisdam.* Brunsbergae: in aedibus E. Peter, 1868.
Tracy, Robert E. *American Bishop at the Vatican Council.* New York: McGraw-Hill Company, 1966.
von Aretin, Karl Otmar. *The Papacy and the Modern World.* Translated by Roland Hill. New York: McGraw-Hill Company, 1970.
Ward, Leo R., ed. *The American Apostolate.* Westminster, Md.: Newman Press, 1952.
Wills, Garry. *Bare Ruined Choirs: Doubt, Prophecy and Radical Religion.* New York: Doubleday and Company, Inc., 1972.
――――. *Politics and Catholic Freedom.* Chicago: Henry Regnery Co., 1964.
Wilson, John ed. *Church and State in American History.* Boston: D.C. Heath and Company, 1965.
Wolf, Donald. *Toward Consensus: Catholic-Protestant Interpretations of Church and State.* New York: Doubleday, 1968.
Yzermans, Vincent A. *American Participation at Vatican II.* New York: Sheed and Ward, 1968.
Yzermans, Vincent A., ed. *A New Pentecost: Vatican II, Session I.* Westminster, Md.: Newman Press, 1963.
Zwierlein, Frederick. *Letters of Archbishop Corrigan to Bp. McQuaid and Allied Documents.* Rochester: The Art Print Shop, 1964.

Unpublished Dissertations

Goerner, Edward A. "John Courtney Murray and the Problem of Church and State." Unpublished Ph.D. Dissertation, University of Chicago, 1959.
Reher, Margaret M. "The Church and the Kingdom of God in America: The Ecclesiology of the Americanists." Unpublished Ph.D. dissertation, Fordham University, 1972.

Articles

Baum, Gregory. "Declaration on Religious Freedom—Development of its Doctrinal Basis," *The Ecumenist,* IV (September-October, 1966), pp. 121-26.

Blanshard, Paul. "Religious Liberty, Limited: A Report from Vatican II," *The Register Leader* (February, 1966), p. 4.
Broderick, A. "Tribute to John Courtney Murray, Symposium: From a Friend Who Never Met Him," *America*, CXVII (September 9, 1967), pp. 246-49.
Burghardt, Walter J. "A Eulogy," *Woodstock Letters*, CXVI (Fall, 1967), pp. 416-20.
———. "From Certainty to Understanding," *Catholic Mind* (June, 1969), pp. 13-27.
"City of God and Man," *Time*, LXXVI (December 12, 1960), pp. 64-70 + cover.
Cogley, John. "Fr. Murray's Death, Great Loss to American Catholicism," *The Catholic Messenger*, August 23, 1964, p. 4.
———. "In Praise of Father Murray," *Commonweal*, LXV (December 7, 1956), p. 253.
———. "Person to Person," *Commonweal*, LXIX (January 9, 1959), p. 385.
Congar, Yves M.J. "The Theological Conditions of Any Pluralism." In *Tolerance and the Catholic*, a symposium. Translated by George Lamb. New York: Sheed and Ward, 1955, pp. 166-99.
Deutsch, Bernard F. "Common Law," *The Jurist*, XXVII (January-October, 1967), pp. 37-57.
Hughes, Emmet John. "A Man For Our Season," *The Priest*, XXV (July-August, 1969), pp. 389-402.
Kuttner, Stephan. "The Code of Canon Law in Historical Perspective," *The Jurist*, XXVII (January-October, 1968), pp. 129-48.
Lindbeck, George A. "John Courtney Murray, S.J.: An Evaluation," *Christianity and Crisis*, XXI (November 27, 1961), pp. 213-16.
Love, Thomas T. "John Courtney Murray, S.J." In *Modern Theologians: Christians and Jews*. Notre Dame, Ind.: University of Notre Dame Press, 1967, pp. 18-39.
McAvoy, Thomas. "Americanism and Frontier Catholicism," *Review of Politics*, V (July, 1943), pp. 275-301.
———. "Americanism, Fact and Fiction," *Catholic Historical Review*, XXXI (July, 1945), pp. 133-53.
———. "The Catholic Minority After the Americanist Controversy, 1899-1907: A Survey," *Review of Politics*, XXI (January, 1959), pp. 53-82.
McAvoy, Thomas. "Liberalism, Americanism, Modernism," *Records* of the American Catholic Historical Society of Philadelphia, LXII (December, 1952), pp. 225-31.
McCarthy, John P. "John Courtney Murray and the American Proposition," *New Individualist Review*, I (November, 1961), pp. 37-40.
O'Malley, John W. "Reform, Historical Consciousness, and Vatican II's Aggiornamento," *TS*, XXXII (December, 1971), pp. 573-601.
Örsy, Ladislas M. "The Problem of Constitutional Law in the Church," *The Jurist*, XXIX (January-October, 1969), pp. 29-56.
Pavan, Pietro. "The Right to Religious Freedom in the Conciliar Declaration." In *Religious Freedom*. Concilium, XVIII, New York: Paulist Press, 1966, pp. 37-52.
———. "Declaration on Religious Freedom." In *Commentary on the Documents of Vatican II*. Ed. by Herbert Vorgrimler. New York: Herder and Herder, 1969, IV, pp. 49-86.
Shannon, James. "Tribute to John Courtney Murray," *Catholic Bulletin*, Archdiocese of Minneapolis-St. Paul, Minnesota Weekly, September 7, 1967, p. 3.
Tinnelly, Joseph T. "The Challenge of John Courtney Murray," *The Catholic Law-*

yer, VII (Autumn, 1961), pp. 270-96.

"Vatican Council: The Uses of Ambiguity," *Time*, November 5, 1965, p. 52.

Vollert, Cyril. " 'Humani generis' and the Limits of Theology," *TS*, XII (March, 1951), pp. 3-23.

Wangler, Thomas E. "John Ireland's Emergence as a Liberal," *Records* of the American Catholic Historical Society of Philadelphia, LXXXI (June, 1970), pp. 67-81.

Wolf, Donald. "The Unitary Theory of Church-State Relations," *A Journal of Church and State*, IV (May, 1962), pp. 47-65.

Yanitelli, Victor R. "A Church-State Anthology: The Work of Father Murray," *Thought*, XXVII (Spring, 1952), pp. 6-42.

—————. "A Church-State Controversy," *Thought*, XXVI (Autumn, 1951), pp. 443-51.

Ziegler, Aloysius K. "Pope Gelasius I and His Teaching on the Relation of Church and State," *The Catholic Historical Review*, XXVIII (January, 1942), pp. 412-37.

Index of Names